Waltham Forest Libraries

Please return this item by the last date stamped. The loan may be renewed unless required by another customer.

Dec 2012 3 0 JAN 2014		

THE
BRITISH
ISLES

THE BRITISH ISLES: A TRIVIA GAZETTEER

Summersdale Publishers Ltd
46 West Street
Chichester
West Sussex
PO19 1RP
UK

www.summersdale.com

Printed and bound in the UK by CPI Group (UK) Ltd, Croydon, CR0 4YY

ISBN: 978-1-84953-322-5

THE
BRITISH
ISLES

A TRIVIA
GAZETTEER

PAUL ANTHONY JONES

summersdale

For my parents, Leon and Maureen

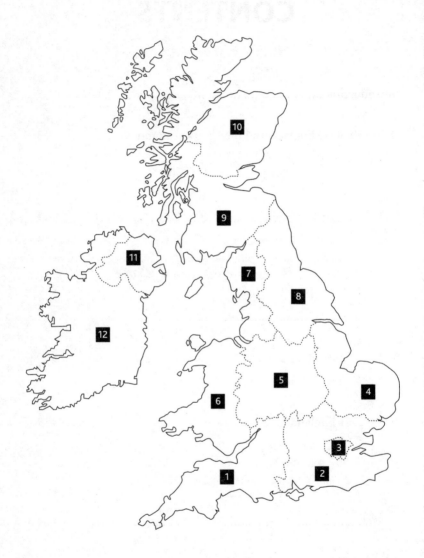

CONTENTS

INTRODUCTION

Chances are that no matter where you were born or where you live, you will know some kind of fact or story about your local area. Perhaps your home town is the birthplace of some celebrated figure, the battlefield of some historical skirmish, the location of some kind of world's first, or the setting for a famous film or book. Perhaps it has made a name for itself more recently through some event or occurrence that made the headlines, or maybe it is – or once was – simply home to the largest, smallest, tallest or earliest of something, or else the northernmost, southernmost, westernmost or easternmost.

Take for instance my home town of South Shields on the coast of South Tyneside – as well as being the finishing line of the internationally renowned Great North Run, South Shields is remarkably the birthplace of one of the earliest prime ministers of New Zealand. Continue onwards down the coast and you'll reach Sunderland, home to the first ship to circumnavigate Australia; then Seaham, constituency of first British Labour Prime Minister Ramsay MacDonald; Whitby, twinned with the capital city of Tonga; and Scarborough, birthplace of Oscar-winning actor Charles Laughton. I could go on, but the fact remains that the British Isles – that is, England, Scotland, Wales, Northern Ireland and the Republic of Ireland, as well as the Isle of Man, the Channel Islands, and all of the other surrounding islands and islets – are home to some extraordinary places indeed, and this is precisely what this book is all about.

In the main, *The British Isles: A Trivia Gazetteer* comprises a region-by-region, location-by-location list of facts, stories, records, histories and biographies like the examples above, each one listed under the town, city or area to which it relates. There are more than 1,100 individual entries featured here, assigned to almost as many different locations ranging from Aberdeen to Zennor, all of which are alphabetically arranged within 12 regional chapters. This regional arrangement comprises the main body of the book, but an alternative approach to the content is offered in the final pages, namely a thematic index that reorganises all of the gazetteer entries into almost one hundred different subject areas, from geography and history to people and culture, and science and nature to the arts and sport. This arrangement enables the book to be browsed by subject rather than location, and in doing so provides an important context for all of the entries, and thus allows for all similarly themed material to be collated and compared.

The British Isles: A Trivia Gazetteer comes from several years' worth of research and reading, but that is not to say that the book in any way attempts to offer an exhaustive guide to the history, culture and geography of the British Isles – far from it, in fact, as this book could easily be ten times as long and still only scratch the surface of what these remarkable islands have to offer. Nonetheless, limits of time and available space mean that regrettably not all of the towns or villages stumbled upon during preparation of the book have since made the final cut, and ultimately if you're disappointed to discover that your home town and its particular claim (or claims) to fame has not been included here, I hope you understand these constraints, and accept my apologies! If, however, you feel that yours is a glaring omission – perhaps you know of some fact or feat so exceptional that it assuredly deserves inclusion in any future edition of *The British Isles: A Trivia Gazetteer* – then please feel free to get in touch in whatever way suits and explain your tale; and remember, you can always follow and comment on the book via Twitter (@TriviaGazetteer). On a similar note, although all of the information here has been double checked and verified as reliably and as thoroughly as possible, with any undertaking as vast as this it is nonetheless feasible that some factual error or misspelling may have slipped through the net; if such a slip or inaccuracy is uncovered in the book then it would of course be of great benefit if you could let us know, so that amendments can be made if necessary.

I would hope that the temptation with this book (as with any book of this type) is to dive straight in to its pages and begin discovering all of the gems of information it contains, but I would lastly here like to draw attention to a few of my own personal favourite entries from the book, if only to highlight their remarkable stories all the more overtly: in compiling *The British Isles: A Trivia Gazetteer*, the stories of Hampton-on-Sea in Kent, Widecombe-in-the-Moor in Devon, Tyneham in Dorset, and Eilean Mòr in Scotland's Flannan Isles were all especially memorable, as were the stories listed here under Harwich in Essex, East Peckham in Kent, Fishguard in Pembrokeshire, Eday in Orkney, and Oughterard in County Kildare.

Happy browsing.

Paul Anthony Jones
May 2012

SOUTH-WEST ENGLAND AND THE CHANNEL ISLANDS

Cornwall and the Scilly Isles, Devon, Somerset, Dorset, Wiltshire, Gloucestershire, Channel Islands

ANDOVERSFORD, GLOUCESTERSHIRE

Grand National winner Mr Frisk

Bought by trainer Kim Bailey in 1986, Grand National winner Mr Frisk was trained at stables in Andoversford in Gloucestershire prior to winning the 1990 National in a record-breaking time of 8 minutes 47.8 seconds, the first ever winning time under 9 minutes, and almost 14 seconds faster than the previous record, set by Red Rum in 1973.

AUST, GLOUCESTERSHIRE

Disappearance of Richey Edwards

The car of former Manic Street Preachers guitarist and lyricist Richey Edwards was found abandoned near the village of Aust in Gloucestershire in February 1995. Edwards had earlier checked out of a London hotel, the day before he and the band were due to embark on a promotional tour of the US, and had apparently travelled to his home in Cardiff and then on to

Newport. On Valentine's Day 1995, his car, which was parked at a service station, was ticketed and three days later was reported as abandoned. Edwards has never been seen since, despite numerous unconfirmed sightings from around the world. It is largely believed that he committed suicide at the nearby Severn Bridge aged just 27, and on 23 November 2008, he was officially presumed dead.

AVEBURY, WILTSHIRE
Avebury Stone Circle

The Avebury Stone Circle in Wiltshire is the largest megalithic site in the British Isles, being both older and larger than Stonehenge, which stands 30 kilometres (18 miles) away. In essence, Avebury actually consists of three stone circles, that is, two smaller circles enclosed by a 400-metre (437-yard) diameter circle of much larger slabs, of which 27 remain in place today. The whole site stands atop a vast circular bank surrounded by a ditch more than –10 metres (–32 feet) deep thought to date from around 3000 BC, and was designated a World Heritage Site in 1986.

BATH, SOMERSET
World Heritage Site

Renowned for being the site of the only naturally hot spring in Britain, Bath was founded by the Romans as the spa town Aquae Sulis in the first century AD. As it continued to grow, Bath was granted official city status by Elizabeth I in 1590 and went on to become a popular resort in the Georgian era, the period from which many of the city's most beautiful buildings originate. Thanks to this long history and stunning architecture, the City of Bath was appointed a World Heritage Site in 1987.

'Get yourself to Bath'

The old phrase 'to get yourself to Bath' or, more fully, 'go to Bath and get your head shaved', was once used as a way of being told not to talk rubbish. The curious phrase derives from the practice of sending people believed to be insane to Bath to be treated in the city's healing mineral waters.

Jane Austen's Northanger Abbey

Both *Northanger Abbey* and Jane Austen's final completed novel

Persuasion are set predominantly in and around the city of Bath, where Austen herself lived in her twenties. The heroine of *Northanger Abbey*, the shortest of Austen's six novels, is 17-year-old Catherine Morland, whose time in the city and the relationships she forges with two gentlemen she meets there, John Thorpe and Henry Tilney, are the focus of the book. Although it was the first novel she completed, *Northanger Abbey* – like *Persuasion* – was not published until after Austen's death in 1817.

BEMERTON, WILTSHIRE
Parish of Welsh writer George Herbert

Born in Montgomery in Powys, Wales, in 1593, the Welsh poet George Herbert studied at Trinity College, Cambridge in the early 1600s and wrote his first published poems there in 1612. After serving as orator for Cambridge University and member of parliament for his home town of Montgomery, Herbert took holy orders in 1630 and served as rector of the parish of St Andrew in Bemerton, Wiltshire, until his death in 1633. Today, Herbert's

poetry may not be particularly well known, but is nonetheless celebrated for its metaphysical and metrical intricacy; his posthumous collection *The Temple* (1633) is his most renowned work.

BERKELEY, GLOUCESTERSHIRE
The life and death of Edward II

The luckless 20-year reign of King Edward II from 1307 to 1327 was marred both by the collapse of his marriage to Isabella of France amidst rumours of homosexual dalliances, and by a series of disastrous military campaigns against Scotland, all of which led to his eventual imprisonment at Berkeley Castle in Gloucestershire at the hands of his estranged wife and her lover, Roger de Mortimer. Deposed, Edward was murdered at Berkeley in 1327, popularly believed to have had a red-hot poker put up him, with the king's ghostly screams still supposedly heard echoing around the castle on the anniversary of his death.

Berkeley Castle itself was fortified in 1154 by Henry II to defend Bristol and the area around the River Severn from invasion by the Welsh. Since its construction, the castle has continued to be held by the Berkeley family and as such is believed to be the only British castle to have been held by a single family for such a great length of time.

Smallpox pioneer Edward Jenner

The English scientist Edward Jenner was born in Berkeley in 1749. Having studied medicine in London, Jenner soon afterwards returned to his home town and opened his own medical practice in 1773. It was here that he began his groundbreaking investigations into smallpox, basing his work on the commonly held notion that local milkmaids were inexplicably unaffected by the virus. Jenner theorised that the cowpox that the maids routinely caught from their animals must somehow protect them against the much more dangerous smallpox virus, testing his theory by injecting a young farmhand with fluid extracted from blisters on the milkmaids' hands. Noting the boy's subsequent immunity to the disease, Jenner published his findings in 1798, eventually leading to an 1840 Act of Parliament that introduced free vaccinations against the disease.

BIDEFORD, DEVON
The Bideford Witch Trial

The Bideford Witch Trial of 1682 was one of the last in England to lead to an execution. The accused were Temperance Lloyd, a local widow who had already been acquitted of the murder of a man by witchcraft in 1671, and both Mary Trembles and Susanna Edwards, two beggars who had reportedly been seen with Lloyd, and who were themselves accused of somehow causing a local woman's illness. Despite a great deal of the evidence brought against the women being nothing but hearsay, all three were found guilty and executed on 25 August 1682 at Heavitree outside Exeter. A plaque commemorating the women displayed on the wall of Exeter's Rougemont Castle, where the trials were held, is dedicated to 'the hope of an end to persecution and intolerance'.

BISHOPS CANNINGS, WILTSHIRE
Moonrakers

A colloquial name for the people of Wiltshire, the term 'moonraker' derives from a local story of a group of Wiltshire men attempting to smuggle contraband brandy through the county in the eighteenth century. Afraid of being caught by excise officers, the smugglers sank the barrels of brandy in a pond so as to return a few nights later to fish them out with rakes. When a group of officers stumbled on the men raking the pond, they were quickly forced to come up with an explanation – pointing to the reflection of the full moon on the water, one of the men promptly claimed that they were trying to catch hold of the cheese that appeared to be in the pond. The officers went away laughing at the men's apparent dim-wittedness, unknowingly leaving the smugglers to their booty. Bishops Cannings is one of several villages and parishes across the county that lay claim to being home to this original moonrakers' pond.

BODMIN MOOR, CORNWALL
The Hurlers

The Hurlers on Cornwall's Bodmin Moor are a series of three Bronze Age stone circles near the village of Minions, thought by local legend to be the remains of

men who were turned to stone as punishment for playing a game of hurling on a holy day. The circles lie roughly in a straight line and, as the northernmost circle is believed to have once been partly paved with granite blocks, are presumed to have once comprised some kind of ceremonial site or meeting place.

BOSCASTLE, CORNWALL
The Boscastle floods

On 16 August 2004, the Cornish village of Boscastle was devastated by flash floods in which a whole month's worth of rain – over 75 millimetres (3 inches) – fell in just two hours. Over 400 million gallons of water swept through the village during the flood, demolishing several buildings and sweeping dozens of cars out to sea. Over a hundred residents and tourists had to be airlifted out of the village by helicopter.

BOURNEMOUTH, DORSET
Lokshin's 1st Symphony

Scored for a full symphony orchestra and chorus and based on the Latin *Dies Irae*, the 1st symphony, known as the *Requiem*, of the little-known twentieth-century Russian composer Alexander Lokshin, debuted in Bournemouth in 1987, some thirty years after it was written, performed by the Bournemouth Symphony Orchestra and Choir. Hailed as a genius by Shostakovich, Lokshin wrote a further 11 symphonies before his death in the same year.

The Bournemouth Puma

In August 2005, a series of reports of a big cat in the Bournemouth area culminated in the supposed sighting of a large lynx- or puma-like animal outside of a hotel in the centre of the town in the early hours of the morning. The sighting led local police to issue an official warning advising holidaymakers to telephone the emergency services should they spot any kind of big cat in the area.

BRIDPORT, DORSET
'Stabbed with a Bridport dagger'

Oddly, to be 'stabbed with a Bridport dagger' was once used as a euphemism for being hanged, as the Dorset town of Bridport was historically a well-known producer of rope for the Royal Navy.

BRISTOL
Twinned with Tbilisi

Amongst many other cities, Bristol is twinned with Bordeaux, Guangzhou, Hanover (in one of the first post-war associations between Britain and Germany) and Tbilisi, the capital of the former Soviet republic of Georgia – indeed, following the dissolution of the USSR, the official charters connecting the two cities were redrafted in Georgian rather than Russian in 1996.

'Bristol fashion'

Originally describing a ship ready to sail, the phrase 'Bristol fashion' – or in full, 'all ship-shape and Bristol fashion' – derives from the city's widely held reputation for seafaring efficiency. Today, it describes anything well organised or fully prepared.

America's first female doctor

Born in Bristol in 1821, Elizabeth Blackwell and her family left England for America in the early

1830s, eventually settling in Cincinnati. After the sudden death of her father in 1838, however, Blackwell resolved to study medicine and was accepted into New York's Geneva College, where, in January 1849, she became the first woman ever to earn a medical degree in the United States, going on to become the country's first practising female doctor. An active abolitionist, Blackwell was also a leading women's rights activist and established both a women's medical college and an infirmary for women and children on New York's Bleecker Street in the 1850s. She eventually returned to England and lived in Hastings until her death there in 1910.

SS Great Western and SS Great Britain

Designed by Isambard Kingdom Brunel, the SS *Great Western* was the flagship of the Great Western Steamship Company, operators of the first regular transatlantic steamer crossing in the early nineteenth century. Built in a specially designed dry dock in Bristol, at the time of its launch in July 1837 the *Great Western* was easily the largest passenger vessel

in the world, yet its successor, Brunel's SS *Great Britain*, was twice its size – launched at Bristol in 1843, it was at least 30 metres (100 feet) longer and 1,000 tons greater than any other ship ever built. Coming in more than £40,000 over budget, however, the *Great Britain* ultimately contributed to the collapse of the Great Western Company after it was damaged and taken out of operation just three years later. Brunel meanwhile went on to build the even larger and more extravagant SS *Great Eastern*, launched from London in 1858, which remained the world's largest passenger ship for the next nine years.

Guys & Dolls premieres

Written by Frank Loesser, *Guys & Dolls* premiered on Broadway in 1950, winning all five of the Tony Awards for which it was nominated. The show's British premiere took place in 1953 at Bristol's Hippodrome Theatre, before the whole production – which featured several of the original cast members, including Vivian Blaine, star of the acclaimed 1955 film adaptation – moved to

London's Coliseum Theatre for its West End debut.

Bristol Island, South Georgia

The British overseas territory of South Georgia and the South Sandwich Islands lies in the southern Atlantic Ocean, almost 1,400 kilometres (870 miles) south-east of the Falklands. The majority of the islands, of which the largest by far is South Georgia itself (3,528 square kilometres/1,362 square miles), are inhospitable and unpopulated and, despite their small size, are treacherously mountainous – even at just 46 square kilometres (18 square miles), an eighth the size of the Isle of Wight, Bristol Island reaches a height of 1,100 metres (3,610 feet). It is the third largest of the South Sandwich Islands, discovered by James Cook in 1775 and named after the naval officer and statesman Augustus Hervey, 3rd Earl of Bristol.

BROWNSEA, DORSET
Population: 31

Brownsea is the largest of the dozen or so islands located in Poole Harbour in Dorset. It is also arguably the most well known, having been the location of Sir Robert Baden-Powell's first Boy Scout camp in 1907, and is also home to a Tudor castle built in the mid 1500s, a church and a pottery both built in the 1850s, and a popular nature reserve established when the island became a National Trust property in 1962. Having recorded a population of 270 in 1881, by the 2001 census the population was just 30 – although in 2010 the first baby born on the island for 83 years took the population to 31.

CALNE, WILTSHIRE
Priestley's isolation of oxygen

Now the home of the Marquis and Marchioness of Lansdowne, Bowood House near Calne in Wiltshire was also the site where, on 1 August 1774, the British scientist Joseph Priestley isolated oxygen for the first time by concentrating sunlight on a tube containing mercuric oxide. Priestley noted that the resultant gas, which he termed 'dephlogisticated air', made candles burn brighter and made his chest feel 'peculiarly light and easy' when he inhaled it. He published his findings in his landmark *Experiments and Observations on Different Kinds of Air* in 1775, beating fellow scientist Carl Wilhelm Scheele – who also, independently, isolated oxygen – by two years.

CHEDZOY, SOMERSET
The Chedzoy Candle Auction

Every 21 years, an auction is held in the village of Chedzoy in Somerset to determine the leasing of a field given to the village's St Mary's Church by a local landowner in the late 1400s. Traditionally, the length of the auction is determined not by the bidding, but by a burning candle – once lit, the auction lasts for as long as it takes a half-inch of the candle to burn down, and ends when the flame is extinguished. The winning bidder gains tenancy of the field until the next auction takes place 21 years later, with proceeds from the sale going to the church. Remarkably, the Chedzoy candle auction is thought to be the oldest recorded public auction in England.

CHELTENHAM, GLOUCESTERSHIRE
The Minotaur and the Hare

Sculpted by the artist Sophie Ryder, *The Minotaur and the Hare* is a 2.75-metre (9-foot) bronze statue on the Promenade in the centre of Cheltenham. Originally part of a temporary exhibition of Ryder's work in 1995, the piece was subsequently purchased for the town and has been a permanent, if controversial, fixture there since 1998.

CHIPPING CAMPDEN, GLOUCESTERSHIRE
The Cotswold Olimpicks

The tiny market town of Chipping Campden in the far north of Gloucestershire plays host each spring to the Cotswold Olimpick Games, an annual festival of sports and games established by a local lawyer named Robert Dover in the early 1600s. Like the modern Olympic Games, Gloucestershire's own 'Olimpicks' were inaugurated to honour those of Ancient Greece, but down the years have featured a much more unusual range of disciplines including shin-kicking contests, dancing, 'singlestick'

stick-fighting, hammer-throwing and 'spurring the barre', a feat of strength akin to tossing the caber. After an absence of many years the games were re-established in the 1960s and have happily continued ever since.

CIRENCESTER, GLOUCESTERSHIRE
The Epiphany Rising

In 1399, Henry Bolingbroke returned from exile in France to claim the English throne from his cousin, Richard II. With Henry now crowned king as Henry IV however, a group of noblemen who had gained titles from Richard in reward for their involvement in his plot to murder the Duke of Gloucester now all had their titles repealed. As a result, in January 1400, the men plotted to murder the new king and reinstate Richard in what became known as the Epiphany Rising, yet before the plot could come to fruition the rebels were betrayed to Henry who promptly raised an army and quashed the attempt on his life. The Earls of Kent and Salisbury, two of those who had helped instigate the plot, fled to Cirencester but were imprisoned

there by those loyal to the new king and, following an attempt to escape, were both executed. Within weeks, Richard too was dead – originally imprisoned in the Tower of London, it is believed he was starved to death at Pontefract Castle, perhaps at Henry's demand, and died in February 1400.

Remarkable Jane Austen auction

In June 2008, a lock of Jane Austen's hair was sold at auction in Cirencester for £4,800. The hair, thought to be one of several locks kept as a memento after her death by Austen's elder sister Cassandra, had unusually been incorporated into a woven design on the front of a locket, depicting a willow tree with branches hanging over Austen's gravestone. A rare first edition of Austen's debut novel *Sense and Sensibility* was also sold at the same auction, fetching £30,000.

CORFE CASTLE, DORSET
The death of Edward the Martyr

Edward the Martyr, the Saxon King Edward II, had been king of England for less than three years when he was stabbed and killed on horseback at Corfe Castle in Dorset in 978. According to some sources, it was Edward's stepmother Ælfthryth who had arranged the assassination, or, even, it was Ælfthryth who killed Edward herself.

DARTMOOR, DEVON
National park

Dartmoor National Park was created in 1951 and, at 956 square kilometres (369 square miles), was the largest national park in southern England until the creation of the South Downs Park in 2009. Reaching a peak of 621 metres (2,039 feet) at High Willhays near Okehampton, roughly one-tenth of the entire area of Dartmoor stands at a height of more than 450 metres (1,500 feet). The park also contains more so-called 'scheduled monuments' – that is, ancient monuments or sites officially recognised by the Department for Culture – than any other in the UK.

DEVIZES, WILTSHIRE
Twentieth-century disaster memorabilia auctioned

Two unique items of memorabilia from two of the twentieth century's most infamous disasters have been sold at auctions in Devizes, Wiltshire, in recent years. In November 2009, a bottle of Löwenbräu beer found amidst the wreckage of the *Hindenburg* airship disaster of 1937 – one of only six such bottles known to exist – was sold for £11,000, making it the most expensive bottle of beer in the world; and in May 2011, a 10-metre (32-foot) long cross-section drawing of the *Titanic* used during the enquiry into the sinking of the ship in 1912 sold for £220,000, making it the most expensive item of *Titanic* memorabilia ever sold at auction.

DORCHESTER, DORSET
Dickens' business card auctioned

In 2006, a business card advertising the author Charles Dickens' services as a freelance shorthand writer based in Westminster's Fitzroy Square was sold at a rare-books auction in Dorchester for £1,800. A rare first-edition copy of Thomas Hardy's novel *The Trumpet-Major* (1880) fetched £3,600 at the same sale.

DOWN HATHERLEY, GLOUCESTERSHIRE
American statesman Button Gwinnett

Born in *c.* 1732 to Welsh parents in the village of Down Hatherley north of Gloucester, Button Gwinnett was, in 1776, the second signatory of the American Declaration of Independence. Gwinnett and his wife Ann had moved to America in the early 1760s, settling in Savannah, Georgia, where he soon became a successful plantation owner and a prominent local figure, serving in the state's provincial assembly before eventually becoming governor in 1777. He died in the same year from injuries sustained in a duel with local political rival Lachlan McIntosh, later a prominent military leader in the War of Independence.

EAST BUDLEIGH, DEVON
Birthplace of Walter Raleigh

Although little of any certainty is known of his early life, Sir Walter Raleigh is believed to have been born in the tiny Devon village of East Budleigh near Exmouth in *c.* 1554. A favourite in the court of Elizabeth I, Raleigh's marriage to one of the queen's maids of honour without her permission in 1591 led to his imprisonment in the Tower of London. On his release, Raleigh resumed his lengthy career as an explorer, travelling extensively around the Atlantic, South America and the Caribbean in the late 1590s. However, his involvement in a plot to remove Elizabeth's successor James I from the throne led again to his imprisonment in 1603 and his eventual execution in 1618.

EAST KNOYLE, WILTSHIRE
Birthplace of Christopher Wren

Perhaps Britain's most celebrated architect, Sir Christopher Wren was born in the tiny Wiltshire village of East Knoyle in 1632. A noted mathematician and astronomer as well as an architect, it is nevertheless for his work rebuilding London after the Great Fire of 1666 that Wren is arguably best remembered today.

EASTLEACH, GLOUCESTERSHIRE
Parish of writer John Keble

Born in Fairford in Gloucestershire in 1792, the English cleric and poet

John Keble is best known for his work *The Christian Year*, written whilst he was curate of St Martin's Church in the Gloucestershire village of Eastleach, halfway between Gloucester and Oxford, in the early 1800s. A collection of poems written for every significant day of the Christian calendar, *The Christian Year* was published in 1827 and soon became hugely popular, selling more than 350,000 copies over the next 50 years. Keble went on to be appointed chair of poetry at Oxford University in 1831, where Keble College, founded in 1870, was named after him.

EXETER, DEVON
Parliament Street

A plaque at the entrance to Parliament Street in Exeter states that it is 'believed to be the narrowest street in the world'. Although this honour actually belongs to a *Strasse* in the German city of Reutlingen, at a width of just 64 centimetres (25 inches) at its narrowest point, Parliament Street is certainly a contender for the narrowest named thoroughfare in Britain.

Exeter pudding

Although many different variations of the recipe exist, a traditional Exeter pudding is made up of alternating layers of jam-covered sponge cake and almond-flavoured ratafia biscuits, separated by a mixture of suet, egg, breadcrumbs, lemon and rum.

The Siege of Exeter

Following the Norman Conquest of 1066, Exeter – then home to Gytha, mother of King Harold Godwinson, who had fallen in battle at Hastings – refused to accept the new king, William the Conqueror. As a consequence, William and his troops besieged the town for 18 days in 1068, until eventually it was forced to surrender. In the aftermath, William had Exeter's Rougemont Castle built in order to discourage any further uprising.

Exeter Racecourse

As well as being one of the longest, Exeter Racecourse also claims to be Britain's highest, situated as it is on Devon's Haldon Hills, which reach heights in excess of 250 metres (820 feet). Other similarly high-altitude racecourses include Bath, the highest flat course, and Hexham, the only racecourse in Northumberland.

EXMOOR
National park

Officially established in 1954, at 692 square kilometres (268 square miles) Exmoor is one of Britain's smallest national parks yet features the longest coastline (55 kilometres/34 miles) of any national park in the whole of England. Straddling the border between Somerset and Devon, Exmoor also encompasses England's highest cliffs and its longest stretch of coastal woodland, whilst its extensive coastline forms part of the 1,000-kilometre (620-mile) South West Coast Path, the longest National Trail walking route in Britain.

EXMOUTH, DEVON
Base of pirate William Kyd

The pirate William Kyd operated throughout the English Channel from a base at Exmouth on the Devon coast in a career spanning three decades in the mid fifteenth century. Known to have taken ships off the coast of the south-west of England, the Channel Islands and northern France, Kyd is reported as early as 1430 as part of a gang of pirates who seized a ship off the coast of Guernsey. Amongst his many other forays, in 1448 he took a ship named *La Marie* at Queenborough on the Thames, later selling its contents on the Isle of Wight, and in 1453, he captured the Scottish ship *The Marie*, likely the greatest haul of his career, taking it back to Exmouth to be sold.

FILTON, GLOUCESTERSHIRE
The Concorde's final flight

Capable of travelling at a supersonic speed of around 2,170 kilometres per hour (1,350 miles per hour) – so a transatlantic flight would take just three and a half hours – the Concorde was introduced into international air travel in 1976. After 27 years' service, in 2003 British Airways and Air France jointly announced that their Concorde fleet would be taken out of service later that year, citing falling passenger numbers in the wake of the September 11 attacks and the catastrophic crash of a Concorde at Gonesse in Paris in July 2000. Consequently, the last ever flight by a Concorde took place on 26 November 2003 when aircraft Concorde 216 flew from London's Heathrow Airport to Filton Airfield on the outskirts of Bristol to be retired.

FLAX BOURTON, SOMERSET
Britain's first breath test

On 8 October 1967, a motorist on the A370 in Flax Bourton in Somerset became the first British driver ever to be administered with a breath test. The test, known today as the breathalyser but at the time jokingly called the 'drunkometer', was introduced in 1967 by then Minister for Transport Barbara Castle, who also made permanent the 70 miles per hour speed limit on British roads.

FOWEY, CORNWALL
Base of pirate Hankyn Seelander

Of all of the counties of England, it is perhaps Cornwall that is the most famously associated with pirates. Just one of many to have operated from the area over the centuries is the Dutchman Hankyn Seelander who, from a base at Fowey near St Austell in the mid 1400s, is known to have taken ships all along the south coast of England throughout his career, amongst them a British ship, the *Mighell*, taken along with its cargo at Plymouth in December 1443.

GLOUCESTER, GLOUCESTERSHIRE
Founding of Gloucester Cathedral

Previously the site of a Benedictine monastery, work began on what is today Gloucester Cathedral under the direction of a Norman monk named Serlo, appointed abbot of the monastery by William the Conqueror in 1072. The cathedral's foundation stone was laid in 1089 by the bishop of Hereford, and St Peter's Abbey, as it was known at the time, was officially consecrated in 1100. After the dissolution of the monasteries under Henry VIII, the abbey officially became Gloucester Cathedral in 1541.

Robert of Gloucester's Chronicle

Robert of Gloucester, thought to have been a monk at the abbey at Gloucester in the late thirteenth century, completed a famous chronicle of English history there in around 1300. Written in verse and thought to have been partly based on Geoffrey of Monmouth's *Historia regum Britanniae*, a Latin account of the history of Britain, Robert of Gloucester's *Chronicle* is today largely disregarded as a work of much historical or poetic merit, but is renowned in part for its author's views on the ever-growing significance of the French language in England since the Norman Conquest – 'for unless a man knows French,' he states, 'he is held in little regard.'

Last coronation outside of London

The last British monarch to be crowned outside of London – and indeed outside of Westminster Abbey – was Henry III. Having succeeded to the throne on the death of his father, King John, in 1216, Henry was crowned at Gloucester Cathedral, as London was at the time under the control of France. His 'official' coronation at Westminster took place four years later, in 1220.

Vaughan William's epic Fantasia

Ralph Vaughan Williams' famous *Fantasia On a Theme by Thomas Tallis* is one of the composer's most popular and well-known works. Arranged for an extended string orchestra, including a separate string quartet, the piece was written especially for Herefordshire, Gloucestershire and Worcestershire's annual Three Choirs Festival, and premiered in Gloucester Cathedral on 6 September 1910. The 'theme' referred to in the title of the piece is that of *Why Fum'th in Fight*, the third of nine musical settings of psalms written by the sixteenth-century English composer Thomas Tallis for a 1567 work attributed to Matthew Parker, the first Anglican Archbishop of Canterbury.

GUERNSEY, CHANNEL ISLANDS
'Sarnia Cherie'

'Sarnia Cherie' ('Guernsey Dear') is the official national anthem of the Bailiwick of Guernsey. Written in 1911, the song gained even greater recognition as the local anthem during the German occupation of the Channel Islands in World War Two. The song's title makes reference to the traditional Latin name for the island, Sarnia.

The Channel Islands Witch Trials

Throughout the sixteenth and seventeenth centuries, the Channel Islands of Jersey and Guernsey conducted well over 150 witch trials, leading to the executions of almost a hundred people, most of whom were either hanged or, more often than not, burnt at the stake. Not all of those found guilty at the trials were executed, however, as many were either banished from the islands or released with a warning, whilst a Collette Gascoing sentenced on Guernsey in August 1563 was whipped, and had one of her ears 'nailed to the pillory' then cut off and thrown into the sea.

The Nazi occupations

The Channel Islands were the only part of the British Isles – and, indeed, the only part of the British Commonwealth – to be occupied by Nazi Germany during World War Two. On 30 June 1940, just two weeks after the British government resolved to demilitarise the islands, believing them to be of little strategic importance, Germany took control of Guernsey; all of the other islands followed, with Jersey taken the very next day, then Alderney (where they went on to build four concentration camps) the day after that, and lastly Sark on 4 July. A mission to reclaim the islands, 1943's Operation Constellation, was proposed but never executed, and even when food supplies were running perilously low – the D-Day landings of June 1944 understandably disrupted all imports from the mainland – the British government still made no attempt to relieve the islands. In full, the occupation lasted for five years until the Channel Islands were finally liberated the day after VE Day, 9 May 1945.

HARNHAM, WILTSHIRE
Incredible Stone Age site

A prehistoric site dating from the early Stone Age, perhaps some 250,000–300,000 years ago, was unearthed during construction work on a relief road in the village of Harnham near Salisbury in 2003. The site, which contained over forty flint hand-axes, one of the earliest known tools used by man, also contained significant traces of charcoal, suggesting that it may have been one of the earliest sites in all of Europe where prehistoric man constructed fires.

HELSTON, CORNWALL
Helston pudding

The Cornwall town of Helston gives its name to a traditional Cornish steamed fruit pudding. Often made from suet and breadcrumbs, the pudding usually contains raisins, sultanas or similar dried fruits and, uniquely, ground rice.

ILCHESTER, SOMERSET
The Fosse Way

The Fosse Way was one of the longest Roman roads in ancient Britain, and is today the only one still known by its original Latin name (derived from *fossa*, 'ditch'). Linking Exeter (Isca Dumnoniorum) to Lincoln (Lindum Colonia) via Bath (Aquae Sulis) and Leicester (Ratae Corieltauvorum), the Fosse Way also converged with the other Roman roads of Ermin Street and Akeman Street at Cirencester (Corinium). It is perhaps unsurprising, given that Roman roads are renowned for their straightness, that for most of its route the Fosse Way followed an almost perfect straight line, never straying any further than 9 kilometres (6 miles) either side of a direct line all the way from Lincoln to Ilchester in Somerset.

JERSEY, CHANNEL ISLANDS
'Ma Normandie' and 'Island Home'

Written by the nineteenth-century French composer and songwriter Frédéric Bérat, 'Ma Normandie' was the equivalent of the national anthem of Jersey for many years until an open competition in 2007 was launched to choose a new anthem for the island that would replace 'Ma Normandie' and its somewhat outdated allusion to Jersey's former French ownership – its first verse ends: 'Under the beautiful sky of our France... I like to see again my Normandy/ It is the country where I was born.' Consequently, in May 2008 the competition culminated in performances of all shortlisted songs at Jersey Opera House, where 'Island Home' by the local musician Gerard Le Feuvre was chosen as the new official national anthem of Jersey.

Base of pirate Eustace the Monk

Known as the 'Black Monk', Eustace the Monk was a pirate operating throughout the English Channel in the thirteenth century. Born in France, he became a Benedictine monk at St Samer Abbey near Calais before turning to piracy at the turn of the thirteenth century after a bitter quarrel with the Count of Boulogne, in whose court he was employed. From his base on Jersey, as a pirate Eustace all but dominated the eastern stretches of the English Channel, working first as an agent of King John and raiding the French coast, before switching allegiance to Philip II of France and leading a terrible attack on Folkestone in 1212. He was eventually captured and executed in 1217.

Milestone language bill passed

On 2 February 1900, a bill was passed allowing the English language to be used instead of French in debates in the States of Jersey, the parliament of the Bailiwick of Jersey in the Channel Islands. This was a controversial milestone in the adoption of English on the island, and the States went on to draft their first law wholly written in English in 1928.

KENIDJACK, CORNWALL
Vagrant American bird spotted

When a North American yellow-throated vireo was spotted in Kenidjack Valley in Cornwall in 1990, it was not only a first for the UK but also the first such sighting this side of the Atlantic.

LACOCK, WILTSHIRE
Photography pioneer Fox Talbot

William Henry Fox Talbot, one of the earliest pioneers of photography, was born on 11 February 1800 to a wealthy family in Lacock Abbey in the Wiltshire village of Lacock. Talbot was educated at Harrow School and Cambridge University, publishing the first of several papers detailing his research into optics shortly after graduating in 1821. In 1835, he successfully captured a photographic image on silver chloride paper and, prompted by the newly announced work of the French photographic pioneer Louis Daguerre, presented his work to the Royal Society in 1839. Within two years, he had created and patented his groundbreaking calotype process, the first to use a paper negative to reproduce a photographic image, before going on to outline his work in *The Pencil of Nature* from 1844 to 1846.

LAND'S END, CORNWALL
The End of England

Land's End is the westernmost point in mainland England, lying a whole 5 degrees west of the Greenwich Meridian. Despite what its name may suggest, however, Land's End is neither the westernmost point in Great Britain, nor the westernmost nor southernmost point in all of England, the latter of which both lie offshore in the Isles of Scilly. Nor, indeed, is Land's End the southernmost point on the English mainland, which is instead found at nearby Lizard Point on Cornwall's Lizard Peninsula.

LAVERSTOCK, WILTSHIRE
Former royal residence Clarendon Palace

Clarendon Palace near Laverstock on the outskirts of Salisbury is thought to have been initially used as a hunting lodge until both Henry II and Henry III vastly developed the site into one of the most significant royal residences of the Middle Ages. Abandoned by the crown after the execution of Charles I in 1649, Clarendon soon fell into disrepair and today only ruins of the former stronghold remain in fields to the east of Salisbury.

LES MINQUIERS, JERSEY
The end of the British Isles

As part of the Bailiwick of Jersey, Les Minquiers – taking their name from a Breton word meaning 'sanctuary' – comprise by far the southernmost point of the entire British Isles, a title contested in the International Court of Justice in the 1950s when the islands' ownership was disputed with France. Little more than a collection of small, uninhabited shallow islands and rocky islets (the largest, Maîtresse, is barely

50 metres – 164 feet – long), only a handful of which remain permanently above the surface of the English Channel, 'The Minkies', as they are affectionately known, stand roughly 15 kilometres (9 miles) further south of the island of Jersey itself.

LES PLATONS, JERSEY
The peak of the Channel Islands

Reaching a height of 143 metres (469 feet), Les Platons in the north of Jersey is the highest point in the Channel Islands. Elsewhere, the highest point in the Bailiwick of Guernsey is found on the smaller island of Sark.

LOSTWITHIEL, CORNWALL
Restormel Castle

One of only a handful of Norman castles in the south-west, Restormel Castle north of the Cornish village of Lostwithiel was constructed in 1100. Surrounded by a moat and situated atop a deliberately steepened hill spur on the River Fowey, Restormel is defensively one of the most invulnerable castles of its type and has only seen conflict once in its 900-year history, during the Civil War in 1644. Once owned by Simon de Montfort, Earl of Leicester, the castle has been the property of the Duchy of Cornwall for over 600 years.

LUNDY, DEVON
Population: 28

At 3.4 square kilometres (1.3 square miles), Lundy is the largest island in the Bristol Channel, lying 19 kilometres (12 miles) off the north coast of Devon. Despite its relative isolation and small size, Lundy nevertheless has its own pub, its own church and shop, produces its own stamps, and has a resident population of 28. It is also one of the most ecologically important of the smaller islands in the British Isles as it is home to several species, both native and introduced, which are found in only a handful of other locations. Appropriately, it was designated a Site of Special Scientific Interest in 1987, and in January 2011 was made Britain's first Marine Conservation Zone.

LYME REGIS, DORSET
Plesiosaur discovered

The Dorset coastline comprises one of the most prolific fossil beds in the entire British Isles, and consequently many species of dinosaur have been unearthed amongst its rocks over the years. In December 1823, the renowned fossil collector Mary Anning discovered the remains of a 2.75-metre (9-foot) long plesiosaur, a carnivorous prehistoric sea-dwelling dinosaur with large flippers, an elongated neck and tiny 12-centimetre (5-inch) head. Whilst the similar ichthyosaur had already been known to science, Anning's discovery was to prove the first plesiosaur ever found.

LYNMOUTH, DEVON
The Lynmouth floods

On 16 August 1952, an intense storm over the south-west of England deposited over 23 centimetres (9 inches) of rain on Exmoor in just 24 hours. As a result, the Devon village of Lynmouth, which stands in a valley downstream from two rivers that drain from Exmoor, was devastated by a flash flood which destroyed more than a hundred buildings and left 34 people dead.

MARLBOROUGH, WILTSHIRE
Marriage of King John

John, Earl of Cornwall, married Isabel, Countess of Gloucester, at Marlborough Castle in Wiltshire in 1189. Shortly before John's accession to the throne in 1199, however, the marriage was annulled at John's request by the Archbishop of Canterbury on the grounds of consanguinity – both descended from Henry I, John and Isabel were second cousins. John remarried in 1200, taking Isabella of Angoulême as his second wife; she was more than twenty years younger than John and aged just 16 at the time of their wedding. Nonetheless she bore John five children, including Henry III of England and Joan, consort of Alexander II of Scotland.

MELKSHAM, WILTSHIRE
Titanic victim Sidney Goodwin

Born on 9 September 1910 in the Wiltshire town of Melksham, Sidney Leslie Goodwin was just 19 months old when he died in the sinking of the *Titanic* in 1912. Buried in a grave dedicated to 'the memory of an unknown child' in

Fairview, Nova Scotia, DNA tests in 2007 finally identified Goodwin as one of the *Titanic*'s youngest victims.

MINCHINHAMPTON, GLOUCESTERSHIRE
Proceratosaurus unearthed

Although only the skull and partial lower jaw of a *Proceratosaurus* dinosaur has ever been discovered – near Minchinhampton in central Gloucestershire in the early 1900s – it can nevertheless be assumed even from these meagre remains that the creature was carnivorous, perhaps 3–4 metres (9–13 feet) in length, and had a single shallow crest or horn in the centre of its snout. As its name may suggest, the *Proceratosaurus* was once believed to be an ancestor of another dinosaur, the much larger *Ceratosaurus*, although today it is considered more closely related to the *Coelurosauria*, a group of dinosaurs which included the tyrannosaurs, the infamous velociraptor, and, later, the archaeopteryx and other primitive bird-like creatures.

MINEHEAD, SOMERSET
The South West Coast Path

The South West Coast Path is the longest official National Trail route in the British Isles. Beginning at Minehead in Somerset, the path heads west to encompass the entire coastlines of Devon and Cornwall, before coming to an end at Poole in Dorset some 1,014 kilometres (630 miles) away. The path passes through Exmoor National Park, and includes all of Devon and Dorset's Jurassic Coast World Heritage Site.

MORWENSTOW, CORNWALL
'The Song of the Western Men'
writer Robert Stephen Hawker

Born in Plymouth in 1803, the poet and writer Robert Stephen Hawker is today perhaps best known as the author of the popular anthem 'Trelawny, The Song of the Western Men'. Also known simply as 'Trelawny', the song is generally considered the unofficial anthem of the Cornish people, commemorating a supposed march on London in 1688 by Cornish people angry over the imprisonment of Jonathan Trelawny, a former bishop of Bristol and rector of St Ives, who had objected to James II's apparent tolerance of Catholic worship. Trelawny was imprisoned at the Tower of London before eventually being acquitted at his trial three weeks later.

Hawker, meanwhile, was a local cleric who, having taken Anglican holy orders in 1831, became vicar of the Church of St Morwenna and St John the Baptist in Morwenstow in 1835, serving until 1874. He died the following year, converting to Catholicism on his deathbed.

NANJIZAL, CORNWALL
Vagrant American bird spotted

In October 2008, the first alder flycatcher ever seen in Britain – and only the second ever recorded in Europe – was spotted at Nanjizal, near Land's End. Ordinarily found in the Americas, the bird migrates from Canada and the northern US to South America in the winter.

NETHERAVON, WILTSHIRE
Parish of writer Sydney Smith

Born in Essex in 1771, Sydney Smith studied at New College, Oxford, before taking holy orders and becoming curate of Netheravon in Wiltshire in 1794. The curacy lasted just two years until Smith was invited to tutor a local squire's son, with whom he spent some time travelling Europe. Subsequently, Smith settled in Edinburgh, where he helped found and contributed to *The Edinburgh Review*, before moving to London in 1803. It was here that he wrote his most famous work, *Peter Plymley's Letters*, a series of satirical open letters, which, despite Smith being an Anglican minister, supported Catholic emancipation.

OWLPEN, GLOUCESTERSHIRE
Ghost of Margaret of Anjou

Margaret of Anjou was the wife and consort of Henry VI, whom she married in 1445. She stayed at Owlpen Manor in central Gloucestershire on the eve of the Battle of Tewkesbury in May 1471, and the ghost of a lady in a fur-trimmed gown identified as Margaret is said to haunt the castle especially around the time of the anniversary of the battle, which effectively ended her family's Lancastrian claim to the English throne.

PAUNTLEY, GLOUCESTERSHIRE
Dick Whittington

Born in Pauntley in the Forest of Dean in the mid 1350s, Sir Richard Whittington MP was the real-life inspiration for the eponymous pantomime hero Dick Whittington. Like his fictional counterpart, in 1397 Richard was made Lord Mayor of London and, in 1402, married his wife Alice. Aside from this, he was elected to parliament in 1412 and, having always been one of the city's most dedicated benefactors, on his death in 1423 bequeathed a huge amount of money to several projects in London, including rebuilding and establishing a library at the city's Guildhall.

PENZANCE, CORNWALL
The Exchange

Opened as part of a £4 million scheme to refurbish and extend Newlyn Art Gallery in Cornwall, Penzance's Exchange is the largest contemporary art exhibition space in the whole of the West Country. Housed inside the town's former telephone exchange building, the gallery features a dramatic exterior made up of a series of illuminated glass columns, its striking design garnering The Exchange numerous accolades, including a 2008 RIBA Award.

Remarkable Churchill auction

In June 2006, an invitation to attend the funeral of Winston Churchill, sent by Queen Elizabeth II to a former Downing Street aide in 1965, was sold at auction in Penzance for £180. Several other Churchillian items went under the hammer at the same sale, including one of his cigars, sold for £70, and a custom-built coffee table once owned by Churchill and made partly from an old cigar box lid, which fetched £250.

PLYMOUTH, DEVON
Janners

Although particularly associated with Plymouth, the term 'Janner' can be used as a nickname for any inhabitant of the West Country, particularly the coastal reaches of Devon and Cornwall. The word is thought to derive simply from the first name John.

Voyages of Edmond Halley

At the end of the seventeenth century, the astronomer Edmond Halley set out on two voyages of exploration aboard the ship HMS *Paramore*, aiming not only to further explore the extremes of the Atlantic Ocean, but, more importantly, to examine magnetic variation, that is, the effect of the Earth's magnetism on compass readings at different points across the globe. Leaving England in October 1698, Halley's first voyage was cut short by a series of disputes with his crew, who resented working under a civilian rather than a more experienced naval officer, and as a result Halley returned home prematurely the following April. His second voyage, however, proved much more successful – departing in September 1699, the *Paramore* sailed almost as far south as South Georgia, a latitude of 52 degrees south, in January 1700, and throughout the trip Halley was able to make twice as many observations of the compass as he had the first time. Returning via the Caribbean and Newfoundland, the *Paramore* docked at Plymouth in September 1700 before heading back to the Thames, whilst Halley went on to publish his groundbreaking *General Chart of the Variation of the Compass* the following year.

The first transatlantic flight

Eight years before Charles Lindbergh's pioneering transatlantic flight, in 1919 the US aviator Albert Read and his crew piloted a US Navy *NC-4* flying boat across the Atlantic, which, although it made several stops along the way, was the first ever to complete the journey. The flight took 23 days in all, departing from New York's Rockaway Beach on Long Island on 8 May and arriving in Plymouth on 31 May, via stops in Newfoundland, the Azores, Portugal and Spain.

Charlie Chaplin costume auctioned

In May 2005, the iconic tramp outfit worn by Charlie Chaplin in the 1914 short film *Kid Auto Races at Venice* fetched £3,100 at an auction in Plymouth. The film was one of the first to feature Chaplin's 'Little Tramp' character, whose trademark scruffy black

SOUTH-WEST ENGLAND AND THE CHANNEL ISLANDS

suit, tie, bowler hat and tattered boots went on to become one of the most familiar images of the silent movie era.

Sense and Sensibility film set

Built in the eighteenth century, Saltram House in Plympton, Plymouth, was used as the home of the Dashwood family in Ang Lee's acclaimed 1995 film adaptation of Jane Austen's *Sense and Sensibility*. The film was nominated for 11 BAFTAs and seven Oscars (including Best Picture and Kate Winslet's first ever Oscar nomination), and Emma Thompson famously won the Best Adapted Screenplay Academy Award for the script, which she took four years to write.

Plymouth, Montserrat

The tiny Caribbean island of Montserrat has been a British territory almost continuously since 1632. Its capital and largest port is named Plymouth, although following a devastating two-year series of eruptions of the island's Soufrière Hills volcano in the mid 1990s, the capital has since been all but destroyed – finally abandoned

in 1997, much of what was once Plymouth now lies beneath more than a metre of volcanic ash. As a result, since 1998 the government of Montserrat has been based in the village of Brades at the opposite end of the island, which is now considered its de facto capital.

POSTBRIDGE, DEVON
The Grey Wethers

The impressive megalithic site at Grey Wethers near the Devon village of Postbridge on Dartmoor features two almost identically sized granite stone circles, comprising 20 stones and 29 stones respectively, both roughly 33 metres (108 feet) in diameter. The centres of the circles, standing roughly 40 metres (131 feet) apart, are aligned north to south.

PUCKLECHURCH, GLOUCESTERSHIRE
Death of Edmund I

King of England from 939, Edmund I was reportedly killed at a banquet in Pucklechurch near Bristol by an exiled thief named Leofa in 946. He was buried at Glastonbury and was succeeded by his younger brother Edred, who ruled until 955.

QUEEN CHARLTON, SOMERSET

Catherine Parr

The name of the tiny Somerset hamlet of Queen Charlton, lying between Bristol and Bath, commemorates Catherine Parr, who was given a manor house there by her husband Henry VIII. Catherine married Henry in July 1543, becoming the king's sixth and final wife, and one of just two of his former wives to outlive him at the time of his death in 1547. Ahead of her own death a year later, Catherine married Thomas Seymour, the uncle of Edward VI, who was to be her fourth husband – indeed, Catherine remains the most married queen in English history.

SALISBURY, WILTSHIRE

Statue of Ezra Baya Lawiri unveiled

In July 2008 a statue of the Sudanese priest and martyr Canon Ezra Baya Lawiri became the sixty-eighth statue displayed on the west front of Salisbury Cathedral. Born in 1917, Canon Ezra was killed by an artillery shell whilst fleeing violent fighting in Sudan in 1991, having just completed a groundbreaking translation of the Bible in the Sudanese language of Moru. Designed by the artist Jason Battle, Canon Ezra's statue was unveiled to celebrate both the cathedral's 750th anniversary and the thirty-fifth anniversary of a diocesan link between Salisbury and the Episcopal Church of Sudan.

King Lear (II.ii)

Old Sarum is an ancient site north of what is now Salisbury, and likewise the 'Sarum plain' mentioned by the earl of Kent in his mockery of the steward Oswald in the second act of Shakespeare's *King Lear* – 'Goose, if I had you upon Sarum plain, I'd drive ye cackling home to Camelot' – is Salisbury Plain. The reference to Camelot here relates to the belief that what is now Winchester, 30 kilometres (18 miles) to the east of Salisbury, was once perhaps the site of the capital of King Arthur's kingdom.

SAMPFORD COURTENAY, DEVON

The Prayer Book Rebellion

On Whitsunday 1549, Edward VI's Act of Uniformity came into being as the new *Book of Common Prayer* became the standard text used to celebrate Mass in England. Although largely accepted, in the Devon village of Sampford Courtenay the change was met with hostility, as an infuriated group of parishioners demanded a return to the now outlawed Latin text. In the weeks that followed, a rebellion against the new ruling spread throughout Devon and Cornwall, eventually prompting a group of armed protestors eastwards where they besieged the city of Exeter. A series of battles ensued, fought against a mercenary army assembled by the earl of Bedford, until the rebellion was eventually suppressed back where it had begun in Sampford Courtenay, in August 1549.

THE SCILLY ISLES

The ends of the United Kingdom

The Scilly Isles are home to both the most westerly and most southerly points in the entire United Kingdom. The westernmost point is found at Peaked Rock in the Crim Rocks, a handful of tiny islets and outcrops west of the central island of St Mary's, although the Isles' westernmost habitable point is Bishop Rock, which also claims to be the smallest island with a building in the world, as its entire area is taken up by an extraordinary lighthouse built there in the 1850s. The southernmost point, meanwhile, is a tiny unnamed outcrop near the larger islet of Gilstone in, confusingly, the Scilly Isles' Western Rocks, a group of dozens of tiny islands and sea stacks south-west of the main island of St Agnes. St Agnes itself is the southernmost settlement in the UK, as only the Channel Islands – which reside outside of United Kingdom jurisdiction – lie any further south in the British Isles.

A New Voyage to Carolina

As well as offering a detailed insight into life in America's colonies in the early eighteenth century, *A New Voyage to Carolina* by the English naturalist and adventurer John Lawson, later surveyor-general of North

Carolina, remains one of the most celebrated and thorough early accounts of the natural history of the United States. Although little is known of Lawson's early life, the voyage described in his book began back in England in 1700, where a chance meeting with a more experienced traveller in London inspired Lawson to head to America, assured that 'Carolina was the best country I could go to'. Having left the Thames, Lawson's ship stopped off at the Scilly Isles in April 1700 for repairs, before finally departing across the Atlantic on 1 May. After his arrival in Charleston the following August, Lawson set off on an extraordinary 965-kilometre (600-mile) exploration of the South Carolina backcountry, his account of which – including detailed descriptions of animals, birds and plants, as well as the native tribes he encountered there – forms the majority of his book. It was published in 1709.

Refuge of vagrant birds

The relatively isolated location of the Isles of Scilly makes them a prime location for spotting vagrant birds. Amongst the many rare and unusual birds to have been spotted on the islands over the years are Britain's first and only American purple gallinule, a type of water rail, in 1958; a yellow-bellied sapsucker, a type of North American woodpecker, in 1975; a magnolia warbler, usually found in Canada and the north-eastern states of the USA, in 1981; and a short-toed eagle, native to southern and central Europe and Asia, spotted in 1999.

SHAFTESBURY, DORSET
US architect Richard Upjohn

The acclaimed architect Richard Upjohn was born in Shaftesbury in Dorset in 1802. In 1829, he and his family emigrated to Massachusetts, eventually settling in Boston, where he began work as an architectural designer. His work soon proved successful and on moving to New York in 1839, he was called upon to redesign the city's central Trinity Church on Wall Street, Manhattan, which was completed in 1846. Following this success, Upjohn went on to design numerous other churches and cathedrals throughout New York and New England, and helped co-found the

American Institute of Architects in 1857. He died in 1878, and although responsible for many diverse buildings throughout his lengthy career is today best known for his stunning Gothic-revival ecclesiastic designs.

SHEBBEAR, DEVON
Turning The Devil's Stone

Each year on the evening of 5 November, a discordant peal of bells said to ward off evil spirits is rung at St Michael's Church in Shebbear, North Devon. Following this, the bell-ringers go down to the village square where the so-called Devil's Stone lies – a 1-tonne monolith said to have been left in the village by the devil himself. The bell-ringers must turn the stone over, prising it from the ground with crowbars, to guarantee good luck for the village in the year to come.

SLADESBRIDGE, CORNWALL
Vagrant bird sighted

Britain's first recorded sighting of a belted kingfisher, the only species of kingfisher widespread throughout North America, was in Cornwall in 1908. Over 70

years later a second such bird was spotted at Sladesbridge near Padstow in November 1979, remaining there well into the summer of the following year.

ST AGNES, SCILLY ISLES
Population: 73

St Agnes is the fourth largest and southernmost of the principal Isles of Scilly, as well as being the least populous of the five inhabited islands in the group. In 2001, the population was just 73, down from a peak of over 200 in the mid nineteenth century. The island, which also includes the nearby tidal islet of Gugh, is a little under 1.5 square kilometres (0.6 square miles) in area and is served by a pub, a post office and a Grade II listed Anglican church. It is also the site of one of the oldest lighthouses in England, built in 1680.

ST BRIAVELS, GLOUCESTERSHIRE
The Bread and Cheese Dole

After the Whitsunday evening service at the local village church in St Briavels in Gloucestershire, two people stand atop the church wall and throw small pieces of bread and cheese, said to be good luck, into a crowd of so-called 'dole claimers' waiting below. Dating from the twelfth century, the tradition is thought possibly to commemorate King John bestowing land on the villagers.

The life of St Briavel

The name of 'St Briavels', a small village on the English-Welsh border, is thought to be an anglicised version of the Welsh name Brioc, that of a sixth-century Welsh saint who was also one of the seven founder saints of Brittany. St Briavel's feast day is observed on 17 June.

ST COLUMB MAJOR, CORNWALL
Hurling

Hurling – a team game in which players pass a silver ball to each other, aiming to be the first to score a goal against the opposition – has been described as the national sport of the Cornish nation, and as such several locations across the county hold regular or annual matches. The annual town match

played in St Columb Major near Newquay takes place on Shrove Tuesday, and begins with a member of the previous year's winning team lobbing the ball into the air with the words 'Town and country do your best, but in this parish I must rest'. The ball is then passed or thrown from player to player, with the game ending with either the scoring of a goal, or with the ball passed out of the parish boundary. The event is commemorated on the town crest, which shows a hand holding a silver hurling ball.

ST HELIER, JERSEY
Patron saint of Jersey

St Helier was born in Tongeren, Belgium, and lived in northern France before being sent to Jersey by the abbot St Marculf in the early sixth century. Having settled on an islet on the town's coast known today as Hermitage Rock, Helier was killed in c. 555 by invaders to the island who beheaded him – legend has it that Helier was able to pick up his own head and stagger onto the beach before dying.

ST IVES, CORNWALL
The life of St Ia

The Cornish St Ia (also spelt *Ya* or *Eia*) after whom St Ives takes its name was a fifth-century missionary who sailed to Cornwall – as legend has it, on a leaf – from Ireland. She was martyred in *c.* 450 at the mouth of the River Hayle, on which St Ives stands.

ST KEVERNE, CORNWALL
The Cornish Rebellion

In 1497, Henry VII raised taxes across England in order to fund a war against Scotland. In response, a blacksmith from St Keverne in Cornwall named Michael Joseph An Gof instigated a rebellion against the tax, inciting hundreds of Cornish men to march to London in protest. Joining forces with fellow protestor Thomas Flamank and his followers at Bodmin, together the two men led an army of many thousands of Cornish men to the capital, eventually setting up camp at Blackheath in South London. Unfortunately, their army was no match for Henry's troops and the rebellion was swiftly and violently quashed, with both Flamank and An Gof captured and executed.

SWINDON, WILTSHIRE
The Magic Roundabout

Swindon's County Island junction, nicknamed the 'Magic Roundabout', was officially designated one of Britain's scariest road junctions in a 2009 poll. Built in 1972, the junction consists of one central roundabout, surrounded by no less than five mini-roundabouts, one for each of the arterial roads that lead into and out of the junction itself.

The FA's first floodlights

Swindon Town FC's County Ground stadium became, in 1951, the first football league stadium in Britain to install permanent floodlights; Arsenal's Highbury followed on just weeks later.

TEWKESBURY, GLOUCESTERSHIRE
Henry IV: Part 2 (II.iv)

A strongly flavoured blend of mustard and horseradish, Tewkesbury mustard has been made in the Gloucestershire town from which it takes its name since the 1600s. Its distinctively thick consistency is alluded to in Shakespeare's *Henry IV: Part 2*, wherein Falstaff insults Poins, a friend of the young Prince Henry (also called Hal), by stating 'His wit's as thick as Tewkesbury mustard'; he goes on to call him a 'baboon', with 'no more conceit in him than is in a mallet'.

TOLPUDDLE, DORSET
The Tolpuddle Martyrs

The village of Tolpuddle, situated between Poole and Dorchester in central Dorset, is famously associated with the Tolpuddle Martyrs, a band of workers and labourers who formed a union in 1833 for which they were subsequently arrested, tried and transported to Australia. Members of the union, known as the Friendly Society of Agricultural Labourers, routinely met beneath a large sycamore in the centre of the village green, that still remains to this day. In 2005, the National Trust carried out an analysis of the tree and calculated it to be around 320 years old, making it already 150 years old when the Martyrs' meetings were taking place.

TORQUAY, DEVON
Sir Richard Burton and Agatha Christie

The celebrated nineteenth-century explorer Sir Richard Burton was born in Torquay in 1821. In a series of adventures lasting almost forty years, Burton famously became one of the first Europeans to complete a pilgrimage to Mecca in 1853 and, in 1857 whilst on an expedition to find the source of the Nile, discovered Africa's Lake Tanganyika. The crime writer Agatha Christie was also born in Torquay, in 1890. Perhaps the biggest-selling author in literary history, since the publication of her first work *The Mysterious Affair at Styles* in 1920, she has sold an estimated two billion books worldwide.

TYNEHAM, DORSET
Commandeered 'in the national interest'

In 1943, at the height of World War Two, the War Office commandeered the coastal Dorset village of Tyneham on the Isle of Purbeck, forcing its 225 inhabitants out of their homes so that the land could be used to train troops.

In a letter sent to every home in the village, the government were said to 'appreciate that this is no small sacrifice', but that it was 'in the national interest... to move you from your home' – residents were told that they had until 19 December, barely four weeks from delivery of the letters, in which to move out. Although the evacuation was originally intended to be temporary, a compulsory purchase order was issued in 1948 that meant that the village could remain in the hands of the Ministry of Defence, and it has never been inhabited since.

WELLS, SOMERSET
Britain's last trenches survivor

In 2009, the last British survivor of the trenches of World War One died at Wells, Somerset, aged 111. Private Harry Patch, born in 1898, was conscripted into the 7th Duke of Cornwall's Light Infantry at the age of just 18 and fought in the trenches as a Lewis gun operator at the Battle of Passchendaele, the 3rd Battle of Ypres, in 1917. Badly injured by a German shell that killed three other men, Patch was sent back to England for treatment and was still recovering when the war ended in 1918. He was one of just five World War One veterans still alive at the time of his death.

WEST OVERTON, WILTSHIRE
The Ridgeway

The Ridgeway is considered the oldest road in Britain, thought to have been used by travellers for more than 5,000 years as part of a much longer route connecting the Somerset coast to The Wash in East Anglia. Stretching for 139 kilometres (87 miles) from Overton Hill, near the tiny Wiltshire village of West Overton, to Ivinghoe Beacon near Dunstable, today The Ridgeway stretches through Wiltshire, Oxfordshire, Berkshire, Hertfordshire and Buckinghamshire, and passes by both the Avebury Stone Circle and Chequers, the country residence of the prime minister. It was designated an official National Trail in 1972.

WHITEBALL, SOMERSET
Britain's oldest shoe

An Iron Age shoe dating from over 2,000 years ago was discovered during an archaeological excavation at Whiteball Quarry in Somerset in

2005. The equivalent of a modern size 10, the shoe was made of leather and was so well preserved that even the holes through which the laces would once have been threaded were still clearly visible. It is likely that it is the oldest shoe ever found in the UK.

WIDECOMBE-IN-THE-MOOR, DEVON
Rare 'ball lightning' attack

Best known as the eponymous village from the folk song 'Widecombe Fair', on 21 October 1638 the tiny Dartmoor village of Widecombe-in-the-Moor was struck by one of the earliest recorded instances of so-called 'ball lightning', a rare and mysterious atmospheric phenomenon characterised by the sudden appearance, often during a thunderstorm, of vast, luminous and incredibly volatile balls of light. The event at Widecombe centred on the village's church, with contemporary accounts claiming that a huge ball of fire suddenly burst through a window of the church during a storm, reportedly rebounding around the interior of the church, smashing into wooden beams and pews and

hurling masonry to the ground, before dividing into two and vanishing as quickly as it had appeared, leaving behind a thick black smoke and a strong smell of sulphur. The devastating event left four of the congregation dead and some sixty more injured, many of whom were very badly burned.

WIMBORNE MINSTER, DORSET
Ripper suspect Montague Druitt

Montague Druitt was born in Wimborne Minster near Poole in 1857. Having studied at Oxford University, he set up a barrister's practice in London's Inner Temple in 1885, alongside playing cricket for Dorset County Cricket Club and working as a teacher at a boys' school in Blackheath in south-east London. On 30 November 1888, however, Druitt was dismissed from the school and subsequently disappeared until, on 31 December, his body was found in the Thames. As well as his suicide coinciding with the last of the Ripper murders, both the proximity of his legal practice to Whitechapel and the fact that he had probably acquired some knowledge of anatomy from his physician father have led to Druitt's name long being attached to the Ripper case, and indeed, Sir Melville Macnaghten, appointed Chief Constable of the Metropolitan Police shortly after the time of the murders, named Druitt as a suspect in 1894.

ZENNOR, CORNWALL

Matthew Trewhella and The Mermaid of Zennor

According to an old Cornish story, many years ago a mermaid who resided in nearby Pendour Cove overheard a local man, Matthew Trewhella, singing in the local parish church in Zennor and became enchanted by his voice. Dressing herself in a long flowing dress, the mermaid secretly began to attend the church each evening just to hear Matthew's wonderful voice, before returning to the sea when the service was over. One day, Matthew happened to catch the mysterious woman's eye and instantly fell in love with her, pursuing her from the church and down onto the beach. When she told him that she was a mermaid and must return to the sea or else die, Matthew swore nevertheless to remain with her forever and entered the water after her, never to be seen again. His beautiful singing can still supposedly be heard at times in the cove, whilst a pew in the local church now bears the image of a mermaid carved into the wood.

WHAT'S IN A NAME?

Antony, Cornwall
Probably derives from the Old English first name Anna.

Beer, Devon
From the Old English *bearu*, meaning 'grove'.

Box, Wiltshire
The Old English word *box* from which this name derives was used of the box tree, *buxus*.

Charles, Devon
An old Cornish name, derived in part from the word *carn* or *karn*, describing a rock pile or tor.

Chew, Somerset
Although its exact meaning is unclear, the name of Somerset's River Chew is likely Celtic in origin.

Ham, Gloucestershire
A common place name in Britain, 'Ham' derives from the Old English word *hamm* (source of the common suffix -ham, as in 'Birmingham'), which could have once variously denoted an enclosure, an area of high land, or an area of land enclosed in a river bend.

Highway, Wiltshire
A West Saxon name meaning 'road for carrying hay'.

Kelly, Devon
Probably from a Cornish word, *kelli*, denoting a small wood.

Mousehole, Cornwall
Perhaps used literally, for the name of a local cave.

Plush, Dorset
The hamlet of Plush probably takes its name from the Old English *plysc*, 'shallow pool'.

Tone, Somerset
The name of the River Tone is Celtic in origin and likely means 'fire', perhaps alluding to the appearance of the water.

Uphill, Somerset
Means 'above the creek', from a compound of the Old English words *uppan* and *pyll*.

Week, Devon
From the generalised Old English word *wic*, used variously for a farmstead, a dwelling, or a trading post, amongst many other meanings.

Wool, Dorset
In fact comes from an Old English word for a spring, *wiell*.

Zeals, Wiltshire
Means 'sallow-trees', deriving from the Old English word *sealh*.

SOUTH-EAST ENGLAND

Bedfordshire, Hertfordshire, Buckinghamshire, Oxfordshire, Berkshire, Surrey, Hampshire and the Isle of Wight, West Sussex, East Sussex, Kent, Essex

ALBURY, SURREY
William Oughtred's slide rule

The invention of the slide rule, a simple analogue calculating device, is credited to several individuals, of which the sixteenth–seventeenth-century English mathematician and cleric William Oughtred is one. His design, originally for a circular slide rule based on an earlier calculating device called a 'gunter' (named after fellow mathematician Edmund Gunter), comprised two logarithmic rules positioned one inside the other, so that the relative position of the numbers on the rule could be used to perform basic calculations. Oughtred's work on the slide rule, as well as many of his other contributions to mathematics (including the introduction of the multiplication sign) was carried out whilst he was rector of Albury in Surrey in the 1620s and 1630s.

ALDERMASTON, BERKSHIRE
Britain's first petrol station

Although roadside petrol pumps had been in use since the early 1910s, on 2 March 1920 the AA opened Britain's first petrol station at Aldermaston in Berkshire.

AMPTHILL, BEDFORDSHIRE
Henry VIII (III.ii)

Ampthill Castle in Bedfordshire was built in the early fifteenth century by Sir John Cornwall, an uncle of Henry V. As recorded in the third act of Shakespeare's history of *Henry VIII* – 'The Archbishop of Canterbury held a late court six miles off from Ampthill, where the princess lay' – it was here that Catherine of Aragon, Henry's first wife, lived from 1531 until the finalisation of their divorce two years later, at which point she was taken to Kimbolton Castle in Cambridgeshire where she remained until her death in 1536. Although the castle itself no longer stands, a cross erected in nearby Ampthill Park commemorates Catherine's time there.

ARUNDEL, WEST SUSSEX
Marriage of Henry IV

Henry Bolingbroke, later King Henry IV, reputedly married Mary de Bohun at Arundel Castle in West Sussex in July 1380. Mary, who was barely a teenager at the time of the wedding, bore Henry five sons and two daughters including Henry of Monmouth (later Henry V); John, Duke of Bedford; and Philippa of England, later the wife of the Scandinavian King Eric of Pomerania. Mary,

however, never became queen herself as she died giving birth to Philippa in 1394, five years prior to Henry's accession in 1399. As king he married his second wife, Joanna of Navarre, at Winchester Cathedral in 1403, the couple having earlier met when Henry was banished from England by Richard II, and they were together until Henry's death in 1413.

ASHFORD, KENT
Malcolm Sargent and Frederick Forsyth

A former Master of the Queen's Music and a principal conductor with the Hallé Orchestra, BBC Symphony Orchestra and both the London and Royal Philharmonic, Sir Malcolm Sargent was born in Ashford in 1895. Frederick Forsyth, meanwhile, the author of the acclaimed thrillers *The Day of the Jackal, The Fourth Protocol* and *The Odessa File* amongst many others, was born in Ashford in 1938.

AUDLEY END, ESSEX
Former royal residence Audley End House

Originally a monastery, Audley End House outside Saffron

Walden in Essex takes its name from Sir Thomas Audley, a former Lord Chancellor and Speaker of the House of Commons, who was given the manor in 1538 by Henry VIII. Audley's grandson Thomas Howard, Earl of Suffolk, extended the building to a palatial size in the early 1600s, and in 1668 it was bought by Charles II for use whilst attending the Newmarket races. Having fallen into disrepair, however, the house was returned to the Suffolks by William III in 1701.

BANBURY, OXFORDSHIRE
The Merry Wives of Windsor (I.i)

Bardolph, one of Falstaff's followers, insults the dim-witted Abraham Slender in the opening act of Shakespeare's *The Merry Wives of Windsor* by calling him a 'Banbury cheese', referring to a pale, richly textured cheese once produced in Banbury in north Oxfordshire. Bardolph's insult is presumably two-fold, intended to refer both to Slender's pasty complexion and, as in the Elizabethan saying 'as thin as Banbury cheese', to his lean, weedy physique.

BARNET, HERTFORDSHIRE
Gosford Park film set

Robert Altman's acclaimed ensemble-cast drama *Gosford Park* (2001) – which, alongside six other nominations, garnered *Downton Abbey* creator Julian Fellowes a 2001 Oscar for Best Original Screenplay – was partly shot at Wrotham Park, an eighteenth-century country house just outside London near Barnet in Hertfordshire.

BATTLE, EAST SUSSEX
Death of Odo of Canterbury

On 20 January 1200, the English theologian Odo of Canterbury died and was buried at Battle Abbey in East Sussex. Odo was a close friend of Thomas Becket, and an enthusiastic scholar who preached in three languages. Despite being one of the most significant theologians of his time – and despite several nominations throughout his life – Odo was never elected Archbishop of Canterbury, instead spending most of what were to be his final years as abbot of Battle Abbey in East Sussex.

BEDFORD, BEDFORDSHIRE
Bedfordshire clangers

Originally popular amongst nineteenth-century labourers and farmworkers – and described by *The Darling Buds of May* novelist H. E. Bates as 'hard as a hog's back' and 'harder [than] prison bread' – a 'Bedfordshire clanger' is a stuffed suet dumpling, usually elongated in shape. Although different recipes and variations of the dish exist across England, the Bedfordshire example is perhaps the most remarkable as it traditionally contains two fillings, one sweet and one savoury, found at opposite ends of the same dumpling, split by a 'dam' of pastry between the two halves.

BENSON, OXFORDSHIRE
Titanic lookout Reginald Lee

Reginald Lee, born in Benson in 1870, was one of two lookouts in the crow's nest of the *Titanic* when she hit an iceberg at 11.40 p.m. on 14 April 1912. Having previously served on other White Star liners, both Lee and his companion, Liverpool-born Frederick Fleet, were experienced lookouts, yet because the night of the *Titanic*'s sinking was so unusually calm and dark – and as neither man had been equipped with binoculars – their job proved much more difficult than normal. Like all six of the *Titanic*'s lookouts, both Lee and Fleet survived the disaster, yet both men later succumbed to tragedies of their own – Lee died just a year later, whilst Fleet committed suicide in 1965 following the death of his wife and was buried in an unmarked grave in Southampton.

BIDDENDEN, KENT
The Biddenden Maids

Known as the Biddenden Maids, Mary and Eliza Chulkhurst were born in the tiny village of Biddenden in south-west Kent in 1100. One of the earliest sets of conjoined twins known to science, the sisters were born joined at the hip and shoulders, and were never separated throughout their lives – when Mary took ill and died in 1134, Eliza refused to undergo the lifesaving surgery required to be removed from her sister and died six hours later, stating, 'As we came together, we will also go together.'

BLETCHLEY, BUCKINGHAMSHIRE
Enigma machine stolen

On 1 April 2000, a rare Enigma machine was stolen from Bletchley Park in Buckinghamshire. The machine, an *Abwehr* model valued at £100,000, was one of just three such machines in the world and had been used at Bletchley, then known as 'Station X', during World War Two to decipher German communication codes. Curiously, in October 2000 the machine was delivered anonymously to the broadcaster Jeremy Paxman at BBC Television Centre. The following month, Derbyshire antiques dealer Dennis Yates was arrested for the theft and was eventually sentenced to ten months in prison.

BOLDRE, HAMPSHIRE
Parish of writer William Gilpin

Born in Cumbria and educated at Queen's College, Oxford, William Gilpin was headmaster of Cheam School in South London before relocating to Boldre in Hampshire's New Forest in 1777, where he served as vicar of the Church of St John the Baptist until his death in 1804. Today, Gilpin is best remembered as one of the earliest proponents of the innovative 'picturesque' movement, established in his *Observations on the River Wye* published in 1782, which aimed to appreciate nature from an aesthetic viewpoint.

BRIGHSTONE, ISLE OF WIGHT
Eotyrannus unearthed

Discovered on cliffs near the village of Brighstone on the Isle of Wight in 1997, *Eotyrannus* was a 4.5-metre (15-foot) carnivorous dinosaur that lived during the early Cretaceous period, roughly 120 million years ago. *Eotyrannus*, whose name means 'early tyrant', is thought to be an ancestor of the much larger and better known tyrannosaurus, which lived around 65–70 million years ago in the late Cretaceous. *Eotyrannus* is one of over a dozen different species of dinosaur to have been found on the Isle of Wight, making it one of the most important palaeontological locations in the whole of the British Isles.

BRIGHTON, EAST SUSSEX
Birthplace of Gilbert Ryle

One of the foremost philosophers of the twentieth century, Gilbert Ryle was born in Brighton on 19 August 1900. An accomplished linguist and a graduate of Queen's College, Oxford, Ryle worked in intelligence during World War Two before returning to Oxford as professor of metaphysical philosophy in 1945. Perhaps his greatest work, *The Concept of Mind*, in which he coined the phrase 'the ghost in the machine', was published four years later in 1949. He died in 1976.

Former royal residence, The Royal Pavilion

Perhaps one of the most famous former royal residences in England, Brighton's Royal Pavilion was built as a seaside retreat for the then Prince Regent, later George IV, in the early nineteenth century. The striking Indian-influenced appearance of the Pavilion is the work of the architect John Nash, who redesigned much of the palace shortly before the king's death in 1830. It was eventually sold to the town by Queen Victoria in 1850.

Pioneering electric railway

The world's oldest surviving electric railway is Volk's Electric Railway, which runs along the seafront at Brighton. Named after the pioneering British engineer Magnus Volk, the first part of the railway – a quarter-mile section originally intended to be just a temporary attraction – was completed in 1883. Today, the railway has three stations and runs for just under 2 kilometres (1.2 miles) from Brighton's Palace Pier to Black Rock, near Brighton Marina.

BURY, WEST SUSSEX
Nobel Laureate John Galsworthy

Bury House in the tiny village of Bury in West Sussex was, from the mid 1920s until his death in 1933, the home of the English writer John Galsworthy, who was awarded the Nobel Prize for Literature in 1932. Born in Kingston Hill in Surrey in 1867, Galsworthy is best remembered for the collection of works comprising his *Forsyte Saga*, the first of which was published in 1906.

CAMBERLEY, SURREY

British Olympian Malcolm Cooper

The sport shooter Malcolm Cooper was born in Camberley in Surrey in 1947. Having made his Olympic debut at Munich in 1972, Cooper won gold in the men's 50-metre (164-foot) three-position rifle event at both Los Angeles (1984) and Seoul (1988), setting a world record in the 1984 games. He died in 2001.

CANTERBURY, KENT

The Pilgrim's Way

Stretching roughly 192 kilometres (120 miles) from Winchester to Canterbury, the Pilgrim's Way was an ancient English trackway at the foot of the North Downs, taking its name from the many Christian pilgrims who used the route in the Middle Ages to reach the shrine of Thomas Becket. Today, the Pilgrim's Way is all but subsumed by the longer North Downs Way National Trail, which connects Farnham in Surrey to Dover in Kent.

Marriage of Henry III

Henry III was nine years old when he became king following the death of his father, King John, in 1216. The eldest of John's five children, Henry was crowned at Gloucester Cathedral and married Eleanor of Provence, the second daughter of Ramon Berenguer IV, Count of Provence, at Canterbury Cathedral in 1236. Despite having never seen each other prior to the wedding (indeed, Eleanor had never before visited England), the couple were married for almost forty years and had five children, including Henry's eventual successor, Edward I.

Murder of Thomas Becket

The assassination of Thomas Becket, Archbishop of Canterbury, is arguably one of the most infamous and most widely disputed in all of English history. Becket was murdered during preparation for vespers inside Canterbury Cathedral on 29 December 1170 by four knights of Henry II: Richard de Brito, Reginald Fitzurse, William de Tracy, and Hugh de Morville, Lord of Westmoreland. Whether the king himself intentionally ordered Becket's killing remains open to considerable debate to this day.

CARISBROOKE, ISLE OF WIGHT
Former royal residence, Carisbrooke Castle

Carisbrooke Castle in the village of Carisbrooke near Newport on the Isle of Wight became the property of the crown in 1293 when Isabella de Fortibus, Countess of Devon, granted the Isle of Wight to Edward I on her deathbed. Greatly developed over the centuries by many of its owners – Henry I added the castle keep, Elizabeth I the extensive outer defences – the castle remained an official royal residence until the death of Princess Beatrice, Governess of the Isle of Wight and a daughter of Queen Victoria, in 1944.

CHAILEY, EAST SUSSEX
Sussex pond pudding

Sussex pond pudding is an unusual traditional English suet pudding, at the centre of which is a whole lemon surrounded by butter and brown sugar. Because the butter and sugar mixture melts and caramelises during the lengthy cooking process, when the pudding is cut open the mixture pours out to create the distinctive 'pond' that gives the dish its name. Although the dish's origins are largely unclear, one of the earliest recorded recipes is attributed to the East Sussex village of Chailey.

CHATHAM, KENT
HMS Victory

Constructed over seven years from the timber of 6,000 trees, Admiral Nelson's flagship HMS *Victory* was built at Chatham on the River Medway in Kent and launched in 1765. Nelson became the ship's captain in 1803, and it was on board the *Victory* that he was killed by a single musket shot during the Battle of Trafalgar on 21 October 1805. The *Victory*, meanwhile, ended her active service in 1812, and today is moored in a dry dock in Portsmouth Harbour.

CHELMSFORD, ESSEX
Former royal Palace of Beaulieu

The former Tudor palace of Beaulieu near Chelmsford in Essex began life as New Hall, a manor house owned by Thomas Boleyn, father of Anne, who sold the hall to Henry VIII in 1516. The king spent a small fortune improving and vastly extending the house (renaming it Beaulieu, 'beautiful place', in the process) and it remained in the possession of the crown until 1573 when it was granted to Thomas Radcliffe, 3rd Earl of Sussex, by Elizabeth I. In the decades that followed, the Palace of Beaulieu changed hands several more times until, in 1798, it was finally acquired by a group of nuns who established a Catholic school there the following year.

The Peasants' Revolt and execution of Thomas Baker

A landowner in the Thurrock village of Fobbing in Essex, Thomas Baker was one of the earliest instigators of the Peasants' Revolt. In May 1381, he led a group of fellow villagers in a refusal to pay poll tax, subsequently running the king's tax collectors out of the town and attacking the local chief justice when he was sent to investigate the situation. In the months that followed, the revolt became increasingly violent as it spread throughout the south-east, with Kent's Wat Tyler eventually leading a march on London. It is unclear how much of a role Baker had in the remainder of the

uprising, but nonetheless he was apprehended soon afterwards and hanged, drawn and quartered at Chelmsford on 4 July 1381.

CHICHESTER, WEST SUSSEX
Peter Shaffer's The Royal Hunt of the Sun debuts

Completed ten years after his first play, Peter Shaffer's *The Royal Hunt of the Sun*, portraying the Conquistador Pizarro's role in the destruction of the Incan Empire, debuted at Chichester's Festival Theatre before transferring to London's Old Vic for its official world debut in December 1964. Critically praised on its opening, the production soon moved to Broadway starring Christopher Plummer and David Carradine, Plummer also starring in a 1969 film adaptation.

The greater mouse-eared bat

Widespread throughout continental Europe, the greater mouse-eared bat had always been something of a rarity in the British Isles until finally, in January 1990, the last few known individuals disappeared and the species was declared extinct in Britain. In recent years, however, the bat has begun to reappear in a handful of sites in southern England, and in 2002 a single male was discovered hibernating near Chichester in West Sussex.

CHIPPING NORTON, OXFORDSHIRE
The King's Men

Dating from *c*. 3000 BC, the King's Men is a stone circle in Oxfordshire, just north of Chipping Norton near the border with Warwickshire. Roughly 33 metres (108 feet) in diameter, the site comprises over seventy individual stones and forms part of the much larger megalithic system known as the Rollright Stones. Stretching from Oxfordshire into Warwickshire, the Rollright system also includes the nearby King Stone, an extraordinary 2.5-metre (8-foot) monolith, and the Whispering Knights, the remains of an ancient Neolithic burial chamber marked by four large standing stones leaning inwards around a fifth fallen stone, probably the remnants of the chamber's roof. Legend has it that the Rollrights are in fact the remains of an ancient king, along with his army and his knights, all of whom were turned to stone by witchcraft.

COLCHESTER, ESSEX
Ripper suspect Sir William Gull

One of the most celebrated of all nineteenth-century physicians – and renowned for being the first to describe anorexia – Sir William Gull was born in Colchester in 1816. In an illustrious 60-year career, Gull was made a Fellow of the Royal Society and held several significant medical positions, including governor of Guy's Hospital in London and Physician-in-Ordinary to Queen Victoria, before his death in 1890. His alleged involvement in the Jack the Ripper killings essentially developed from later elaborate conspiracy theories involving both the Freemasons and the royal family, with Gull's medical expertise often used to account for the gruesome surgical procedures performed on some of the victims who had had their internal organs removed.

COMPTON, BERKSHIRE
Grand National winner Foinavon

Originally owned by Anne, Duchess of Westminster, the

notorious 100/1 Grand National winner Foinavon was bought by Cyril Watkins and trained by John Kempton at his yard in Compton, Berkshire, in preparation for the 1967 race. A jockey himself, Kempton chose not to ride Foinavon in the National, leaving John Buckingham to take victory in his (and his horse's) first ever appearance. His unlikely victory was famously brought about by a melee at the twenty-third fence caused by a riderless horse crossing in front of the race leaders. Foinavon, whose name is now shared by the fence that secured its victory, went on to a convincing win with all 17 of the other finishing horses having to be remounted; it was only the fourth time that a horse at odds of 100/1 had won the National in its entire history.

COOLING, KENT
Dickens' Great Expectations

Several locations in Kent appear in Charles Dickens' works, amongst them the North Kent Marshes, near the village of Cooling on the Hoo Peninsula. Both the marshes and the nearby churchyard of St James' Church in Cooling inspired the gloomy and atmospheric opening chapters of Dickens' *Great Expectations*, wherein the protagonist Pip first meets the dangerous escaped convict Abel Magwitch.

CROWMARSH GIFFORD, OXFORDSHIRE
Jethro Tull's seed drill

The farmer and agricultural scientist Jethro Tull was born in Basildon in 1674. Following studies at St John's College, Oxford and a period travelling the continent, Tull returned to England to begin working on his father's farm in Oxfordshire shortly after his marriage in 1699. It was during this time, when he was living in the tiny village of Crowmarsh Gifford, that Tull invented the seed drill, a wheeled device designed to plant seeds in the soil at regular, specified intervals and depths. This, along with several other successful inventions and ideas which Tull conceived, would eventually help to launch England's agricultural revolution.

DEAL, KENT
Invasion of Perkin Warbeck

On 3 July 1495, the pretender to the English throne Perkin Warbeck landed at Deal on the Kent coast hoping to summon up support in England for his uncorroborated and somewhat dubious claim to the throne. Warbeck alleged that he was Richard of Shrewsbury, Duke of York and son of Edward IV, who had been one of the infamous 'Princes in the Tower', whose mysterious disappearance in 1483 had eventually led to the accession of Richard III. Having gained some considerable support for his tale in Europe, at Deal Warbeck found none and instead more than a hundred of his accompanying troops were reportedly slain by local forces before he even had the chance to disembark. Understandably, he fled immediately, heading first to Ireland and then on to Scotland, where support for his cause was somewhat easier to come by. After a second equally disastrous attempt to land in England in 1497 at Whitesand Bay near Land's End, however, Warbeck was captured and imprisoned by Henry VII, and eventually executed in London in 1499.

DOVER, KENT
'When Dover and Calais meet'

Something said to happen 'when Dover and Calais meet' will, proverbially, never happen at all.

Marriage of James II

Following the death of his first wife Anne Hyde (the mother of both Mary II and Queen Anne), James II married his second wife Mary of Modena at Dover in November 1673. Together, James and Mary had seven children, of whom five died in infancy; when James was deposed in the Glorious Revolution of 1688, the couple's son became recognised in France and Scotland as James III, the Jacobite pretender to the throne, following his father's death in 1701.

Arnold's 'Dover Beach'

'Dover Beach' is perhaps the most famous work by the poet and social critic Matthew Arnold, as well as one of the most popular short poems of the Victorian era. In it, Arnold addresses an anonymous companion (thought to be his wife, as Arnold spent his honeymoon in Dover in 1851), first describing a moonlit scene looking out over the English Channel to France, before going on to use the retreating tide as a metaphor for the decline of faith in society. Published in 1867, the poem was set to music by Samuel Barber in 1931, is mentioned in Joseph Heller's *Catch-22*, Ian McEwan's *Saturday* and Ray Bradbury's *Fahrenheit 451*, and furthermore inspired poems by both W. B. Yeats and US Poet Laureate Anthony Hecht.

Dover, Delaware

Dover shares its name with one of the longest-serving state capitals in the entire United States, founded in 1683 by William Penn, founder also of Pennsylvania, and made capital of Delaware in 1777. It is the state's second-largest city after Wilmington, yet with a population of just 36,000 it remains one of the smallest of all state capitals in the whole of the USA. Appropriately enough, like its namesake, the Delawarean Dover also stands in a county called Kent.

DUNGENESS, KENT
Vagrant gull spotted

Named after the French naturalist Jean Victoire Audouin, Audouin's gull is one of the rarest species of gull in the world – usually found around the coasts of the Mediterranean, Britain's first example of the species was sighted at Dungeness in 2003.

DUNSTABLE, BEDFORDSHIRE
'Downright Dunstable'

Anything or anyone said to be 'downright Dunstable', or 'as plain as the road to Dunstable', is simple, straightforward or straight-talking. The phrase alludes to a stretch of the Roman road Watling Street, extending from London to Dunstable in Bedfordshire, which is notoriously straight.

EAST COWES, ISLE OF WIGHT
Former royal residence, Osborne House

Osborne House in East Cowes on the Isle of Wight was purchased by Queen Victoria and Prince Albert in 1845. Following Albert's sudden death from typhoid in 1861, Victoria increasingly spent more time at the house right up until her own death there in 1901. Her eldest son and successor, Edward VII, did not share his parents' liking for the house, however, and donated it to the nation soon after becoming king.

EAST PECKHAM, KENT
Britain's first speeding ticket

On 28 January 1896, Walter Arnold of East Peckham near Tonbridge in Kent became the first motorist ever to be charged with speeding, having been caught driving at 8 miles per hour (12.8 kilometres per hour), far exceeding the then 2 miles per hour speed limit for towns. Arnold, who was fined one shilling, was caught by a policeman on a bicycle.

EGHAM, SURREY
The Founder's Building

Designed by William Henry Crossland, the impressive Founder's Building of London's Royal Holloway College was opened by Queen Victoria in 1886. Originally a women's college founded by the entrepreneur Thomas Holloway, Holloway College became part of the

University of London in 1900 and admitted its first male students in 1945.

EPPING, ESSEX
Prime Minister Winston Churchill's constituency

Sir Winston Leonard Spencer Churchill represented five different parliamentary constituencies during his political career, but was member of parliament for Epping (1924–45) during his first term as prime minister from 1940 to 1945. During his second term (1951–55), Churchill was MP for Woodford in Essex, a seat he held for nearly twenty years until 1964. He died on Sunday, 24 January 1965, exactly 70 years to the day after his father.

EPSOM, SURREY
The suffragette movement

Following decades of largely ineffectual political lobbying by different women's suffrage organisations, the activist Emmeline Pankhurst formed the Women's Social and Political Union in 1903. Renowned for using much more militant tactics in promoting their cause than ever before, over the years that followed various WSPU members chained themselves to railings, threw stones through the windows of Downing Street, planted bombs, set fire to buildings, and even slashed a painting in the National Gallery; when arrested, many, including Pankhurst herself, went on hunger strike. But in perhaps the most infamous of all of these demonstrations, on 4 June 1913 Emily Davison, wrapped in a WSPU banner, stepped out in front of George V's horse Anmer at the Epsom Derby – trampled and knocked unconscious, Davison died four days later of a fractured skull. Although the WSPU went on to cease activity following the outbreak of World War One, in 1918 all women in Britain over the age of 30 were given the right to vote.

ETON, BERKSHIRE
Eton mess

Named after Eton College in Windsor where it is said to have been first served, Eton mess is a dessert of whipped cream mixed with chunks of meringue and strawberries, although bananas and other soft fruits are also often used. The original dish, comprised just of strawberries and cream, dates from the nineteenth century.

FARNBOROUGH, HAMPSHIRE
The Great Storm

Perhaps the most infamous weather-related disaster of recent times, the Great Storm of 1987 saw an extraordinarily powerful low-pressure system travel upwards from the Bay of Biscay towards the southern half of the British Isles, bringing with it extreme conditions and hurricane-force winds – in the UK alone, the disaster claimed 18 lives. Throughout, winds regularly remained above 70–80 knots (130–148 kilometres per hour/80–92 miles per hour) for hours on end, whilst a single record-breaking gust of 106 knots (196 kilometres per hour/122 miles per hour) was recorded on the Norfolk coast; yet of all of the extremes recorded during the storm, an incredible rise in temperature from 8.5 °C (47 °F) to 17.6 °C (64 °F) in just 20 minutes, recorded at Farnborough in Hampshire, is perhaps one of the most staggering.

Britain's first powered flight

On 16 October 1908, the aviator Samuel Cody is credited with having completed the first powered flight on British soil. Cody, who had earlier toured America as a Wild West showman, began his career in aviation by designing kites in the early 1900s, exhibiting a collection at London's Alexandra Palace in 1903. Soon afterwards, he began designing aircraft for the military, beginning with gliders and dirigibles before moving on to aeroplanes in 1907. The following year, his British Army Aeroplane 1, a motorised biplane known as the *Cody 1*, flew almost 425 metres (1,400 feet) at Farnborough in Hampshire, thereby completing Britain's first powered flight.

FARNCOMBE, SURREY
Titanic victim Jack Philips

Born in Farncombe in 1887, John 'Jack' Philips was one of two telegraphists on board the *Titanic* and, as such, was responsible for transmitting the ship's distress signals. When the ship's fate became apparent, both Philips and his assistant Harold Bride were officially released from their duties by the ship's captain and, despite separating as they fled, are thought to have ended up on the same lifeboat. Philips, however, who had celebrated his twenty-fifth birthday on the second day of the *Titanic*'s voyage, died of hypothermia before being rescued.

FARNHAM, SURREY
Gladiator film set

The thrilling opening battle sequence of Ridley Scott's acclaimed epic *Gladiator* (2000) saw Bourne Woods outside of Farnham in Surrey transformed – for three weeks' filming at least – into Ancient Germania. The film went on to be nominated for more than a hundred major cinematic awards worldwide, picking up the 2000 Best Picture and Best Actor Oscars along the way.

FORD END, ESSEX
Parish of writer Arthur Shearly Cripps

Born in Tunbridge Wells in 1869, Arthur Shearly Cripps studied at Charterhouse School and Trinity College, Oxford before being ordained as a priest in 1893 and beginning his service as rector of the parish of Ford End in Essex the following year. From 1900 onwards, however, Cripps spent much of his life as a missionary in Africa, returning for only a short period to his old parish at Ford End in 1926, before retiring to Africa in 1930, where he remained until his death in 1952. As well as writing numerous poems and essays – including the treatise *Africa for Africans* (1927) – today Cripps is perhaps best known as a prolific short story writer, with many of his most famous and popular works comprising the collection *Cinderella in the South: South African Tales*, published in 1918.

THE GOODWIN SANDS, KENT
The Merchant of Venice (III.i)

Aptly described in Shakespeare's *Merchant of Venice* as 'fatal, where the carcasses of many a tall ship lie buried', the 16-kilometre (10-mile) Goodwin Sands off the coast of Kent, at the entrance to the Strait of Dover, is one of Britain's – and indeed the world's – most treacherous sandbanks. The many hundreds of ships lost to the sands over the years have included the transatlantic liner SS *Montrose*; the

MV *Ross Revenge*, once famously home to Radio Caroline; and over fifty military craft lost in one night during the Great Storm of 1703. Nevertheless, despite the danger, an annual cricket match was traditionally held on the sands for more than 150 years until 2003.

GOSPORT, HAMPSHIRE
Hawkey vs Seton

What is believed to be one of the last fatal duels ever fought on English soil (and almost certainly the last fought between two Englishmen) took place between Lieutenant Henry Charles Hawkey and Captain Alexander Seton in 1845. Earlier, Hawkey had confronted Seton over his burgeoning relationship with his wife, whom Seton had secretly been pursuing whilst Hawkey was away on duties. Infuriated, he challenged Seton to a duel and, on 20 May 1845, the men met in Gosport. Whilst an initial shot proved inconclusive – Seton missed his target whilst Hawkey's gun misfired – both men fired a second time; Seton again failed to hit, but in return Hawkey shot him in the hip, and he died from the injury several days later.

GREAT DUNMOW, ESSEX
'To eat Dunmow bacon'

The unusual phrase 'to eat Dunmow bacon' means to be happily married, and derives from an unusual centuries-old custom in which anyone coming to the village of Great Dunmow in Essex that could truthfully swear an oath claiming not to have 'had a household brawl or wished himself unmarried' in the last year would be awarded with a side of bacon.

HAMBLEDEN, BUCKINGHAMSHIRE
Sleepy Hollow film set

When existing towns suitable for filming Tim Burton's acclaimed 1999 adaptation of Washington Irving's folk tale *The Legend of Sleepy Hollow* could not be found in the USA, production switched to England where an entire replica village was constructed around a duck pond at Hambleden in rural Buckinghamshire. The production design team went on to win an Oscar for their work on the film.

HAMPTON-ON-SEA, KENT
Lost to the sea

The north Kent village of Hampton-on-Sea thrived in the mid nineteenth century at the hands of a local oyster-dredging company that invested thousands of pounds in developing the town as a base for its employees. However, construction of a pier as part of the village's development in 1865 inadvertently disrupted the strong sea currents which naturally flowed along the shore at Hampton, breaking them up to create a series of powerful eddies which consequently began to erode the shoreline. Within a matter of decades, land was being lost to the sea at an astonishing rate of 2 metres (6.5 feet) per year, and the town was finally abandoned in the 1910s.

HARWICH, ESSEX
The Great Storm

The Great Storm of 1703 remains, in terms of fatalities, the worst on record for the British Isles, with estimates at the number of lives lost during the storm – in which hurricane-force winds blew across southern England

and the English Channel for over a week from 24 November to 2 December – ranging from 8,000 to 15,000. Amongst the hundreds of buildings that were damaged or destroyed by the storm were Westminster Abbey, which lost most of its lead roof, and the original lighthouse at Devon's Eddystone Rocks, which collapsed, killing the six men inside. Most of the fatalities, however, were at sea – dozens of ships returning from conflict in the War of the Spanish Succession were wrecked in the Channel, and in total the Royal Navy lost 13 vessels, taking more than 1,500 lives with them. One of the most remarkable reports, however, is that of the navy's HMS *Association*, which, having been moored at Harwich in Essex, was blown right across the North Sea to Gothenburg in Sweden.

HASLEMERE, SURREY
Oscar-winner Rachel Portman

Born in Haslemere, Surrey, in 1960, the composer Rachel Portman became the first woman ever to win the Oscar for Best Original Score for her work on Douglas McGrath's acclaimed adaptation of *Emma* in 1996.

She has since been nominated a further two times, for *The Cider House Rules* (1999) and *Chocolat* (2000).

HATFIELD, HERTFORDSHIRE
Death of Edmund, son of Henry VII

Having taken the throne from Richard III at the Battle of Bosworth Field in 1485, the following year Henry VII married his consort Elizabeth of York at Westminster. Together, the couple had seven children, amongst them Henry Tudor, later Henry VIII, and his elder brother Arthur, Prince of Wales. Tragically, Arthur died in 1502 aged just 15, whilst another three of Henry and Elizabeth's children died in infancy – Edmund, Duke of Somerset, died at Hatfield in Hertfordshire in 1500, aged just 16 months. He was buried at Westminster Abbey.

The Queen Elizabeth Oak

Built in the late fifteenth century, Henry VIII's Royal Palace of Hatfield – some of which still stands in the grounds of Hatfield House today – was the childhood residence of Elizabeth I. On 17

November 1558, the 25-year-old Lady Elizabeth Tudor was sat beneath an oak tree in the palace's gardens when she received word that, following the death of her elder sister Mary, she had now acceded to the throne and was henceforth queen of England. The tree, now appropriately known as the Queen Elizabeth Oak, still stands in the centre of the gardens at Hatfield House, and can also be found on the Hatfield coat of arms.

HENLEY-ON-THAMES, OXFORDSHIRE
The Oxford-Cambridge Boat Race

The University Boat Race between Oxford and Cambridge has been held since 1829, and once every year, with the exception of during the two world wars, since 1856. Although today the race takes place over a 4-mile, 374-yard (6,779-metre) length of the River Thames, westwards from Putney Bridge to the finish line at Mortlake, the first race was in fact held at Henley-on-Thames in south Oxfordshire. The current course was first used in 1845.

HIGH WYCOMBE, BUCKINGHAMSHIRE
The Beast of Bucks

In 2001, a set of paw prints found on a golf course in Loudwater in High Wycombe was confirmed by experts to be those of a young puma. Since then, a number of sightings of the creature, dubbed the 'Beast of Bucks', have been reported in and around the Wycombe area, including one in January 2006 when the feline was spotted in the grounds of the Chequers Estate.

HITCHIN, HERTFORDSHIRE
Birth of the Queen Mother

Several members of the extended British royal family were born in 1900. Amongst them were five of Queen Victoria's 87 great-grandchildren, including Prince Henry, Duke of Gloucester, the third son of George V and an uncle of Elizabeth II, born at Sandringham on 31 March, and Louis Mountbatten, 1st Earl Mountbatten of Burma and an uncle of Prince Philip, the Duke of Edinburgh, born at Frogmore House in Windsor on 25 June. Perhaps the most significant royal birth of 1900, however, was that of Elizabeth Bowes-Lyon, consort of George VI, who took the title of Queen Mother on the accession of her daughter, Elizabeth, in 1952. Born on 4 August, the exact location of the Queen Mother's birthplace is uncertain, but nonetheless her birth was later registered as Hitchin, Hertfordshire. One of the most popular and respected members of the royal family in recent years, she died in 2002 at the age of 101.

HORSHAM, WEST SUSSEX
The Rising Universe

Known locally as 'Shelley's Fountain', Horsham's *Rising Universe* is a massive spherical sculpture in the town centre, intended as a memorial to the English poet Percy Bysshe Shelley, who was born nearby in 1792. Designed by the artist Angela Conner, the sculpture is essentially a massive water feature, comprising a large concrete globe, over which water cascades, standing atop a pillar in the centre of a pool. Unveiled to commemorate the bicentenary of his birth, the piece is inspired by Shelley's poem 'Mont Blanc'

(1817) – 'The everlasting universe of things/Flows through the mind, and rolls its rapid waves'.

ISLE OF WIGHT
French invasion and the Siege of Carisbrooke

During the course of the Hundred Years' War (1337–1453), French forces carried out dozens of raids against England, although few – if any – could be classed as full-scale invasions. At the height of the conflict, however, in 1377 the French, under the command of the powerful Admiral of France Jean de Vienne, launched a series of devastating attacks on ports along the English Channel which crippled the English Navy and allowed for a subsequent and much more invasive attack on the Isle of Wight. De Vienne and his forces entered the Solent in late August, and soon landed on the north-west coast of the island, seizing town after town en route to the island's stronghold, Carisbrooke Castle. The castle, however, remained impenetrable to the invading force and after a brutal siege lasting several frustrating weeks, de Vienne and his men eventually abandoned the island.

ISLIP, OXFORDSHIRE
Birthplace of Edward the Confessor

The penultimate English monarch ahead of the Norman Conquest, Edward the Confessor was born in the village of Islip in Oxfordshire in *c.* 1004, the first child born of Æthelred the Unready's second marriage to Emma of Normandy. Edward's own marriage to Edith of Wessex, from 1045 until his death in January 1066, produced no children and consequently led to a dispute over who should succeed him. Eventually, it was decided that Harold Godwinson, Earl of Wessex, should be Edward's replacement, yet his reign lasted just nine months until his death at the Battle of Hastings.

KEMPSTON, BEDFORDSHIRE
Devastating Home Counties tornado

On 21 May 1950, a massive thunderstorm and tornado caused chaos throughout the north of London, Bedfordshire, Buckinghamshire, Cambridgeshire and the Fens. The tornado, which touched down near Linslade in Buckinghamshire, left a 107-kilometre (66-mile) path of destruction right across the south-east of England to the Cambridgeshire village of Coveney; in Kempston, near Bedford, the storm claimed its only two fatalities when two men were struck by lightning whilst trying to find shelter.

KINGS LANGLEY, HERTFORDSHIRE
Former royal residence, Kings Langley Palace

Situated on the outskirts of the historic village of Kings Langley near St Albans, Kings Langley Palace in Hertfordshire was a major royal house of the Plantagenets, built by Eleanor of Castile in the thirteenth century. All but destroyed by fire in 1431, the only original building still standing is that of a Dominican friary, established by Edward II in 1308, which today stands in the grounds of a private school opened on the site in 1949.

LANGSTONE, HAMPSHIRE
The Langstone longboat

A longboat dating from some 1,500 years ago was discovered

protruding from mudflats in Langstone Harbour between Portsmouth and Chichester in 2002. Two years later, an ancient stone carved head, around 13 centimetres (5 inches) in length and thought to be over 20,000 years old, was found in the same harbour, and is perhaps the oldest such artefact ever found in Britain.

LEDBURN, BUCKINGHAMSHIRE
The Great Train Robbery

Bridgego Bridge in the tiny hamlet of Ledburn in Buckinghamshire was, on 8 August 1963, the location of the Great Train Robbery. A sum of £2.6 million in used bank notes was stolen in the incident, in which a post office mail train travelling from Glasgow to London's Euston Station was stopped by a rigged signal and hijacked by a gang of 15 men. Having uncoupled one of the train's carriages, the men ordered its driver to continue on to Bridgego Bridge where 120 sacks of cash were dropped down to cars waiting below. In the huge police search that ensued, the gang's hideout at nearby Leatherslade Farm was discovered and several of the gang's members were caught

and sentenced to a total of 300 years in prison between them. Bruce Reynolds, a known burglar who had masterminded the robbery, was caught after five years on the run in 1968 and sentenced to ten years, whilst Ronnie Biggs (whose birthday was 8 August) escaped from Wandsworth jail in 1965 just 15 months into his sentence and fled the country. Aged 71, and after having spent some 35 years in Brazil, Biggs voluntarily returned to the UK and was imprisoned in 2001.

LEIGHTON BUZZARD, BEDFORDSHIRE
The Wilkes Walk

Each Rogationtide – 25 April and the three days before Ascension Thursday in the Christian calendar – a procession of the local clergy and choristers sets out from All Saints Church in Leighton Buzzard heading across town to the local almshouses. Held in memory of Edward Wilkes, who founded and financed the houses in the mid 1600s, at the end of the so-called 'Wilkes Walk' a section of Edward's will is read aloud whilst, at the unusual request of Edward's son Matthew, one of the church's choristers is held upside-down, presumably in an attempt to make his father's words more memorable to the town's residents.

LEWES, EAST SUSSEX
Devastating avalanche

The winter of 1836–37 was particularly severe in the UK, with relentless heavy snowfall and gale force winds reportedly affecting vast areas of the country. In Lewes, the wintry conditions led to perhaps the deadliest avalanche ever recorded in Britain when, on 27 December 1836, a vast overhanging cornice of snow on a clifftop overlooking the town collapsed onto a row of cottages below, killing eight people.

LONG CRENDON, BUCKINGHAMSHIRE
Death of Ruth Pitter

Born in Ilford in 1897, the English poet and writer Ruth Pitter died at her home in Long Crendon near Aylesbury on 29 February 1992. During her lifetime, Pitter was a popular and well-known poet, often appearing on television and radio arts programmes. A close friend of C. S. Lewis, she published nearly twenty volumes of verse over a career of 70 years, and received the Queen's Gold Medal for Poetry in 1955, becoming the first woman ever to do so. Her works *A Trophy of Arms* (1936) and *The Ermine* (1953) both won literary awards, and in 1979 she was awarded a CBE for her contribution to English literature.

LUTON, BEDFORDSHIRE
Joe Payne and his ten-goal game

Kenilworth Road Stadium has been home to Luton Town FC since 1905 and was, on Easter Monday 1936, the site of a league match between Luton and Bristol Rovers in which Joe Payne scored ten goals in a single match, with the home side going on to win 12–0. Remarkably, Payne was just 22 at the time, had never played as centre forward before, and was a last-minute addition to the starting line-up due to two of Luton's strikers being injured.

MALDON, ESSEX
The Battle of Maldon

Although the Battle of Maldon took place between East

Saxons and Viking raiders in August 991, a celebrated poem commemorating the skirmish is estimated to have been written in *c.* 1000, and is today considered amongst the most significant examples of Anglo-Saxon verse dating from the time. Tragically, the original manuscript was all but destroyed in a fire at Westminster's Ashburnham House in 1731, yet even this original copy contained just 325 lines of what must have once been a considerably longer work. Most of what is known of the poem today comes from a translation of 1724, whilst precisely who wrote the poem and where will almost assuredly never be known.

MARLOW, BUCKINGHAMSHIRE
British Olympian Steve Redgrave

Hailed as Britain's greatest Olympian, Sir Steve Redgrave was born in Marlow in Buckinghamshire in 1962. Having won his first gold medal in the coxed four rowing class at the 1984 Los Angeles Games, Redgrave took bronze at the 1988

Seoul Games before winning gold at every Summer Olympics until 2000, the year he also won BBC Sports Personality of the Year. Awarded an MBE in 1987 and a CBE in 1997, he was knighted in 2001.

MIDDLESEX
Middlesex, Belize

Middlesex shares its name with that of a village in the Central American country and former British colony of Belize, situated roughly 40 kilometres (25 miles) south-east of the national capital, Belmopan. The village lies just south of the Sibun Forest Reserve, one of the country's largest nature reserves.

MIDGHAM, BERKSHIRE
Rare Beatles album auctioned

A rare early vinyl copy of The Beatles' 1968 self-titled album, also known as *The White Album*, was sold at auction in Midgham, Berkshire, for £5,600 in March 2008. The vinyl, numbered 0000007, was bought by an anonymous telephone bidder in Chicago.

MIDHURST, WEST SUSSEX
WOTTON UNDERWOOD, BUCKINGHAMSHIRE
Deaths of Alec Guinness and John Gielgud

The year 2000 saw the deaths of two of Britain's greatest ever actors, namely Sir Alec Guinness and Sir John Gielgud. Born in London in 1914, Alec Guinness' career spanned seven decades, during which time he was nominated for five Oscars (winning Best Actor for *The Bridge on the River Kwai* in 1957), received a knighthood in 1959, and in the late 1970s gained a whole new generation of fans thanks to his role in the original *Star Wars* trilogy. He died aged 86 in Midhurst, on 5 August 2000.

Described by his biographer Sheridan Morley as 'the best actor of all time', John Gielgud died at his home in the village of Wotton Underwood near Aylesbury on 21 May 2000, aged 96. Knighted in 1953, Gielgud played every male Shakespearean lead role throughout a 70-year career that also saw London's Globe Theatre renamed in his honour. Almost as prolific on film as he was on the stage, he remains one of only a handful of performers – and the only Briton – ever to have won an Oscar, Emmy, Tony and Grammy Award.

MILTON KEYNES, BUCKINGHAMSHIRE
Extraordinary Harry Potter pre-orders

Staff at the main distribution centre of the online retailer Amazon in Milton Keynes were required to work through the night on 8 July 2000 in order to meet unprecedented demand for *The Goblet of Fire*, the latest of J. K. Rowling's *Harry Potter* series of books. Some 400,000 copies, almost one-third of the book's initial UK print run, had been pre-ordered through the website, leaving Amazon the unenviable task of delivering a staggering 53 tonnes of books to UK households on its day of release.

NEWENDEN, KENT
Edward II's game of 'creag'

On 10 March 1300, Edward, youngest son of Edward I and the future King Edward II, is recorded as playing a game called *creag* at

Newenden in Kent with his long-time friend and companion Piers Gaveston, later Earl of Cornwall. It is thought, albeit uncertainly, that this game of *creag* was the earliest known mention of what would eventually become modern-day cricket, and if this assumption is true then this game was the earliest recorded game of cricket in history.

THE NEW FOREST, HAMPSHIRE
National park

The New Forest National Park is one of the most recently established in Britain, opened in March 2005 as England's first official national park for more than fifty years. It is also one of the smallest, at just 570 square kilometres (220 square miles), yet is home to a remarkable diversity of animals and plants, including all native British reptile species, six different kinds of deer, all three British species of newt, and even its own unique species of cicada beetle, discovered in 1912.

Stronghold of Britain's reptiles

The New Forest is one of only a handful of places in the British Isles where all of Britain's native terrestrial reptile species – the adder, grass snake, smooth snake, slow worm, common lizard and sand lizard – can be found in the wild. As such, it is an invaluable area in terms of conservation as all of these species are listed as either vulnerable or endangered. The sand lizard in particular is Britain's rarest reptile, with its population having drastically declined in recent years due to extensive habitat loss. A successful scheme to reintroduce the lizard to the sandy heathlands of the New Forest began in 1989, and the site has since become one of the creature's most important strongholds.

NEWHAVEN, EAST SUSSEX
Disappearance of Lord Lucan

On the evening of 7 November 1974, Veronica, the wife of Richard John Bingham, 7th Earl of Lucan, ran into a pub near their London home with several serious head wounds, claiming that she had just fled from an attacker in her home who had killed the family's nanny. When police arrived at the house, they found the front door locked and the back door open, a bloodied length of lead piping lying on the hallway floor and, in a room at the back of the house, a blood-stained sack containing the body of the Lucans' nanny, Sandra Rivett, who had apparently been beaten to death; the family's three young children, meanwhile, remained unharmed in their bedrooms upstairs. Although a man's footprints could be seen in a pool of blood on the floor, there was no sign of Lord Lucan, and Lady Lucan soon named her husband as both her attacker and the murderer. Three days later, his abandoned Ford Corsair – reportedly containing traces of two types of blood and a length of pipe similar to that found at the house – was discovered at Newhaven on the Sussex coast. Despite several unconfirmed sightings in destinations as diverse as Ireland, the Netherlands, South Africa and Australia, Lucan has never been seen since. He was officially declared dead in 1999.

NEWPORT, ISLE OF WIGHT
Henry Sewell, first premier of New Zealand

Born on the Isle of Wight in 1807, Henry Sewell emigrated

to New Zealand following several personal upsets in his life in Britain, and arrived at Christchurch in 1853. Having been instrumental in the success of the British-run Canterbury Company, which promoted colonisation of the New Zealand territory of Canterbury, Sewell was elected to the inaugural New Zealand Parliament in May 1854 as MP for Christchurch, and became the country's first premier (the precursor to prime minister) on the position's creation two years later. However, like many premierships in the early days of the parliament, Sewell's term was startlingly short, lasting only 13 days, and indeed remains the shortest in the country's history.

OTTERSHAW, SURREY
H. G. Wells' War of the Worlds

Amongst the last and perhaps most well known of H. G. Wells' works, *The War of the Worlds* is set in various locations throughout England in the early twentieth century. At the beginning of the novel, an unnamed narrator and protagonist is asked by a noted astronomer, Ogilvy, to visit his observatory at Ottershaw in Surrey, to 'take a turn with him... in scrutiny of the red planet'. Whilst there, the narrator witnesses a 'jetting out of gas from the distant planet... A reddish flash at the edge, the slightest projection of the outline', which turns out to be one of numerous Martian spacecraft setting off on their way towards Earth.

OXFORD, OXFORDSHIRE
Stephen Hawking and Jacqueline du Pré

Born in Oxford just three years apart, Stephen Hawking and Jacqueline du Pré both went on to achieve worldwide recognition – Hawking, born in 1942, remains one of the most highly respected scientists of recent times, whilst du Pré, born in 1945, became known as a world-class cellist in a career tragically curtailed by multiple sclerosis. She died aged just 42 in 1987.

Early performance of Hamlet

Although much of William Shakespeare's life is largely unknown (including the dates of many of his plays), by 1600 it is believed that he had been based in

London for a little under a decade, and had already completed some of his most well-known and popular works, including *Richard III*, *Romeo and Juliet*, *The Merchant of Venice*, and *A Midsummer Night's Dream*. From 1600 onwards, many of his works received their earliest performances at Southwark's Globe Theatre, which had opened the previous year, but is it possible that one of the first performances of his masterpiece *Hamlet* took place at Oxford University in 1600, prior to a later performance at The Globe the following year.

Former royal residence, Beaumont Palace

No longer standing today, Beaumont Palace in Oxford was built by Henry I in the early twelfth century and remained a royal residence until 1318 when it was granted to the Carmelites by Edward II for use as a friary. Following the dissolution of the monasteries under Henry VIII, Beaumont was dismantled, its stones being used in the construction of Oxford's Christ Church and St John's Colleges in the mid 1500s.

Orlando Gibbons' baptism

Although the exact date of his birth is unknown, the composer Orlando Gibbons was baptised at St Martin's Church, Oxford, on Christmas Day 1583. Born into a musical family, Gibbons studied music at King's College, Cambridge (where he was also a chorister) before moving to London in the early 1600s as organist of the Chapel Royal and later Westminster Abbey. A favourite musician of James I, he played at the king's funeral in 1625 just months before his own sudden death at Canterbury aged just 41. Despite his relatively short life, Gibbons' diverse body of work – including madrigals and other choral pieces, several fantasias for viol, and some of the most complex keyboard work of his time – is today considered that of one of the most significant and popular of all early English composers.

Rare signed books auctioned

A charity book auction in Oxford raised £20,000 for Oxfam in June 2009. Amongst the most remarkable lots sold were a signed first edition of Jack Kerouac's On The Road, a signed first edition of Sebastian Faulks' Birdsong, and a copy of The History of the Second World War uniquely signed by Winston Churchill.

Lewis Carroll's early religious studies

Born Charles Lutwidge Dodgson in Daresbury, Cheshire, in 1832, the author Lewis Carroll began studying at Christ Church College, Oxford in 1851, gaining a first class degree in mathematics three years later. Dodgson stayed on at Christ Church as a senior student and mathematics lecturer from 1855, during which time, in 1861, four years before the publication of Alice's Adventures In Wonderland, he was ordained as a deacon. Going against what was expected of senior students of the college at the time, however, Dodgson opted not to continue into the clergy (likely owing in part to his stammer) and was never fully ordained as a priest.

Nobel Laureate Sir John Hicks

Born in Warwick in 1904, Sir John Richard Hicks studied at Oxford

University before a lifelong academic career led to teaching positions at the London School of Economics and both Cambridge and Manchester universities. Hicks returned to Oxford, however, in 1946 as a fellow of Nuffield College, and received a knighthood whilst professor of political economy there in 1964. As a research fellow at All Souls' College, he became the first British winner of the Nobel Prize in Economics in 1972, sharing the award with the American academic Kenneth Arrow. Other Oxford University Nobel Laureates include biochemist and anti-nuclear campaigner Linus Pauling (Chemistry, 1954; Peace, 1962), theoretical physicist Erwin Schrödinger (Physics, 1933), animal behaviourist Nikolaas Tinbergen (Medicine, 1973), and Oxford graduates John Galsworthy (Literature, 1932), T. S. Eliot (Literature, 1948), William Golding (Literature, 1983) and Aung San Suu Kyi (Peace, 1991).

Bacon's early optical research

Perhaps the most significant English thinker of his time, Roger Bacon was born in Ilchester, Somerset, sometime around 1214. Educated at both Oxford and Paris, Bacon became a Franciscan friar before taking up a teaching position back at Oxford, and it was here that he began carrying out a series of groundbreaking experiments into all manner of subjects, including, most notably, optics – indeed, Bacon is considered one of the first scientists to propose the use of corrective lenses to mend problems of vision. Instructed to report all of his findings to the Vatican, Bacon sent his *Opus Majus*, an epic seven-part discussion of all of his work, to Pope Clement IV in *c.* 1267.

Eustreptospondylus dinosaur discovered

Eustreptospondylus, a name meaning 'well-curved vertebra', was amongst the earliest of all dinosaurs discovered in Britain, unearthed in a brick pit near Oxford in 1871. *Eustreptospondylus* was carnivorous, stood around 2 metres (6.5 feet) tall, and lived during the Middle Jurassic period, roughly 160 million years ago.

Oxford, Ohio

More than twenty US states are home to towns and cities named Oxford, of which the largest by far is in Ohio, whose Oxford – like its UK namesake – is a successful university city, built up around the campus of the misleadingly named University of Miami, alma mater of former US President Benjamin Harrison. Other famous Oxfords across the United States include those in North Carolina, home to the world's largest cosmetics factory; in Connecticut, which made headlines in 2001 when a 94-year-old resident inexplicably died of anthrax poisoning; and in Georgia, whose college, part of the state's Emory University, was the location of the final famous jump by the 'General Lee' in the title sequence of the television series *The Dukes of Hazzard*.

PEMBURY, KENT
British Olympian Dame Kelly Holmes

Born in Pembury in 1970, Kelly Holmes spent several years in the army before turning to athletics and winning her first Olympic medal in 2000, taking bronze in the women's 800 metres at Sydney. Four years later, at Athens, she put a career dogged by injury behind her to become only the third female runner in Olympic history to win both the 800 metres and the 1,500 metres at the same games. Her two Olympic golds were matched by a damehood awarded in the 2005 New Year Honours.

PEVENSEY, EAST SUSSEX
Invasion of William of Normandy

Although nearby Hastings is by far the location most closely associated with the Norman Conquest, it was actually at Pevensey on the Sussex coast that William the Conqueror – then just William, Duke of Normandy – first landed in England on 28 September 1066. He arrived with the intention of taking the crown from Harold Godwinson, who had succeeded Edward the Confessor as king on his death in January; William had been Edward's cousin and, according to some sources, had been promised the throne by Edward in the event of his death, so when Harold was instead proclaimed king – with the full backing of the Witenagemot, the highest assembly of English nobles at the time – William saw an English invasion as his only recourse. The two rivals met in battle near Hastings on 14 October, where after more than nine hours of fighting William overcame Harold's exhausted army (who were still recovering from the Battle of Stamford Bridge, barely three weeks earlier) and Harold was killed, popularly believed to have been struck by an arrow in his eye. William was ultimately free to take the throne.

PORTSMOUTH, HAMPSHIRE
Brunel and Dickens

Remarkably, Portsmouth can claim to be the birthplace of two of the most celebrated Britons ever to have lived – the engineer Isambard Kingdom Brunel was born there in 1806, whilst just six years later in 1812 Charles Dickens was born in the city's Landport district.

Marriage of Charles II

Following the restoration of the Portuguese monarchy in the mid 1600s, a new-found British-Portuguese alliance was cemented by the marriage of Catarina Henriqueta, the second surviving daughter of John IV of Portugal, to the British King Charles II. Married by proxy in Lisbon in April 1662, Catarina, known as Catherine of Braganza, arrived at Portsmouth the following month and wed Charles in two separate ceremonies, the first a secret Catholic ceremony, the second an Anglican ceremony at Portsmouth's thirteenth-century Domus Dei, now the Royal Garrison Church.

Assassination of the Duke of Buckingham

A close friend of James I – and, according to some, his lover – George Villiers, 1st Duke of Buckingham, was stabbed and killed in Portsmouth by a man named John Felton on 23 August 1628. A year earlier, Felton had been wounded in a disastrous military venture led by Buckingham at La Rochelle in France, which had seen the loss of 4,000 lives.

Aspex Gallery

Aspex in Portsmouth is the city's largest contemporary art gallery, and has been based in the Vulcan Building – a nineteenth-century former naval storehouse on the city's quayside – since 2006. The regeneration of the building took over two years to complete, and it was awarded a RIBA regional award in 2007.

James Lind's experimental voyage

When HMS *Salisbury* set sail from Portsmouth on a defensive tour of English waters in March 1747, on board was the Scottish naval physician James Lind, the ship's surgeon. In the course of the voyage, Lind administered several substances to the crew – amongst them garlic, citrus fruit, vinegar and even seawater – which he believed would be effective in preventing scurvy. Having cleverly given a different treatment to separate groups of the crew, Lind could compare the relative effectiveness of each of the treatments, rightly noting that those crewmembers given citrus were best protected against the condition. Although not the first scientist to propose the benefits of citrus fruit, Lind's experiment on board HMS *Salisbury* is

nonetheless considered the first strictly observed clinical trial of its type in medical history.

Portsmouth, Dominica

Portsmouth shares its name with the second-largest town and former capital of the island of Dominica in the Windward Islands of the eastern Caribbean. The island's current capital, Roseau, replaced Portsmouth in 1760 following a devastating outbreak of malaria in the town.

QUEENBOROUGH, KENT
Philippa of Hainault

The town of Queenborough on Kent's Isle of Sheppey flourished in the mid fourteenth century at the design of Edward III, who wanted the town to become a defensive port protecting English ships sailing up the River Swale at the height of the Hundred Years' War. Edward chose to name the town, which was granted its royal charter in 1368, after his wife, Philippa of Hainault, whom he had married in 1328. The couple were together for over forty years until Philippa's death in 1369.

READING, BERKSHIRE
Wilde's 'Ballad of Reading Gaol'

In 1895, Oscar Wilde was convicted of homosexual offences (classed as 'gross indecency' in Victorian law) and sentenced to two years' hard labour in Reading Prison. Following his release, he left England for France, where he went on to write one of his best known and most celebrated works, *The Ballad of Reading Gaol*, in 1898. The poem – published anonymously under his prisoner identification number C33 – was inspired by and dedicated to one of Wilde's fellow inmates, Charles Thomas Wooldridge, who was hanged in 1896 for the murder of his wife; the poem features the famous line, 'Yet each man kills the thing he loves'.

The Maiwand Lion memorial

Reading's Grade II listed Maiwand Lion commemorates the Battle of Maiwand of 1880, and is a memorial to the 329 men from the 66th Berkshire Regiment who lost their lives during the Second Anglo-Afghan War; the names of all of those killed in the conflict are inscribed on the plinth beneath, along with a short inscription stating 'History does not afford any grander or finer instance of gallantry... than that displayed by the LXVI Regiment at the Battle of Maiwand.' The lion, which is made of cast iron and weighs around 16 tonnes, stands in Reading's Forbury Gardens and was erected in 1886. In more recent years, it has become something of an unofficial emblem of the town, and today features on the local football team's crest and on the masthead of the *Reading Post*.

Football mascot sent off

During a match at Reading's Madejski Stadium on 30 April 2007, Kingsley Royal, a 2.5-metre (8-foot) tall smiling lion, the mascot for Reading FC, was sent off by referee Mike Riley for looking too much like a Reading player, considered a potential source of confusion for Reading's opponents, Newcastle United. Reading went on to win 1–0.

RICHBOROUGH, KENT
Roman invasion of Britain

Following on from Julius Caesar's somewhat diplomatic forays into

Britain in 55–54 BC (as well as a later disastrous invasion overseen by the insane Emperor Caligula), the first truly successful Roman invasion of Britain took place during the reign of Emperor Claudius in AD 43. Under the pretext of going to the aid of the Atrebates – a Celtic British tribe allied with Rome who had recently been conquered by the neighbouring Catuvellauni tribe – Claudius ordered his general Aulus Plautius to take command of four legions of men and launch an invasion on Britain. Plautius and his forces most likely landed at Richborough (Roman Rutupiae) on the Kent coast, but were faced with widespread resistance from the offset, largely led by the British chieftain Caractacus, leader of the Catuvellauni. The ensuing unrest eventually compelled Emperor Claudius himself to travel to Britain – along with some 38 war elephants – and soon much of the resistance was quashed, allowing Claudius to return home to Rome a hero, and a Roman capital to be established at Camulodunum (Colchester).

ROCHESTER, KENT
Viking raids

Having earlier held off an attack by Danish invaders in 884, in 999 Rochester was the site of one of the last Viking raids of the tenth century, as once again Danish forces sailed up the River Medway and attacked the town. In 1000, the Vikings who had been raiding the south coast of England moved on to Normandy, and did not return to England until the following year.

RUNNYMEDE, BERKSHIRE
The Ankerwyke Yew

The Ankerwyke Yew is possibly one of the most important trees in the entire history of Britain, as it is thought that it was here, near Ankerwyke Abbey in 1215, that King John was taken to sign the Magna Carta; it is also believed that the tree often served as a meeting place for Henry VIII and Anne Boleyn in the 1530s. In any case, it is now known the tree was already well over 1,000 years old by the time of King John, and has since grown to a circumference of over 9 metres (30 feet).

RYDE, ISLE OF WIGHT

Remarkable waterspout recorded

An astonishing mile-high waterspout – essentially a tornado formed at sea – thought to be the largest ever recorded in Britain appeared at midday on 21 August 1878, roughly 3.5 kilometres (2.2 miles) offshore from Ryde on the Isle of Wight. The waterspout was measured by sextant to be over a mile (1,600 metres) in height, and approximately 100 yards (90 metres) in diameter.

SEVENOAKS, KENT

Death of John Morton, Archbishop of Canterbury

Born in Dorset *c.* 1420, throughout his life John Morton held several important posts in Tudor England, being made Archbishop of Canterbury (1486) and Lord Chancellor (1487) by Henry VII and appointed Chancellor of Oxford University in 1494. He held all three posts until his death in 1500 at Knole House in Sevenoaks, Kent.

SLOUGH, BERKSHIRE

Herschel discovers infrared

In 1800, the acclaimed astronomer and scientist William Herschel discovered what we now know as infrared radiation at Observation House, his home in Slough. On 11 February, whilst experimenting with different coloured glass filters so that he could observe sunspots through his telescope, Herschel noted that certain colours appeared to let through more of the sun's heat than others. With this in mind, he shone sunlight through a prism to create a spectrum, used thermometers to record the temperature of the different colours and, to his surprise, recorded a higher temperature just outside of the spectrum, beside the red light, than within it. After some further experimentation, Herschel named his discovery 'calorific rays', demonstrating for the first time the existence of light beyond that which is visible to the human eye.

Betjeman's 'Slough'

John Betjeman's poem 'Slough', which famously calls for the destruction of the town, was written by the former Poet Laureate in response to the destruction of rural land around the ever-expanding town, partly used here as a metaphor for what Betjeman saw as a more widespread disregard for our environment. Although Betjeman's daughter later revealed that her father regretted having ever written the poem and in fact never wanted it published, its scathing content has nevertheless helped to make it one of his best remembered works.

Automated train system developed

A train crash at Slough Station in which five people were killed on the afternoon of 16 June 1900 is seen as being instrumental in the development of so-called 'automatic train control' (ATC) systems on British train lines. The crash involved a London express and a stationary local train, and because it had been caused by the express driver failing to notice two trackside signals, the Great Western Railway company went on to develop a system for automatically slowing and stopping trains which pass through 'danger' signals. The system remained in use in Britain until replaced in the 1970s.

SNODLAND, KENT
Roman hoard unearthed

A hoard of 3,600 Roman coins or *nummi*, some displaying the head of the Emperor Constantine, were unearthed by workmen on a building site in Kent's Medway Valley in 2006. Dating from the mid fourth century, the coins were believed to have come from all across the Roman Empire and had presumably been stashed away in an urn by their owner when they ceased to be legal tender in AD 348.

THE SOLENT
Execution of Admiral John Byng

Having joined the navy at the age of 13, by 19 John Byng had been made lieutenant, and by 23 was captain of HMS *Gibraltar*, spending many years' service throughout the Mediterranean. In 1756, at the onset of the Seven Years' War, Byng was put in charge of a fleet of ships and ordered to prevent a French invasion of the then British-controlled island of Minorca. The fleet, however, was both poor quality and poorly manned and arrived too late to prevent the invasion, so, holding back from a confrontation with a French squadron, Byng instead made the questionable decision to head back to Gibraltar to repair his ships and subsequently return better prepared. By holding back, however, Byng was deemed not to have done his utmost in battle against the enemy, and as such was reckoned to have been in breach of the navy's strictly enforced rules, known as the Articles of War. All in all, the incident was enough to see Byng court-martialled and controversially sentenced to death, executed by firing squad on board HMS *Monarch* in The Solent on 14 March 1757.

THE SOUTH DOWNS
National park

The UK's most recently created national park, the South Downs was set aside in March 2009 and officially came into being on 1 April 2011. Stretching for 140 kilometres (90 miles) from Winchester to Eastbourne, the park is Britain's sixth largest, covering some 1,634 square kilometres (634 square miles), and is home to more than 120,000 people, more than any other national park in the whole of the British Isles.

ST ALBANS, HERTFORDSHIRE
The life of St Alban

Known to the Romans as Verulamium, St Albans is named after the first known Christian martyr, who was executed in the town sometime around the third/ fourth century. According to Bede's monumental *Ecclesiastical History of the English People*, Alban was a pagan who converted to Christianity after allowing a cleric fleeing from persecution to shelter at his home. Consequently, he was tortured and sentenced to death by beheading, his feast day of 22 June still commemorating his death today.

Female Ripper suspect Mary Pearcey

The most likely female suspect in the Jack the Ripper case, Mary Pearcey was born Mary Eleanor Wheeler in *c.* 1866, probably in St Albans in Hertfordshire, where her father Thomas worked as a farmer. Thomas was convicted of murder and hanged in 1880, and in 1890 Pearcey herself (who had since taken the name of one of her previous lovers) was convicted of the murder of Phoebe Hogg, the wife of her lover and the mother of his child, whom Pearcey bludgeoned to death with a poker having invited her to her home. She was later hanged at Newgate Prison. The violent nature of Pearcey's crime soon led to her name being associated with the Ripper killings.

Tree disrupts play at football match

St Albans City FC was founded in 1908 and the club have played their home games at Clarence Park ever since. However, as Clarence Park stands within the grounds of a larger public park donated to the town in the nineteenth century, the stadium had been built around a great oak tree which ultimately stood in the middle of the terraces directly behind one of the goals, overhanging the pitch. When the club was offered promotion to the Football Conference at the end of the 1992/93 season, Conference rules demanded that the tree be removed, but the club refused to cut it down and eventually lost out on their promotion. Sadly, the tree

was later found to be infected with a disease and had to be destroyed.

STOKE MANDEVILLE, BUCKINGHAMSHIRE
The Stoke Mandeville Games

In 1948, the Buckinghamshire town of Stoke Mandeville held the first ever Stoke Mandeville Games, a series of multi-discipline sporting events especially intended for athletes with a disability. The games, also known as the World Wheelchair and Amputee Games, are rightly considered to have been the precursor of the now internationally renowned Paralympic Games and in respect of this the seventh official Paralympics in 1984 were divided between Stoke Mandeville and New York. Indeed, 1984 remains the last time that the Paralympics were not held in the same city as the Summer Olympic Games, which had taken place in Los Angeles earlier that year.

STOKE POGES, BUCKINGHAMSHIRE
Gray's 'Elegy'

St Giles' Church in the Buckinghamshire village of

Stoke Poges is thought to be the eponymous location of Thomas Gray's *Elegy Written in a Country Churchyard* – indeed, Gray himself is buried in the cemetery of St Giles', with a monument inscribed with the poem erected nearby. The *Elegy* remains by far Gray's most famous work, and has maintained continual popularity since it was first published in 1751. Interestingly, the poem is the source of both the phrase 'kindred spirit' and 'far from the madding crowd', the latter of which Thomas Hardy famously took as the title of his novel of 1874.

SUNNINGDALE, BERKSHIRE
Disappearance of Agatha Christie

Following an argument with her husband at their home in Sunningdale near the Berkshire-Surrey border, the crime writer Agatha Christie disappeared for 11 days in December 1926. She eventually reappeared over 200 miles away at the Swan Hotel in Harrogate, North Yorkshire, where she was registered under the name Teresa Neele. She could give no explanation for her disappearance and was subsequently diagnosed with amnesia by several doctors,

who claimed that the condition had been brought on by the shock and emotional distress of discovering that her husband had been having an affair.

Former royal residence, Fort Belvedere

An official royal residence from 1750 until 1976, Fort Belvedere near Sunningdale in Berkshire – but in fact located across the border in Surrey, in Windsor Great Park – was given to Edward, Prince of Wales, by his father, George V, in 1929. Following George's death in 1936, Edward became King Edward VIII, but his intention to marry the American socialite Wallis Simpson was met with such great opposition that he was eventually compelled to renounce the throne. He signed the official Instrument of Abdication at Fort Belvedere on 10 December 1936, which, ratified by parliament's specially created Declaration of Abdication Act, came into effect the very next day. Edward VIII remains not only the last British monarch to have abdicated, but was also the first to have done so since Richard II in 1399, and is the only monarch in British history ever to have voluntarily given up the throne.

SUTTON, SURREY
Quentin Crisp

The controversial writer, actor and raconteur Quentin Crisp was born Denis Charles Pratt at Sutton on 25 December 1908. A well known and colourful figure in London for much of his early adult life, it was the publication of his autobiography *The Naked Civil Servant* in 1968 – and the subsequent television adaptation starring John Hurt – that made Crisp an international star. He toured the UK with a sell-out one-man show in the 1970s, taking it to America in 1975, and in 1981 he moved to New York, where he remained for much of the rest of his life. On the eve of another UK tour at the age of 90, Crisp died in Manchester in 1999.

TERLING, ESSEX
Discovery of argon

When the father of the British scientist John William Strutt died in 1873, Strutt became 3rd Baron Rayleigh and inherited Terling Place in the village of Terling

in Essex. Whilst also working at London's Royal Institute, it was at Terling that Rayleigh carried out much of the principal experimentation that would lead to his isolation of the chemical element argon in 1895.

TIDE MILLS, EAST SUSSEX
Eighteenth-century village abandoned

The village of Tide Mills near Newhaven on the East Sussex coast grew up around a water-driven flour mill built on the site in the late 1700s. When the mill closed in 1883 the village for a time remained unchanged, but as the twentieth century progressed Tide Mills fell victim to a landmark parliamentary Housing Act of the 1930s, the first in Britain to confer on local authorities the power to condemn housing as 'unfit for human habitation'. Amidst reports of appalling sanitation, a total absence of street lighting, and a non-existent sewerage system – all vividly described in a damning report printed in the *Daily Mail* that branded Tide Mills a 'hamlet of horror' – in 1937 the local council forcibly rehomed the village's few remaining inhabitants and by 1939 Tide Mills was abandoned.

TITCHFIELD, HAMPSHIRE
Marriage of Henry VI

Henry VI's marriage to Margaret of Anjou was arranged as a means of fostering peace between Britain and France following the Hundred Years' War, with the additional condition, established by the French King Charles VII in the Treaty of Tours, that the French lands of Maine and Anjou be returned to France. The treaty was signed on 22 May 1444 and Henry and Margaret married the following year at Titchfield Abbey in Hampshire. Their only son, Edward of Lancaster, remains the only Prince of Wales ever to die in battle, killed at Tewkesbury in 1471 attempting to regain his right to the throne.

TONBRIDGE, KENT
Securitas robbery

On 22 February 2006, a gang of 14 armed robbers made off with more than £53 million in used banknotes from a Securitas depot in Tonbridge, Kent. The previous day, the manager of the depot,

along with his wife and young son, had all been kidnapped and held hostage at gunpoint by members of the gang; at around 1 a.m. the following morning, they were driven to the depot where several members of staff were being held captive. When the alarm was finally raised around two hours later, the gang had managed to escape with the largest amount of cash ever stolen in a robbery in British history.

TUNBRIDGE WELLS, KENT
Record-breaking penalty shoot-out contested

When an FA Cup replay between Tunbridge Wells FC and Littlehampton Town at Kent's Culverden Stadium ended 2–2 after extra time in August 2005, a penalty shoot-out of 43 spot kicks was required to bring the final score to 16–15 in Tunbridge Wells' favour.

UFTON NERVET, BERKSHIRE
The Ufton Dole

On Maundy Thursday in the Berkshire village of Ufton Nervet near Reading, gifts of bread and linen are traditionally handed out to the villagers through a window at Ufton Court, a local Tudor manor house. The tradition dates back to the sixteenth century, when a Lady Elizabeth Marvyn became lost in woodland on her way back to the house and had to be rescued by villagers. After her death, Elizabeth left money for the gifts, known as the 'Ufton Dole', in her will and it has remained an annual tradition ever since.

UPPER CANTERTON, HAMPSHIRE
Death of William II

On 2 August 1100, William II of England – William Rufus, third son of William the Conqueror – was killed in a hunting accident in the New Forest. Although the exact circumstances of the king's demise are uncertain, it appears that William was struck in the chest by a stray arrow shot by Sir Walter Tyrell, one of his companions. Fearing that he would be accused of murder, Tyrell supposedly fled the scene, leaving the king's body to be discovered by peasants the following day – legend has it that a local charcoal-burner carried William's body to Winchester Cathedral on his cart. The Rufus Stone, a memorial to William near the village of Upper Canterton in Hampshire, was erected on the approximate site of his death in 1745.

WALLISWOOD, SURREY
Baryonyx dinosaur discovered

The first ever specimen of a *Baryonyx*, a 10-metre (32-foot), 2-tonne dinosaur which lived around 125 million years ago, was discovered in a clay pit south of the village of Walliswood in Surrey in 1983. The find was to prove remarkable on several counts as not only was it the first and most complete specimen of its type, but moreover *Baryonyx* seems to have been piscivorous, making it apparently one of the few land-dwelling dinosaurs now believed to have fed primarily on fish. *Baryonyx* was also physically exceptional as its crocodile-like head contained almost one hundred teeth and, as its name (meaning 'heavy claw') suggests, each of its 'hands' was armed with an extraordinary foot-long curved claw that was presumably used to thrash and haul its prey from the water.

WALMER, KENT
Invasion of Julius Caesar

During his reign as emperor, Julius Caesar led two attempted Roman invasions of Britain. For the first attempt in 55 BC, it appears he had intended to land at Dover, but facing a horde of curious Britons looking down from the clifftops he instead opted to head further down the coast and likely landed at nearby Walmer. By some, this first effort is considered to have been more of a reconnaissance mission rather than an outright invasion and was likely intended merely to pave the way for a second and far more successful venture that followed a year later. Both of Caesar's two invasions, however, are seen as more diplomatic than suppressive, and unlike later Roman incursions were largely concerned with simply establishing another trade partner for Rome.

WANTAGE, OXFORDSHIRE
Birthplace of Alfred the Great

The town of Wantage in Oxfordshire was the birthplace of Alfred the Great in *c.* 849. As king of Wessex from 871 to 899, Alfred is fêted for his defence of the kingdom from the Viking raids that had ravaged much of the rest of England, even establishing an agreement with the Viking leader Guthrun in 878. He died at Winchester in 899.

WARE, HERTFORDSHIRE
Twelfth Night (III.ii)

The Great Bed of Ware is an oversized, ornately decorated oak four-poster bed built in the Hertfordshire town of Ware in the late sixteenth century. The extraordinary object – more than 11 square metres (118 square feet) and over 2.6 metres (8.5 feet) in height – is currently housed in London's Victoria and Albert Museum. Shakespeare's reference to it in *Twelfth Night* – '… and as many lies as will lie in thy sheet of paper, although the sheet were big enough for the bed of Ware in England, set 'em down' – appears in the bawdy Sir Toby Belch's advice to his underdog companion Sir Andrew Aguecheek, as he instructs him how to make a letter demanding a duel as provocative as possible.

WATFORD, HERTFORDSHIRE

Oscar-winner T. E. B. Clarke

In 1952, Thomas Ernest Bennett Clarke became the first British writer to win an Oscar when he took the Best Original Screenplay award for the Ealing comedy *The Lavender Hill Mob*, beating both Terrence Rattigan and John Steinbeck to the prize. Born in Watford in 1907, Clarke wrote the scripts to several well-known Ealing comedies throughout his career, including *Passport To Pimlico*, *Hue And Cry* and *Barnacle Bill*, Alec Guinness' final film with the studio.

WHERWELL, HAMPSHIRE

Death of Queen Ælfthryth

Although the exact date is unknown, it is nevertheless believed that Queen Ælfthryth of England, wife of the English King Edgar, died at Wherwell in Hampshire in 1000. Edward was Ælfthryth's second husband, following her earlier marriage to Æthelwald, an ealdorman of East Anglia. According to the twelfth-century historian William of Malmesbury, in looking for a suitable queen Edgar had sent Æthelwald to meet Ælfthryth to find out whether reports of her beauty were true. Having met her, however, Æthelwald married Ælfthryth himself and falsely reported back to the king that she would not make a suitable queen. When Edgar finally arranged his own meeting with her in 962, he discovered Æthelwald's betrayal and killed him, finally taking Ælfthryth as his wife in *c.* 964. Soon afterwards, she gave birth to their son Æthelred, who himself went on to become king in 978.

WICKFORD, ESSEX

Remarkable Stone Age camp unearthed

In November 2008, Mesolithic – Middle Stone Age – remains were unexpectedly unearthed at Wickford in Essex. Fragments of stone artefacts and what is thought to be the remains of an ancient camp dating from sometime between 8500 and 4000 BC were found on scrubland near the A127 which was otherwise due to be flooded and converted into wetlands.

WINCHESTER, HAMPSHIRE
Birthplace of Matilda and Henry III

It could be argued that two English monarchs have been born at Winchester Castle, namely Henry III in 1207 and Matilda, the eldest daughter of Henry I, in 1102. Rightfully, Matilda should have succeeded Henry I to the throne on his death in 1135, but instead she was usurped by her cousin, Stephen of Blois. Consequently, the years following Henry's death were marked by Matilda's lengthy and largely futile struggle to claim the throne, and although she managed to capture (and thus effectively depose) Stephen at the Battle of Lincoln in 1141, she was never crowned and he was released after just a few months' incarceration to continue his reign.

Troilus and Cressida (V.x)

Winchester is referred to by name in two of Shakespeare's plays, namely *Henry VI, Part 1*, which features the bishop of Winchester as a character, and here in *Troilus and Cressida* – 'Some galled goose of Winchester would hiss'. In this instance, the city's name appears as part of the old slang term 'Winchester goose', a phrase alluding to the twelfth-century bishop of Winchester's licensing of brothels on his land in Southwark, London, and ultimately referring to either a prostitute or else sexually transmitted disease. Precisely which one of these two rather unappealing meanings is the one intended here in *Troilus and Cressida* is unclear, but given that the play is set in ancient Troy the reference is certainly somewhat anachronistic.

WINDSOR, BERKSHIRE
Herne the Hunter

According to legend, Herne the Hunter had been one of the best huntsmen in the court of Richard II, but was killed one day defending the king from an attack by a white stag. Luckily, a local wizard is said to have brought Herne back to life and the delighted king soon made him one of his closest companions. The king's other huntsmen, however, became jealous and ultimately framed Herne for poaching. When the king was forced to dismiss him, Herne hanged himself from an oak tree in Windsor Great Park. One of the most famous ghost stories in English folklore – Shakespeare even retells it in Act IV of *The Merry Wives of Windsor* – the ghost of Herne the Hunter is still said to haunt the park.

Ripper suspect Prince Albert Victor

Prince Albert Victor was born at Frogmore House in Windsor in 1864, the eldest son of the Prince of Wales, later Edward VII, and a grandson of Queen Victoria. The prince was second in line to the throne, and had relationships with many potential suitors, yet was rumoured to be gay or bisexual and was even implicated in the Cleveland Street Scandal of 1889 that exposed a network of male prostitution in upper-class London. His engagement to Princess Mary of Teck in 1891 ended years of scandal regarding his private life, but soon afterwards he died of pneumonia at Sandringham House, six days after his twenty-eighth birthday. The somewhat salacious theory that he was responsible for the Jack the Ripper murders – or that he had fathered a child with one of the victims and had those who

knew killed in order to cover up the indiscretion – is today largely considered fantasy, as the prince was not in London at the time of any of the killings.

Death of William, Duke of Gloucester

Born at Hampton Court in 1689, Prince William Henry Oldenburg, Duke of Gloucester, was the only one of Queen Anne's 17 children to survive infancy. Nevertheless, the young prince was a sickly child and, having taken ill on his eleventh birthday, died just a few days later at Windsor Castle on 30 July 1700. As Anne's only surviving child, William's death threatened the Protestant claim to the throne that had been secured by the Glorious Revolution of 1688, and as a result parliament was forced to pass the Act of Settlement the following year, arranging for the throne to pass to the Protestant children of Sophia of Hanover, a granddaughter of James I, rather than the offspring of the deposed Catholic King James II. Consequently, on Anne's death in 1714, King George I took to the throne as the first monarch of the newly formed House of

Hanover, which would go on to rule Great Britain and Ireland until 1901.

Ghosts of Henry VIII, Charles I, and many more

Built by William the Conqueror, Windsor Castle has been an official royal residence for almost 1,000 years and consequently is considered the oldest continually occupied castle in the world, as well as being almost assuredly the largest. The castle is reputed to be haunted by several of its former residents, amongst them Henry VIII, George III, Charles I and William of Wykeham, the castle's architect. Indeed, several of Windsor's ghosts have supposedly been seen by members of the royal family over the years, including the ghost of Elizabeth I, said to haunt the Royal Library, and allegedly glimpsed by Princess Margaret during one of her stays at the castle.

Popularisation of the Christmas tree in Britain

In 1848, a hand-drawn picture of Queen Victoria and Prince Albert standing with their children around a Christmas tree at Windsor Castle appeared in *The Illustrated London News*. Until then, in Britain at least, the traditional Christmas tree had primarily been a royal custom, but with the publication of this picture it became a fashionable and much more widespread practice throughout Victorian society. Two years later, the same image – although doctored to remove Victoria's crown and Albert's moustache – appeared in print in America, helping to establish the tradition of the Christmas tree there too.

WOKING, SURREY
Tripod

In April 1998, a statue of one of H. G. Wells' Martians – the giant silver 'tripods' that feature in his novel *The War of the Worlds* – was unveiled in Woking town centre. The statue commemorated the centenary of Wells' groundbreaking novel, much of which was both written and set in Woking, where Wells spent a number of years. Designed by Michael Condron, the chrome-plated statue stands 7 metres (23 feet) tall, and is positioned so as to appear to be walking towards the town from Horsell Common, where the Martians first land in Wells' novel.

WOOTTON, KENT
Britain's shortest racetrack

The tiny east Kent village of Wootton near Folkestone is home to Lydden Hill Race Circuit, the shortest motor racing circuit in the UK. Founded in 1955, the track, today mainly used for rallycross, is just one mile (1.6 kilometres) in length.

WOTTON UNDERWOOD, BUCKINGHAMSHIRE
see under Midhurst, West Sussex

WHAT'S IN A NAME?

Battle, East Sussex
From the French *bataille*, literally meaning 'battle'.

Chess, Buckinghamshire
Buckinghamshire's River Chess likely takes its name from the town of Chesham near its source, which is itself derived from the Old English word *ceastel*, meaning 'mound of stones'.

Cooling, Kent
Perhaps derives from an Old English first name, Cul or Cula.

Crow, Hampshire
Listed as Croue in the *Domesday Book* of 1086, Crow perhaps derives from the Celtic word *crou*, meaning 'sty'.

Deal, Kent
Derives from an Old English word, *dæl*, for a hollow or valley.

Dean, Hampshire
A very common place name, Dean usually derives from the Old English word for a valley, *denu*.

Easter, Essex
Shared by several villages in rural Essex, the name Easter derives from the Old English word *eowestre*, meaning 'sheep-fold'.

Lake, Isle of Wight
The village of Lake is one of the so-called Seven Wonders of the Isle of Wight, alongside 'The Needles you cannot thread', 'the Cowes you cannot milk' and 'the Newport you cannot bottle'. The name of 'the Lake with no water' actually derives from the Old English word *lacu*, meaning a stream or brook.

Loose, Kent
Comes from an Old English word for a pigsty, *hlose*.

Send, Surrey
Actually derives from the Old English word for sand, *sende*.

Sheering, Essex
Likely derives from an ancient first name, Sceara.

Sheet, Hampshire
From the Old English *sciete*, describing a corner of land.

Stock, Essex
From the Old English word *stoc*, describing an outlying or secondary settlement.

Thong, Kent
Derives from the Old English *thwang*, denoting a narrow stretch of land.

Tiptoe, Hampshire
Likely derives from the old family name Typetot, recorded in the area from the 1200s.

Worth, West Sussex
A common English place name, from an Old English word meaning 'enclosure'.

LONDON

30 ST MARY AXE, CITY OF LONDON

The Gherkin

Partly designed by Sir Norman Foster, 30 St Mary Axe is more commonly known as The Gherkin, a jocular reference to its somewhat unusual shape and colouring. Not only the most expensive tower block in Britain, at 180 metres (591 feet) The Gherkin also ranks amongst London's – and indeed the British Isles' – tallest buildings. Completed in 2004, it has since won several significant architectural awards, amongst them a Regional RIBA Award and the 2004 Stirling Award, and in 2003 was named the World's Best Skyscraper by the real estate firm Emporis.

ALDGATE

'Aldgate draught'

Although somewhat obsolete today, the phrase 'Aldgate draught', or 'a draught on the pump at Aldgate', was once used to describe a bad cheque, a pun on the words 'draught' (drink) and 'draft' (money order). It alludes to the old water pump at Aldgate in East London that traditionally marked the start of London's East End.

BANKSIDE

The Tate Modern opens

London's Tate Modern art gallery was officially opened on 11 May 2000. Housed inside the former Bankside Power Station, on its opening the Tate was the largest modern art gallery in the world, exhibiting works by dozens of renowned twentieth-century artists including Dali, Matisse, Warhol, Rothko, Lichtenstein, Monet and Picasso.

BAYSWATER
British Olympian Kitty McKane

Kathleen 'Kitty' McKane remains one of the most successful of all Britons at the Olympic Games, with the five medals she won in her career remaining the most ever won by a female tennis player. Born in Bayswater in 1896, McKane made her first Olympic appearance at the Antwerp Games in 1920, where she won three medals: gold in the doubles, silver in the mixed doubles, and bronze in the women's singles. In 1924, she won a further two medals at the Paris Games, as well as the first of her two Wimbledon singles titles – she went on to win her second in 1926, the same year that she and her husband, Leslie Godfree, became the first and to date only married couple ever to win the mixed doubles title at Wimbledon.

BEXLEY
Prime Minister Ted Heath's constituency

Born in Broadstairs in Kent, Sir Edward Richard George Heath was leader of the Conservative Party for ten years (1965–75) and prime minister for four (1970–74) whilst serving as MP for Bexley in London from 1950 until the seat's dissolution in 1974. As prime minister, Heath was both preceded and succeeded by Harold Wilson.

BRENTFORD
The Merry Wives of Windsor (IV.ii)

In this scene from *The Merry Wives of Windsor*, the pompous Falstaff has been trying to woo the eponymous Mistress Ford, but when her husband unexpectedly returns home she convinces Falstaff to disguise himself as her aged aunt, 'the fat woman of Brainford' (i.e. Brentford in London). Knowing full well that her husband despises her aunt, Mistress Ford thus sets the hapless Falstaff up for a beating, and he is unceremoniously thrown from the house with the words, 'Out of my door you witch, you rag, you baggage, you polecat, you ronyon!'

BRIDGE, CITY OF LONDON
Pudding Lane

Unsurprisingly, London contains dozens of famous streets, roads and other notable thoroughfares, of which Pudding Lane in the ward of Bridge in the City of London is just one. It is also perhaps one of the most infamous, having once been the site of Thomas Farriner's bakery where, shortly after midnight on 2 September 1666, the Great Fire of London broke out – within three days the fire had destroyed around four-fifths of the entire city.

THE BRITISH MUSEUM, BLOOMSBURY
Discovery of niobium

When a forgotten sample of the mineral columbite sent from America to the British Museum in Bloomsbury in the mid eighteenth century was re-examined by the British physicist Charles Hatchett in 1801, it was found to contain a metal which had never been identified before, which Hatchett

named 'columbium'. In the years that followed, considerable debate ensued amongst the scientific community as to whether Hatchett's discovery was in fact identical to a similar metal, tantalum, which had been discovered the following year by the Swedish scientist Anders Gustaf Ekeberg. It was not until the 1840s that the two were finally proven to be distinct materials by the German mineralogist Heinrich Rose, who renamed Hatchett's discovery 'niobium', the name by which chemical element number 41 has been officially known since 1950.

BROMLEY
Prime Minister Harold Macmillan's constituency

One of three twentieth-century prime ministers to have been born in London, Macmillan was prime minister from 1957 to 1963 whilst member of parliament for Bromley. Having earlier served the constituency of Stockton-on-Tees (1924–29, 1931–45), Macmillan was made earl of Stockton in 1984, two years before his death at the age of 92.

BUCKINGHAM PALACE

Fathers 4 Justice

The controversial activist group Fathers 4 Justice have staged several high-profile protests in recent years to raise awareness of the rights of fathers denied access to their children. In one of their most infamous stunts, one of their activists managed to climb onto a Buckingham Palace balcony dressed as Batman in September 2004, before being removed by police.

CAMDEN

William Camden

Although the London Borough of Camden can trace its name back to William Camden, a sixteenth-century scholar famed for compiling *Britannia*, the first great geographical survey of Britain and Ireland, the connection is far from a direct one. The borough takes its name from Camden Town, which in turn is named after the eighteenth-century lawyer and politician Sir Charles Pratt – when he was made a peer in 1765, Pratt created for himself the title 'Baron of Camden', in reference to his home in Chislehurst in Kent which was the former residence of the great William Camden. In 1791, Pratt, who was then 1st Earl of Camden, leased the construction of the buildings that would eventually become Camden Town itself.

Ripper suspect Walter Sickert

Born in Munich in 1860, Walter Sickert moved to London with his family when he was eight years old. He attended London's Slade School of Fine Art and was appointed assistant to both James Whistler and then Edgar Degas in Paris before returning to England in the early 1900s, where he set himself up on Mornington Crescent, Camden, as a prolific and often controversial painter and writer, and later as a private tutor, counting a young Winston Churchill amongst his many pupils. His attachment to the Ripper case has been asserted by several high-profile investigations, including those of the writers Patricia Cornwell and Stephen Knight, but seems merely to have developed from nothing more than Sickert's own interest in the case and others like it – indeed, amongst his works are a painting of *Jack the Ripper's Bedroom* (*c.* 1907) and *The Camden Town Murder* (1908), a group of four paintings based on the murder of a prostitute in 1907.

CHRISTIE'S, WESTMINSTER
On the Origin of Species auctioned

In 2009, marking the 150th anniversary of its publication, several rare first edition copies of Charles Darwin's masterpiece *On the Origin of Species* went on sale at auctions across Britain. In Edinburgh, a copy was sold for £15,625; at Aylsham in Norfolk another fetched £35,000; but at Christie's auction house in St James's, Westminster, an astonishing price of £103,250 was reached. Only 1,250 copies of the book were published on its first print run in 1859.

CROYDON
Croydon Airport

Opened in 1920, Croydon Airport was Britain's first airport terminal and, the following year, became one of the first in the world to introduce air traffic control. Prior to its eventual closure in 1959, the airport gained a certain amount of recognition in the years between the world wars as the starting point for both the world's first solo flight from England to Australia in 1928, and aviator Amy Johnson's solo flight to Australia in 1930.

Oscar-winners David Lean and Peggy Ashcroft

Born in Croydon in 1908, Sir David Lean remains the most successful British-born director at the Oscars, having won two Best Director awards (for *The Bridge on the River Kwai* and *Lawrence of Arabia*) from a total of seven nominations. Dame Peggy Ashcroft, one of Britain's finest ever actresses, was also born in Croydon, in 1907. The pair worked together just once throughout their careers, in what would be Lean's last film, *A Passage To India*; Ashcroft won the 1984 Best Supporting Actress Oscar for her performance.

EAST FINCHLEY
Jerry Springer

Gerald Norman Springer was reputedly born in East Finchley

tube station on 13 February 1944. Five years later, his parents – Jewish refugees escaping Nazi Germany – emigrated with their family to Queens in New York City. Springer studied political science at New Orleans' Tulane University, earned a doctorate in law at Illinois' Northwestern University and worked as a political campaign aide for Robert Kennedy before joining a law firm in Cincinnati, where he was elected mayor in 1977. Subsequent work in radio and as a local news anchor led to the notorious *Jerry Springer Show*, first broadcast in 1991.

EAST INDIA HOUSE, CITY OF LONDON
East India Company founded

One of the most powerful corporations in British history, the East India Company was officially founded in London by Royal Charter on 31 December 1600. Over the next 250 years the company forged a monopoly on trade between England and the Indian subcontinent, dealing in cotton, spices, opium, silk and tea, amongst a great many other commodities. As it grew increasingly powerful, the company's role in India became much more authoritative and administrative, and by the 1800s the company, by then based at East India House on Leadenhall Street in the City of London, effectively ruled over vast areas of the country. A rebellion against its control in 1857 eventually brought about its downfall, however, and in the following year the company's role in India was assumed by the British Raj.

ELTHAM
US entertainer Bob Hope

Born Leslie Townes Hope in Eltham on 29 May 1903, Bob Hope grew up in Weston-super-Mare and Bristol before his family moved to Cleveland, Ohio, in 1908; he became a US citizen aged 17. Originally a successful vaudeville performer, Hope made his film debut in the short *Going Spanish* in 1934, and went on to become one of America's most popular entertainers. In a career lasting 70 years, Hope was awarded four honorary Oscars and in 1997 was uniquely made an 'Honorary Veteran' by Act of Congress for his work entertaining troops in World War Two, Korea, Vietnam and the Gulf. Having just celebrated his hundredth birthday, Hope died at his home in Toluca Lake, California, on 27 July 2003.

ENFIELD
Broadcaster Ross McWhirter murdered

An outspoken critic of the IRA, the broadcaster and co-founder of the *Guinness Book of Records* Ross McWhirter was shot and killed at his home in Enfield on 27 November 1975. McWhirter had earlier offered a reward of £50,000 for information leading to the arrest of IRA bombers.

FARRINGDON STREET, CLERKENWELL
Labour Party founded

Following limited success with his Independent Labour Party at the 1895 general election, party leader Keir Hardie reasoned that to achieve success in parliament, his and several other small, independent left-wing organisations should amalgamate into one much larger political

body. Consequently, at a TUC meeting in London's Memorial Hall on Farringdon Street on 27 February 1900, a vote was held on Hardie's proposal among 129 socialist and trade union delegates, leading to the formation of the so-called Labour Representation Committee. After considerable success in the subsequent 1906 election, the LRC adopted the new name of the 'Labour Party', going on to elect their first prime minister, Ramsay MacDonald, in 1924.

FINCHLEY
Prime Minister Margaret Thatcher's constituency

Born Margaret Hilda Roberts in Grantham, Lincolnshire, on 13 October 1925, Baroness Thatcher of Kesteven remains Britain's only female prime minister, holder of the longest continuous period in office since Lord Liverpool in the early nineteenth century, and the only British prime minister ever to have held office for an entire decade. She was member of parliament for Finchley in north London from 1959 until 1992.

FLEET STREET, CITY OF LONDON

Early printing press established

Born Jan van Wynkyn sometime in the mid fifteenth century in Wœrth, Alsace, Wynkyn de Worde was an associate of the printing pioneer William Caxton. After Caxton's death in *c.* 1491, de Worde took over his press, moving it from Westminster to Fleet Street in the City of London in 1500. As such, de Worde is often credited with instigating the centuries-long association of Fleet Street with the printed word. Thought to be the first person to use italic type in English books, he died in 1534.

GOLDSMITHS' HALL, CITY OF LONDON

Hallmarking established

In 1300, a statute introduced by Edward I decreed that all silverware made in England should meet a newly defined standard, and as such must comprise at least 92.5 per cent solid silver. The statute also ensured that no silver could be sold in England until it had been taken to the headquarters of the guild of goldsmiths in London and had its quality officially assessed. Only if it passed all of the tests administered by the guild could it then be sold as so-called 'sterling' silver and stamped with the king's own mark, that of a leopard's head, to confirm its quality. Consequently, Edward can be said to have introduced the assay tests that all precious metals are put through to this day, as well as beginning what would eventually become known as 'hallmarking', taking its name from Goldsmiths' Hall in the City of London where England's first assay office was sited.

GREENWICH

First marriage of Henry VIII

Henry VIII married his first wife Catherine of Aragon in a small ceremony at Greenwich shortly after his coronation in 1509. Catherine was the youngest daughter of Ferdinand and Isabella of Spain, and had earlier been married to Henry's elder brother Arthur, until his sudden death in 1502. Henry had had to be granted papal permission to marry his brother's widow, which was outlawed by Catholic canon law, but eventually went even further against the wishes of the Church by having his marriage to Catherine annulled in 1533. Nevertheless, during their 24 years together, Catherine became pregnant several times, but only her daughter Mary Tudor, later Mary I of England, survived past infancy.

Greenwich, South Shetland Islands

The South Shetland Islands is a group of 11 islands and several smaller islets in the Drake Passage, an arm of the Southern Ocean between Antarctica and South America. Although the islands have been claimed by Britain since 1908, and are today considered part of the British Antarctic Territory established in 1962, officially they do not belong to any one nation and can legally be used by any of the 12 original signatory nations of the 1959 Antarctic Treaty; indeed, Greenwich Island, one of the smallest and centremost in the group, is home to scientific bases used by both Chile and Ecuador.

GUY'S HOSPITAL, SOUTHWARK
Impressive hospital tower

Forming part of University College London, Guy's Tower – or officially, the Tower Building of Guy's Hospital – was completed in 1974. Its highest point stands 143 metres (469 feet) tall and contains 34 storeys, placing it amongst the tallest buildings in London and making it the tallest hospital building in the world.

HACKNEY
US actress Jessica Tandy

Jessica Tandy was born in Hackney on 7 June 1909. Originally a successful stage actress, Tandy moved to New York in 1940 and made her US film debut two years later in *The Seventh Cross* (1944) opposite her second husband Hume Cronyn, with whom she would also star in – amongst many others – *Cocoon* (1985), **batteries not included* (1987) and her last film, *Camilla* (1994). A US citizen from 1952, Tandy won the first of three Tony Awards for her role as Blanche DuBois in a Broadway production of *A Streetcar Named Desire* in 1948, and also appeared in the films *The Birds* (1963), *Still of the Night* (1982) and *Fried Green Tomatoes* (1991) before becoming the oldest woman to win the Best Actress Oscar for her title role in *Driving Miss Daisy* (1989).

HAGGERSTON
Nobel Laureate Randal Cremer

The first individual winner of the Nobel Peace Prize, Sir William Randal Cremer served as member of parliament for Haggerston in London's East End from 1885 to 1895 and from 1900 until his death in 1908. Cremer was a noted pacifist, and served as general secretary of the Workmen's Peace Association before his election to parliament. He was awarded the Nobel Prize in 1903, partly on the recommendation of the 1901 winner Frédéric Passy, for his work in international arbitration.

HEATHROW
The village cleared for the airport

One of the busiest airports in the world, London's Heathrow takes its name from the old Middlesex hamlet of Heathrow, which was demolished in the 1940s to make way for its construction. A mainly agricultural settlement dating back hundreds of years – its name is first recorded in a document dating from the early 1400s – the village stood where the airport's Terminal 3 building stands today. Controversial plans in recent years to build a third runway at Heathrow Airport would have led to the nearby village of Sipson in Hillingdon sharing a similar fate, but the planned expansion was quashed by the newly elected coalition government in 2010.

HEATHROW AIRPORT
Brink's-MAT robbery

The Brink's-MAT robbery, which resulted in the theft of 6,800 gold bars – weighing roughly three tonnes, and worth an estimated £26 million at the time – took place at the Heathrow depot of the security company Brink's-MAT at 6.40 a.m. on 26 November 1983. Six armed robbers broke into the depot, tied up the security guards and doused them with petrol, threatening to set them alight unless they revealed the depot's security codes. Expecting to find cash, the robbers were reportedly surprised to find gold bullion

instead, and took almost two hours to collect it all.

THE HOUSES OF PARLIAMENT, WESTMINSTER
Assassination of Prime Minister Spencer Perceval

The only British prime minister ever to have been assassinated, Spencer Perceval was shot through the heart in the lobby of the House of Commons on 11 May 1812 by a merchant, John Bellingham, who had just been released from prison in Russia. The Conservative politician Airey Neave, meanwhile, was killed by an IRA bomb in the House of Commons car park on 30 March 1979.

HOXTON
Ben Jonson vs Gabriel Spenser

Perhaps one of the most famous duels in British history, on 22 September 1598 the renowned English playwright Ben Jonson stabbed and killed Gabriel Spenser, an actor, in a duel at Hogsden (now Hoxton) in central London. Found guilty of manslaughter, Jonson escaped hanging through so-called 'benefit of clergy', an obsolete loophole in

English law in which the accused could be excused the death penalty by reciting a Latin biblical verse, thereby demonstrating their literacy. As a result, despite the charge of manslaughter being upheld, Jonson was merely branded on his hand and briefly imprisoned in Newgate.

HYDE PARK
The Great Exhibition

Opened by Queen Victoria on 1 May 1851, London's Great Exhibition was the first of a number of international cultural and technological expositions popular during the nineteenth century. Located in Hyde Park and housed in the specially built Crystal Palace designed by Joseph Paxton, when the exhibition finished the palace was relocated to Sydenham in south London, where it was once more opened by Victoria on 10 June 1854. Tragically, it was destroyed by fire in 1936.

ILFORD
Oscar-winner Maggie Smith

Dame Maggie Smith remains the most successful British actress at the Oscars, having won two awards from a total of six nominations. Born in Ilford in 1934, Smith earned her first nomination (Best Supporting Actress for *Othello*) in 1965, before going on to win the award for Best Actress in 1969 for her lead role in *The Prime of Miss Jean Brodie* and then Best Supporting Actress for *California Suite* in 1978. Most recently, she was nominated again for Best Supporting Actress in 2001 for her role in Robert Altman's *Gosford Park*.

KENSINGTON
Actor Joss Ackland

The actor Joss Ackland was born Sidney Edmond Jocelyn Ackland in North Kensington on 29 February 1928. His 60-year career has included appearances in over 100 films, including *The Hunt for Red October* (1990) and *Lethal Weapon 2* (1989), as well as roles in the classic television series *The Avengers, Z Cars, The Persuaders!, The Sweeney* and *Tinker, Tailor, Soldier, Spy*. In 1985 he portrayed C. S. Lewis in the original television production of *Shadowlands*, and was awarded a CBE in 2000.

KENSINGTON PALACE
London's last royal days

Since 1066, 18 British kings and queens have died in London, amongst them Edward VII (the only monarch to have died at Buckingham Palace, in 1910), Elizabeth I (at Richmond Palace, 1603), Henry VIII (at Whitehall Palace, 1547), and both Henry VI and Edward V (killed at the Tower of London in 1471 and 1483 respectively). London was also the site of the executions of Charles I, beheaded at Whitehall Palace in 1649, and Lady Jane Grey who, although never crowned nor fully accepted as queen, was executed at the Tower of London in 1554. Of all locations across the capital, however, an unsurpassed four kings and queens have seen out their days at Kensington Palace, namely George II (1760), Anne (1714), and both Mary II (1694) and William III (1702). In more recent times, Princess Alice, Duchess of Gloucester, died at Kensington Palace in 2004 and was at the time of her death the oldest member of the British royal family in history, aged 102.

The ghost of George II

Kensington Palace in London has been an official royal residence since the 1600s and has played host to several monarchs over the years. In 1760, George II died at Kensington and as such his is one of several ghosts often recorded at the palace, seen either staring at a weathervane on the palace roof, or else standing gazing out of one of the palace's bedroom windows.

KNIGHTSBRIDGE
Knightsbridge safe deposit robbery

In 1987, a hoard estimated to be worth £40–60 million was stolen from a safe deposit centre in Knightsbridge. On 12 July that year, two men entered the centre requesting to rent a deposit box, but on being shown into the vault the men held the staff there at gunpoint whilst other members of their gang were let in and broke open many of the boxes inside. One of the criminals behind the theft, Valerio Viccei, was sentenced to 22 years in prison for his organisation of the gang responsible, but in 2000 was shot and killed by police for acting suspiciously whilst on day release from prison in Italy where he was serving the final years of his sentence.

LIMEHOUSE
Prime Minister Clement Attlee's constituency

Following Churchill's defeat in the 1945 election, Clement Attlee became Britain's second Labour prime minister and the first to hold both a full term and a parliamentary majority. He was born in London, served his entire political career as member of parliament for London constituencies (Limehouse, 1922–50, Walthamstow West, 1950–55), and died in London in 1967. His ashes are buried in Westminster Abbey.

LONDON BRIDGE
Death of Georgi Markov

A pellet containing the poison ricin was injected into Georgi Markov's calf by a man who had seemingly accidentally jabbed him with an umbrella as he waited for a bus near London Bridge on 7 September 1978. Markov, a writer and Bulgarian dissident whose assassination was linked to the KGB, died in hospital four days later.

LONDON

The Great Smog

London's Great Smog of 1952 is estimated to have claimed the lives of at least 4,000 people, all of whom died as a result of just five days of bad weather from 5 to 9 December. The smog was caused by a combination of several meteorological conditions, including a thick bank of freezing fog, a prolonged period of light winds, and an area of high pressure which, mixed with the pollutants from an increased use of coal fires, led to a dangerous level of air pollution that remained trapped directly above the city by a mass of cold air.

Cockneys

As well as being one of the most familiar regional nicknames, 'Cockney' is also one of the oldest, probably dating from the fourteenth century. Most likely derived from the Middle English words *cokene* and *ey* (literally 'a cockerel's egg'), the term first appeared in the mid 1300s, where it was probably used for any bad or misshapen hen's egg. By the turn of the fourteenth century, however,

the term began to be used for any weak or overly pampered child (appearing as such in Chaucer's *Canterbury Tales*), before describing the effeminate, foppish inhabitants of towns and cities in the 1500s – it was not until a century later that 'Cockney' finally gained the unique association with London which it retains today.

Britain's first traffic lights

Throughout the years, London has seen the implementation of several firsts in British transportation. Britain's first traffic signals, for instance, were installed outside of the Houses of Parliament on 10 December 1868, using a similar 'semaphore' system to that of the railways – red, amber and green lights would not appear until 1926, when they were first used in Piccadilly, although at the time they were still manually operated. Britain's first specially designed cycle lane was trialled on Western Avenue in Merton in 1934, and the following year Londoner Mr J. Beene became the first Briton ever to pass a driving test, three months before the test was made mandatory for all new drivers. Parking meters made their way to Britain from America in 1958 when they were installed outside of the American Embassy, and on 16 May 1983, wheel clamps were introduced in the capital, with over 22,000 cars recorded as being clamped across the city over the following six months alone. More recently, in June 2010, eight London road junctions became the first in the country to trial special 'countdown' pedestrian crossings, uniquely fitted with numerical displays showing how many seconds pedestrians have left to cross the road.

George Orwell's 1984

Winston Smith, the central character of George Orwell's iconoclastic dystopian novel *1984*, lives in the ruined city of London, the principal city of what is known as Airstrip One – whilst Airstrip One, Orwell writes, 'had always been called England, or Britain... London, he felt fairly certain, had always been called London.'

The London Olympics

When it was awarded the 2012 Olympic Games in 2005, beating Moscow, New York, Madrid and Paris, London assured its status as the first city to host the modern Summer Olympic Games on three separate occasions, having already hosted them in 1908 (when the eruption of Mount Vesuvius forced Rome, the original host city, to pull out) and 1948 (which compensated for the cancellation of London's 1944 games due to the war). London is also one of just three cities worldwide to have hosted both the Olympic and Commonwealth Games, alongside Sydney and Melbourne.

London, Kiribati

As well as being the capital of the UK, London is also the name of the principal town and port on Christmas Island, an atoll in the Line Islands of the central Pacific Ocean, discovered on Christmas Eve 1777 by Captain Cook. At around 320 square kilometres (120 square miles), Christmas Island – or Kiritimati as it is known locally – is the largest coral atoll in the world and, despite being one of some 32 islands to comprise the Pacific Republic of Kiribati, makes up over two-thirds of the country's entire land area. It is also amongst the easternmost places in the world, and as such is one of only a handful of locations to lie an unsurpassed 14 hours ahead of GMT.

London, Ohio

There are towns named London in several American states including Arkansas, Texas, Minnesota, Kentucky and California. The largest, however, is found in Ohio and has been the capital of Ohio's Madison County (named after US President James Madison) since 1811. With a little under 8,000 inhabitants, however, the population of London, Ohio, is equivalent to just 0.1 per cent of that of the English capital.

THE MILLENNIUM DOME, GREENWICH
'Millennium Star' attempted robbery

On 7 November 2000, the Metropolitan Police foiled the attempted theft of the Millennium Star, a 203-carat diamond on display at London's Millennium Dome, worth £200 million. The gang of five men responsible for the plot smashed through a wall at the Dome in a stolen JCB digger

and had planned to escape up the Thames in a speedboat, but having been under police surveillance for several months, the gang were instead apprehended in the middle of the robbery and arrested.

NEWGATE
'Newgate fashion'

To go 'Newgate fashion' means 'two by two', the term alluding to inmates of Newgate Gaol who would be led there shackled together in pairs. The phrase appears in Shakespeare's *Henry VI, Part 1*.

OLD FORD
Spring-heeled Jack

More than forty years before the Jack the Ripper murders, a sinister character known as Spring-heeled Jack terrorised London in the 1800s. Described by many of his victims as a tall, slender gentleman with a devilish face, Jack was blamed for dozens of attacks across the capital in which he often ambushed people or escaped from capture by leaping extraordinary heights over fences, walls and across rooftops. Several of his victims even claimed that Jack could breathe fire, and was armed with sharp metal claws on his fingertips – one such incident was reported in *The Times* in February 1838 in which a young woman was attacked outside of her home in London's Old Ford by a man who had knocked on her door dressed as a policeman, claiming to have caught Spring-heeled Jack out in the street. Although a handful of arrests were made at the time, many of the crimes attributed to Spring-heeled Jack are for the most part unsolved and he remains something of an eerie urban legend.

OLD TEMPLE HOUSE, HOLBORN
Death of Hugh of Lincoln

St Hugh of Lincoln was one of the most important ecclesiastic figures of the late twelfth century. Born in Avalon in Isère, France, Hugh came to England in 1179 to take over the position of prior at Witham Priory in Somerset. In 1186, having come to the attention of Henry II, he was elected bishop of Lincoln, a position he held until his death from a fever at his London residence, Old Temple House in Holborn, in 1200.

During his time at Lincoln, Hugh gained a considerable charitable reputation and ordered the reconstruction and expansion of the cathedral building following damage from an earthquake in 1185. He was canonised 20 years after his death, becoming the first Carthusian monk to be made a saint; St Hugh's College, Oxford, is named after him.

PICCADILLY
Murder of Alexander Litvinenko

In 2006, former Russian State security officer Alexander Litvinenko, an outspoken critic of Russian leader Vladimir Putin's presidency, was poisoned with polonium-210, probably whilst dining at a sushi restaurant in Piccadilly, and died 22 days later on 23 November.

POPLAR
US actress Angela Lansbury

One of the most popular stage and screen actresses of her generation, Angela Lansbury was born in Poplar in the Borough of Tower Hamlets in 1925. Having emigrated to America with her mother in the early 1940s,

Lansbury soon starred in her first film, *Gaslight*, in 1944, for which she gained the first of her three Best Supporting Actress Oscar nominations. In a career spanning eight decades, Lansbury has since been awarded a CBE, won six Golden Globes and five Tony Awards, and between 1985 and 1996 was nominated for a record 12 consecutive Emmy Awards for her role as Jessica Fletcher in the popular television series *Murder, She Wrote*. In March 2012, at the age of 86, she returned to the Broadway stage once more in an acclaimed production of Gore Vidal's *The Best Man*.

RICHMOND-UPON-THAMES
Maids of honour

Maids of honour are a type of curd cheese tart associated with Richmond and are thought to date from the sixteenth century. Various accounts of their origin have been suggested, with many claiming a connection to Henry VIII – one account states that the cakes were notably baked for Henry's first wife Catherine of Aragon by her maid of honour, Anne Boleyn, at Hampton Court in Richmond.

Richmond, Virginia

Founded in 1737, Richmond was made the state capital of Virginia in 1780. Also the capital of the Confederate States during the American Civil War, Richmond is the sixth-oldest city in the state and the fourth largest by population, with around 204,000 residents – indeed, it was once the most densely populated city in the whole of the USA. It is both named after and twinned with the London Borough of Richmond-upon-Thames, once part of Surrey, which is itself named after Richmond in North Yorkshire.

THE ROYAL ALBERT HALL, KENSINGTON
The Central Hall of Arts and Sciences

Following the success of the earlier Great Exhibition, Prince Albert proposed using the profits to develop a number of arts and cultural venues across London, of which the so-called Central Hall of Arts and Sciences was one. Albert, however, died suddenly of typhoid in 1861, long before work on the hall began on 20 May 1867, when Queen Victoria laid the first stone and renamed the building in honour of her husband – The Royal Albert Hall took almost three years to build, and was officially opened on 29 March 1871. Victoria is said to have been too distraught to speak at the inauguration ceremony, leaving her son Edward, Prince of Wales, to instead announce that 'the Queen declares this hall now open'.

THE ROYAL COURTS OF JUSTICE, WESTMINSTER

The English High Court

Situated on the Strand, The Royal Courts of Justice house the Court of Appeal and High Court of Justice for England and Wales. Designed by George Edmund Street, work began on the courts in the 1870s, and the building was officially opened by Queen Victoria in December 1882.

THE ROYAL INSTITUTION, MAYFAIR

Humphrey Davy's chemical elements

One of the greatest British scientists of all time, Sir Humphrey Davy became professor of chemistry at the Royal Institution in Mayfair in 1801. During his time there he pioneered electrolysis, using it to isolate and identify the elements sodium, potassium, calcium and magnesium in 1807–08. Davy also contributed to the isolation of boron, barium and strontium, and carried out further research into the elements chlorine, discovered by Carl Wilhelm Scheele in 1774, and iodine, discovered by Bernard Courtois in 1811.

THE ROYAL OPERA HOUSE, COVENT GARDEN

Vaughan Williams' The Pilgrim's Progress debuts

Taking almost fifty years to complete, the final and perhaps most well known of Ralph Vaughan Williams' five operas, *The Pilgrim's Progress*, was first performed at the Royal Opera House on 26 April 1951. Vaughan Williams himself wrote the libretto for the work, basing it on John Bunyan's allegory of the same title, although he chose to alter the title character's name from 'Christian' to simply 'Pilgrim' in an attempt to universalise the story.

SHARD LONDON BRIDGE, SOUTHWARK
Britain's tallest building

Built in 1991, the 50-storey One Canada Square – more familiarly known as Canary Wharf – was, at 230 metres (770 feet), the tallest habitable building in the British Isles until construction of London's striking Shard building surpassed its height in 2010. Now complete, The Shard stands at 310 metres (1,017 feet) tall, making it the second-tallest free-standing structure in the British Isles, and the tallest building in the European Union.

ST BARTHOLOMEW'S, SMITHFIELD
William Harvey's circulatory research

Born in Folkstone in 1578, the pioneering physician William Harvey studied at Cambridge University and at Padua in Italy before taking up a senior position at London's St Bartholomew's Hospital that he would hold for almost fifty years until his death in 1657. During this time, in 1616, Harvey began a series of groundbreaking lectures to the Royal College of Physicians in which he outlined his pioneering theories on the circulation of blood around the body. His extraordinary work, based on a long series of experiments and dissections, was outlined in his *De Motu Cordis* ('On the Motion of the Heart') in 1628.

ST DUNSTAN-IN-THE-WEST, CITY OF LONDON
Church of St Dunstan founded

The Church of St Dunstan-in-the-West on Fleet Street was founded sometime around 1000. The church has an astonishing history, during which time it has survived the Great Fire of London (which stopped just three doors away), served as the parish church of both John Donne and William Tyndale, and in 1671 installed what is thought to be the first public clock in London to have a minute hand. The present building dates from 1831 and, despite having a fairly commonplace Gothic-style exterior, boasts a uniquely octagonal interior.

Parish of English poet John Donne

Considered perhaps the greatest of the metaphysical poets, John Donne worked as a lawyer and served as chief secretary to the Lord Keeper of the Great Seal and as member of parliament for Brackley before being ordained into the Anglican Church in 1615. As a clergyman, Donne was vicar of London's Church of St Dunstan-in-the-West on Fleet Street from 1624 until his death in 1631, whilst also serving as Dean of St Paul's Cathedral and later Royal Chaplain to Charles I. Although he never published a poem in his lifetime, today Donne's vast body of work, encompassing sonnets, elegies, songs and sermons, is considered one of the most significant in all of English literature.

ST JAMES'S PALACE, WESTMINSTER
London's royal birthplaces

Since the Norman Conquest, 17 British or English monarchs have been born in London, amongst them Henry VIII (at Greenwich Palace in 1491), Victoria (Kensington Palace, 1819), George V (Marlborough House, 1865), and Elizabeth II (born on Brunton Street, Mayfair, in 1926). Overall, however, it is St James's Palace that has seen by far the most royal births of all London venues, and indeed of the whole of Britain – Charles II (1630), James II of England (1633), Mary II (1662), Anne (1665) and George IV (1762) were all born there.

THE THAMES
England's longest river

At 346 kilometres (215 miles), the Thames is the longest river located entirely in England. From its source at the aptly named Thames Head in Gloucestershire, the river flows through eight counties as well as the cities of Oxford, Reading, Windsor and London, before reaching the North Sea at its estuary at Southend. The Thames is fed by more than thirty tributary rivers, is crossed by some two hundred bridges, and contains more than eighty islands.

'Setting fire to the Thames'

'Setting fire to the Thames' is an odd phrase usually appearing in constructions like 'he'll never set the Thames on fire', meaning 'he'll never make a name for himself'. Its origin is unclear, but a similar phrase – 'to set the Seine on fire' – also exists in French.

THATCHED HOUSE LODGE, RICHMOND-UPON-THAMES
Birth of James Robert Bruce Ogilvy

Thirteenth in line to the throne at the time, James Robert Bruce Ogilvy, the first child of Sir Angus Ogilvy and Princess Alexandra, second cousin of Elizabeth II, was born in Thatched House Lodge in Richmond-upon-Thames on 29 February 1964. James' was the first of four royal births in 1964 – those of Prince Edward, Earl of Wessex, Lady Helen Taylor (née Windsor) and Lady Chatto (née Armstrong-Jones) all followed.

THE THEATRE ROYAL, COVENT GARDEN
Attempted assassination of the king

On 15 May 1800, a former soldier named James Hadfield attempted to assassinate George III at the Theatre Royal on London's Drury Lane. Reportedly, Hadfield, who

had earlier served in battle under George's son Prince Frederick, Duke of York, fired one shot into the royal box, narrowly missing the king's head, before dropping the gun with the words, 'God bless your Royal Highness, I like you very well, you are a good fellow.' At his subsequent trial for high treason, Hadfield was deemed insane and spent the rest of his life in an asylum, dying in 1841. King George, meanwhile, was seemingly so unperturbed by the incident that he remained at the theatre for the rest of the performance, even reportedly falling asleep during the interval. He went on to reign for a further 20 years, and, having held the throne for a total of 59 years, remains Britain's longest-serving king.

THE TOWER OF LONDON
The Princes in the Tower

The fate of the so-called 'Princes in the Tower' remains one of the most alluring unsolved mysteries in all of English royal history. Declared illegitimate by the *Titulus Regius* Act of Parliament of 1484, the princes were imprisoned in the Tower of London by their uncle, Richard III, who thus secured his own right to the throne; there is no record of the princes after this date. Whilst it is largely presumed that Edward and Richard died or, as Shakespeare prefers, were killed at the Tower in order to ensure Richard's accession, there is no corroborative evidence to prove it – equally, however, there is no evidence to suggest that they otherwise escaped imprisonment or managed to flee elsewhere.

The Tower of London's first prisoner

On 5 August 1100, Ranulf Flambard became the first prisoner to be held in the Tower of London, on the orders of the newly crowned Henry I. Ranulf had earlier served as an important minister and aide to both William the Conqueror and, most significantly, to William II, who made him bishop of Durham in 1099. Under William, Ranulf had raised vast amounts of money by holding numerous ecclesiastic offices, pursuing lucrative lawsuits and collecting taxes, but when Henry came to the throne he was accused of embezzlement and imprisoned. Not only the Tower's first prisoner, Ranulf was also to become its first escapee, somehow managing to flee to self-imposed exile in Normandy in February 1101.

UNIVERSITY COLLEGE LONDON, BLOOMSBURY
Discovery of the noble gases

The Glasgow-born scientist Sir William Ramsay isolated the noble gases helium, krypton, neon and xenon whilst chair of Chemistry at University College London in Bloomsbury in the late 1800s. Working first with fellow scientist John Strutt, Lord Rayleigh, on his isolation of argon, Ramsay and his associates went on to discover helium at UCL in 1895, and then – under the assumption that both argon and helium were members of a group of comparable gases – discovered krypton, neon and xenon in 1898. Knighted in 1902, Ramsay went on to receive the Nobel Prize for Chemistry in 1904, the same year in which Rayleigh took the prize for physics.

WEMBLEY ARENA
Prime Minister Tony Blair heckled

On 7 June 2000, Prime Minister Tony Blair was memorably

heckled by several members of the Women's Institute during a speech at a WI conference at Wembley Arena. In front of 10,000 WI members, the prime minister was slow hand-clapped and jeered, whilst some members of the audience walked out in protest at Blair's overtly political speech being delivered at the conference of the traditionally impartial WI.

The Beatles' last concert

On 1 May 1966, at what was then the Empire Pool (now Wembley Arena) in north-west London, the Beatles performed their last scheduled British concert at the NME Poll Winners All-Star Party, playing a 15-minute set of five songs – 'I Feel Fine', 'Nowhere Man', 'Day Tripper', 'If I Needed Someone' and 'I'm Down' – to an audience of 10,000. Four months later, on 29 August, the band played their last US concert in San Francisco before a final impromptu concert on the roof of the Apple Corps building in Mayfair on 30 January 1969. The following year, the band announced their decision to split.

WEMBLEY STADIUM
The White Horse Final

An estimated 300,000 spectators watched the FA Cup Final at London's new Empire Stadium (later renamed Wembley) in 1923, easily the largest crowd ever to attend a British football final in history. The match, held just four days after construction of the stadium was completed, became known as the White Horse Final in reference to Billie, one of several police horses used in an attempt to control the immense crowd; a public poll in 2005 fittingly chose to name a footbridge at the new Wembley Stadium the White Horse Bridge.

WEST HAMPSTEAD
Nobel Laureate Doris Lessing

One of the most recent British Nobel Prize winners, Doris Lessing was awarded the Nobel Prize for Literature in 2007. Born in Iran in 1919, Lessing lived in Africa for several years before moving to West Hampstead in London in 1949. The following year, her debut novel *The Grass is Singing* was published, followed by a number of collections of short stories and, in 1962, arguably her most famous novel, *The Golden Notebook*. Having turned down both an OBE and a damehood, Lessing was made a Companion of Honour in 2000. On being awarded the Nobel Prize in 2007 she commented, 'I've won all the prizes in Europe, every bloody one, so I'm delighted to win them all, it's a royal flush', although she later called the award 'a bloody disaster' as the increasing publicity it generated left her little time to write. Lessing remains only the eleventh female winner of the Literature prize since 1901 and, at 87, is the third-oldest recipient of any Nobel Prize.

WESTMINSTER
Death of John Dryden

Born in Aldwincle, Northamptonshire, in 1631, the English writer John Dryden died in London in 1700. Educated at Trinity College, Cambridge, on moving to London Dryden first worked as a government clerk under Oliver Cromwell, publishing his first poem *Heroique Stanzas* in response to Cromwell's death in 1658. In the years that followed, he established himself as one of the foremost writers of his age with plays including *Marriage*

à la Mode (1672) and *All For Love* (1678), and the epic poems *Annus Mirabilis* (1667) and *Absalom and Achitophel* (1681). Made Poet Laureate in 1668, he was removed from office 20 years later for refusing to convert from Catholicism, before going on to complete some of his most significant works in his final years, including groundbreaking English translations of the works of Virgil, Homer and Ovid. He died at his home on Gerrard Street in Westminster on 1 May 1700.

The end of Prince Harry's tour of duty

On 29 February 2008, the British Ministry of Defence announced that the decision had been made to bring Prince Harry home from an otherwise undisclosed tour of duty in Afghanistan. Harry, who was 23 at the time, had been serving with the British Army in Helmand Province since December 2007 and, although a media blackout had been imposed to ensure that his service remained unknown, on 29 February the story was broken by a US website and published in a handful of magazines around the world, greatly compromising the prince's safety.

The platinum metals

The British scientists William Hyde Wollaston and Smithson Tennant met whilst studying at Cambridge University and entered into a partnership in London in 1797, aiming initially to produce a malleable form of platinum. Dissolving platinum ore in aqua regia, however, instead produced the four rare 'platinum metals', namely the elements palladium and rhodium (both discovered by Wollaston, probably at his home laboratory in Westminster), and iridium and osmium (discovered by Tennant). Their findings were presented to the Royal Society in 1804.

WESTMINSTER ABBEY

Coronation of Henry I

Following the death of his elder brother William II, Henry I was crowned king of England at Westminster Abbey on 5 August 1100. Three months later, also at Westminster, Henry married Edith of Scotland, one of two daughters of Malcolm III of Scotland, on 11 November. As queen consort, Edith took the name Matilda, which was also her godmother's name, Henry's mother's name and the name of her only daughter, born in 1102. Matilda died in 1118, leaving Henry to marry his second wife Adeliza of Louvain in 1121.

Coronation of Isabella of Angoulême

Following her marriage to the English King John at Bordeaux in August of the same year, Isabella of Angoulême was crowned at Westminster Abbey by Hubert Walter, Archbishop of Canterbury, on 8 October 1200.

The Coronation Chair

When Edward I brought the Stone of Scone down from Scotland to London in 1296, he commissioned his royal artist, Master Walter of Durham, to produce a new throne to house the stone at Westminster Abbey. Originally Edward intended it to be made of bronze, but he was forced to reconsider his plan for the throne when the sheer expense of the project became clear, and instead it was built from solid oak. Thought to have been completed in 1300, the Coronation Chair as it is now known stands in the abbey and has been used at the coronation of every British monarch since Edward II in 1308.

Death of Chaucer

The greatest of all mediaeval writers, Geoffrey Chaucer is believed to have died in London in 1400. With relatively little known of the final years of his life, several conspiracies have arisen around the exact circumstances of Chaucer's death, amongst them the theory that he was murdered by enemies of the deposed king (and his former financial patron) Richard II, or even on the orders of Henry IV himself. These theories aside, however, late in 1399 Chaucer is known to have taken out a lease on a house within the boundaries of Westminster Abbey, where he was buried after his death on 25 October the following year.

Coronation of William the Conqueror

Following his victory at the Battle of Hastings on 14 October 1066, William the Conqueror soon afterward marched on London, entering the city from the north-west (having been prevented from crossing London Bridge) to accept the surrender of Stigand, the then Archbishop of Canterbury, at Wallingford early in December. A few days later, the young Edgar Ætheling, who had quickly been elected king when the death of King Harold had become known, handed William the crown at Berkhamsted and on Christmas Day 1066 he was finally crowned William I of England at Westminster Abbey.

WHAT'S IN A NAME?

Barking
Likely comes from the Old English first name Berica.

Bow
Derives from the Old English word for an arched bridge, *boga*.

Hook
From Old English *hoc*, meaning 'hook of land'.

Tooting
From the Old English first name Tota.

EAST ENGLAND

Lincolnshire, Cambridgeshire, Norfolk, Suffolk

ALDEBURGH, SUFFOLK
Scallop

Dedicated to the Suffolk-born composer Benjamin Britten, *Scallop* is an eye-catching sculpture by the artist Maggi Hambling located on the Suffolk coast near Aldeburgh. Comprising two broken steel scallop shells, the sculpture is inscribed with the words 'I hear those voices that will not be drowned', a quotation from Britten's 1945 opera *Peter Grimes*. Hambling's striking 4-metre (13-foot) work was unveiled in September 2003, and has proven a controversial addition to the local coastline ever since.

ATTLEBOROUGH, NORFOLK
Bronze Age settlement unearthed

In 2002, a Late Bronze Age settlement was unearthed during work to expand the A11 near Attleborough in south Norfolk. The ancient site, dating from before the first century BC, appeared to show a defined system of fields and drainage ditches and contained several pottery, bone and flint artefacts.

AYLSHAM, NORFOLK
Churchill's ashtray auctioned

In November 2009, a 200-year-old silver butter dish once used as an ashtray by Winston Churchill was sold at an auction in Aylsham for £4,200, almost three times its original £1,500 estimate. Churchill is thought to have flicked cigar ash into the shell-shaped dish during a meeting at London's Savoy Hotel of The Other Club, a political debating society he helped establish in 1911.

BEACON HILL, NORFOLK
Norfolk's highest point

Just over one-tenth the height of England's highest mountain Scafell Pike, Beacon Hill (103 metres/338 feet) near Sheringham is the highest point above sea level in Norfolk, which is otherwise Britain's flattest county.

BLICKLING, NORFOLK
The fate of George Boleyn

The brother of Anne, George Boleyn was born at Blickling Hall in the village of Blickling in Norfolk in *c.* 1500. A former Lord Warden of the Cinque Ports as well as an acclaimed translator and poet, George's loyalty to his sister during her doomed marriage to Henry VIII was to prove his downfall – in an attempt to end their marriage prematurely, Henry

falsely charged Anne with treason and infidelity, implicating George by claiming that they had had an incestuous relationship. Although all of the charges were entirely untrue, the fates of Anne and her brother were nevertheless sealed and they were both executed in 1536. On the anniversary of her death, 19 May, Anne's headless ghost is said to haunt her former home at Blickling, and there are even reports of a ghostly horse-drawn coach driven by a headless driver seen approaching the house.

BOURNE, LINCOLNSHIRE
The Bourne Running Auction

Traditionally, on Easter Monday each year the village of Bourne in Lincolnshire holds an annual 'running auction' to determine the tenancy of a field bequeathed to the village by a local landowner, Matthew Clay, in the eighteenth century. In his will, Clay had stipulated that the auction should last only as long as a simultaneous race run by two local children, coming to an end not when the bidding concluded but rather when the winner of the race crossed the finish line. Clay also stipulated that any rental money made from letting the field over the following year should be used to provide the poor of the parish with white bread, although today it has become customary for any profits to be donated to local charities instead.

THE BROADS

The Broads Authority National Park

Controlled by a separate authority to the other national parks of England and Wales, the Norfolk Broads were nonetheless given equivalent status by an Act of Parliament in 1988. Despite covering an area of just 303 square kilometres (117 square miles), England's smallest national park contains six rivers and some 63 individual broads, which altogether form more than 200 kilometres (125 miles) of navigable waterways. The Broads are also, curiously, the flattest national park in the whole of the British Isles, as at no point do they reach any height above just 12 metres (39 feet).

BURNHAM THORPE, NORFOLK

Birthplace of Admiral Nelson

The Norfolk village of Burnham Thorpe was, in 1758, the birthplace of Horatio Nelson, one of the most accomplished heroes in British history. The sixth of 11 children born to a local clergyman, Nelson's naval career began when he joined his uncle on HMS *Raisonnable* in 1770; within three years he was a lieutenant, and by 1778 he was captain. After one of the most illustrious careers in all British naval history, Nelson was killed at Trafalgar in 1805.

BURY ST EDMUNDS, SUFFOLK

Sir Peter Hall and Bob Hoskins

Two of the entertainment world's most familiar names were both born in Bury St Edmunds – acclaimed theatre director Sir Peter Hall, founder of the Royal Shakespeare Company, was born there in 1930, whilst Bob Hoskins, star of films including *Mona Lisa* (for which he was nominated for an Oscar), *The Long Good Friday* and *Who Framed Roger Rabbit*, was born there in 1942.

The life of St Edmund

St Edmund the Martyr was in fact King Edmund of East Anglia, who was reputedly captured, tortured and killed by Danish invaders in *c.* 870. According to records, Edmund was buried in the town of Beodricesworth, which following his canonisation – and several subsequent tales of miracles supposedly occurring at the shrine – became known as Sancte Eadmundes Byrig in the early eleventh century, and eventually Bury St Edmunds.

CAMBRIDGE, CAMBRIDGESHIRE

Nobel Laureate J. J. Thomson

Joseph John Thomson was born in Manchester in 1856. Having studied engineering at Manchester University, Thomson's postgraduate study took him to Cambridge University, where he later became professor of physics. It was there that he carried out a series of groundbreaking experiments on cathode rays, which led to the conclusion that the rays themselves were in fact formed by streams of minute particles or 'corpuscles', which were smaller than (and thereby components of) the atom itself – thus Thomson suggested both the existence of electrons, as well as the fact that the atom itself was not an indivisible entity. For all of this Thomson was awarded the 1906 Nobel Prize for Physics, and became recognised as one of the foremost scientists of his day – indeed, several of Thomson's own students went on to become Nobel Laureates themselves, including his son George Paget Thomson (1937), as well as Ernest Rutherford (1908) and Max Born (1954).

Mendel's hybridisation rediscovered, 1900

On 8 May 1900, whilst on a train journey from Cambridge to London where he was due to deliver a lecture at the Royal Horticultural Society, the English scientist William Bateson read a copy of *Experiments in Plant Hybridisation* by the nineteenth-century scientist Gregor Mendel, and immediately rewrote his lecture to include Mendel's groundbreaking work on the transmission of hereditary characteristics. Bateson's lecture was to prove the first public account of Mendel's work ever given in English, and contributed to a total redressing of hereditary theory in biology; Bateson went on to coin the term 'genetics' in 1905.

The discovery of pulsars

Pulsars – that is, neutron stars that appear to emit 'pulses' of electromagnetic radiation – were first described by the astronomers Jocelyn Bell Burnell and Antony Hewish at Cambridge University on 29 February 1968. Although initially pulsars baffled the scientific community, it is now understood that the 'pulses' that give the stars their name are caused by their rotation, so that the radiation they emit can only be detected when they are facing towards the Earth. Hewish later became the first astronomer to be awarded the Nobel Prize for Physics in 1974, whilst Burnell – who was one of Hewish's PhD students at the time of their discovery – received a damehood for services to science in 2007.

Darwin statue unveiled

A statue of Charles Darwin was unveiled at Christ's Church,

Cambridge on 12 February 2009, marking the bicentenary of his birth. The bronze statue, designed by sculptor Anthony Smith, was unveiled by the Duke of Edinburgh in the presence of Sarah Darwin, Charles Darwin's great-great-granddaughter, and depicts Darwin as a young man, the age he would have been as an undergraduate student at Cambridge in 1831.

The Cambridge Accordia

Built on a brownfield site in the centre of Cambridge, the Accordia residential development became the first housing project to be awarded the RIBA's Stirling Prize for architecture in 2008. Designed collaboratively by three different architectural firms and comprising more than three hundred contemporary houses and apartments, the development was widely praised for combining high-density housing with high-quality architecture.

Harold Pinter's The Birthday Party debuts

The second and perhaps most well-known play by Harold Pinter,

The Birthday Party debuted at Cambridge's Arts Theatre in April 1958. Although initially well received, the play was a critical and commercial disaster on its premiere in London the following month, and closed after just eight performances – a single positive review in *The Sunday Times* was, alas, printed *after* the production had closed. Since its debut, however, the play has since gone on to be considered arguably one of the greatest dramatic works of the twentieth century, whilst its author went on to achieve international success as a writer, director, actor and poet, and was awarded the Nobel Prize for Literature in 2005.

Importance of vitamins explained

The English biochemist Frederick Gowland Hopkins was appointed lecturer in chemical physiology at Cambridge University in 1898. Here, he carried out several groundbreaking experiments in biochemistry and in the early 1900s became one of the first scientists to propose the existence and importance of vitamins, what he termed 'accessory food factors'. His pioneering work in nutrition led to a knighthood in 1925 and the Nobel Prize for Medicine in 1929.

CAWSTON, NORFOLK
Hobart vs Le Neve

The Norfolk village of Cawston was the site of a duel on 20 August 1698 between Sir Henry Hobart MP, 4th Baronet of Blickling Hall, and Sir Oliver Le Neve, a local lawyer. Hobart had accused Le Neve of spreading rumours that he had acted dishonourably during the Battle of the Boyne in 1690, and although Le Neve denied the accusations, he nevertheless accepted Hobart's challenge. In the resulting skirmish, Hobart was fatally stabbed in the stomach and died of his wounds the following day. Le Neve, meanwhile, fled to the Netherlands and did not return to England for two years. He was eventually acquitted of Hobart's murder.

COTTENHAM, CAMBRIDGESHIRE
The Fen Tiger

The so-called 'Fen Tiger' has been sighted at several locations around Cambridgeshire since 1982, when an account of a large cat was reported in Cottenham. Despite its nickname, however, the creature is certainly not a tiger as reports have always described a large cat with jet-black fur.

EAST DEREHAM, NORFOLK
Parish of English writer William Cowper

One of the foremost poets of his day, William Cowper was born at Berkhamsted in Hertfordshire in 1731. The son of an Anglican clergyman, he converted to Evangelicalism whilst recovering from a severe bout of depression in the 1760s, and soon afterwards collaborated with John Newton, a local Evangelical curate, on the anthology *Olney Hymns* (1779). A collection of his own poems followed in 1782, as well as numerous hymns, English translations of both *The Iliad* and *The Odyssey* (1791), and *The Task* (1785), a monumental six-book poem often considered Cowper's greatest achievement, in which he famously states, 'Variety's the very spice of life.' Having moved to Norfolk in 1795, he died at East Dereham on 25 April 1800.

ELY, CAMBRIDGESHIRE
The King's Speech film set

Nominated for 12 Oscars and 14 BAFTAs in 2011 – and named Best Picture at both – 2010's *The King's Speech* told the story of George VI (Best Actor winner Colin Firth) and his attempts to overcome his stammer with the help of Australian speech therapist Lionel Logue (Geoffrey Rush). It was filmed at a variety of locations across the UK (including Elland Road, home ground of Leeds United, and London's Battersea Power Station, which doubled for the BBC wireless control room), and Ely Cathedral in Cambridgeshire was used as Westminster Abbey in the film.

EMNETH, CAMBRIDGESHIRE
Parish of Thomas the Tank Engine writer W. V. Awdry

The Reverend Wilbert Vere Awdry was born in Hampshire in 1911. The son of a clergyman, Awdry himself was ordained into the Anglican Church in 1936. Having served as curate in Kings Norton, Birmingham, he moved to Cambridgeshire in 1946 and became the vicar of Emneth near the Norfolk border in 1953. The first of Awdry's *Railway Series* books, better known as *Thomas the Tank Engine*, was published in 1945; by the time his last book, *Tramway Engines*, was published in 1972, the series numbered 26 books, with Awdry's son Christopher having subsequently added over a dozen more titles to the series since 1983.

THE FENS, EAST ANGLIA
Britain's lowest point

The Fenlands are easily the lowest point in the entire British Isles, with estimates at their most extreme reaches ranging from between 2 metres (6.5 feet) to 4 metres (13 feet) *below* sea level – indeed, The Fens rank amongst the lowest areas of land in the whole of Western Europe.

FRAMLINGHAM, SUFFOLK
Framlingham Castle built

Although the Suffolk village of Framlingham has probably been the site of a castle since the seventh century, the one that stands today was likely completed sometime around 1200. Built by Roger Bigod, 2nd Earl of Norfolk, to replace his father's castle which had been destroyed by Henry II in 1175, the castle remained the property of the Bigod family until 1306 when it became a possession of the English crown on the death of the 5th Earl of Norfolk. In 1553, Edward VI gave the castle to his sister Mary Tudor, who discovered her accession to the throne at Framlingham in July of the same year.

GAINSBOROUGH, LINCOLNSHIRE
Death of King Sweyn Forkbeard

The son of Harald Bluetooth, Sweyn Forkbeard was born in *c.* 960 and became king of Denmark following his father's death in *c.* 986. In 1013, having led numerous raids along the English coast, Sweyn also took control of the Danelaw region of northern England and, after a successful attack on the south, deposed Æthelred the Unready to claim the English throne. Within months of his accession, however, Sweyn died in 1014 at Gainsborough having attempted to destroy the abbey at Bury St Edmunds – legend has it that Sweyn was killed by the ghost of

St Edmund himself, which came down from the skies with a lance and ran the king through.

GRANTCHESTER, CAMBRIDGESHIRE
Brooke's 'The Old Vicarage, Grantchester'

Rupert Brooke's celebrated poem 'The Old Vicarage, Grantchester' was written in 1912 whilst Brooke was in Berlin recovering from a nervous breakdown he had suffered earlier that year. In the poem, Brooke reminisces about both the England he has left behind and his former home in the village of Grantchester near Cambridge, where he lived for a time following his graduation from Cambridge University in 1909. After travelling America and the South Pacific, Brooke died aged just 27 en route to the Battle of Gallipoli shortly after his return to Europe in 1915.

GRANTHAM, LINCOLNSHIRE
Grantham gingerbread

Several places across Britain are renowned for their own individual gingerbread recipes, yet one of the most distinctive is that which is unique to Grantham –

unlike traditional gingerbread, Grantham gingerbread is made without the addition of syrup or treacle, and consequentially has a characteristic white colour.

'Grantham gruel'

As well as literally describing a very meagre gruel, the phrase 'Grantham gruel' was once used figuratively to describe the needlessly circuitous speech of a person who talks around a main point without ever touching on it. According to the seventeenth-century English historian Thomas Fuller, the full phrase 'Grantham gruel, nine grits and a gallon of water' applied to 'those who in their speeches or actions multiply what is superfluous... either wholly omitting, or less regarding, the essentials thereof'.

GREAT WITCHINGHAM, NORFOLK
The Norfolk Lynx

In 2006 an investigation into the authenticity of a contentious photograph of an adult lynx supposedly shot dead in the Norfolk countryside concluded that the photograph was indeed genuine, with the release of an earlier police report into the mystery revealing that the 26-kilogram (59-pound) body of the lynx had been found in the freezer of a local gamekeeper. The animal, long blamed for killing sheep in the area, had reportedly been shot in the village of Great Witchingham, roughly 15 kilometres (10 miles) north-west of Norwich.

GREAT YARMOUTH, NORFOLK
6.1 magnitude earthquake

An earthquake in 1931 centred somewhere off the east coast of Britain on the Dogger Bank – estimates put the epicentre roughly 120 kilometres (75 miles) east of Great Yarmouth – remains the strongest ever recorded in the British Isles, reaching a magnitude of 6.1 on the Richter scale, almost as powerful as the devastating quake which struck Christchurch, New Zealand, in February 2011. Understandably, the 1931 quake was felt right across Great Britain and caused noticeable damage to several locations along the east coast. The tremor was also felt in Germany, Belgium, the Netherlands and France, and

was even reported as far afield as Ireland, Denmark and Norway.

Dickens' David Copperfield

Charles Dickens used Great Yarmouth as the home town of the Peggotty family in his classic 1850 novel *David Copperfield*. Dickens, who visited and stayed in Yarmouth in the late 1840s, describes the town favourably in the novel, with Clara Peggotty even claiming that 'it was well known... that Yarmouth was, upon the whole, the finest place in the universe'.

Invention of the fire extinguisher

The fire extinguisher was invented by the prolific English inventor Captain George William Manby in 1813 whilst he was master of the Yarmouth Barracks. Manby's extinguisher, which he called the 'Extincteur', comprised a copper cylinder containing three gallons of a solution of potassium carbonate or 'pearl ash', which could be sprayed onto a fire using compressed air. As well as this, Manby also invented a type of harpoon gun, a device for saving people who have fallen through ice, and an early breeches buoy, an onshore mechanism similar to a zip wire used to rescue people from sinking ships.

HAXEY, LINCOLNSHIRE
The Haxey Hood

Each year on the afternoon of the twelfth day after Christmas, 6 January, the Lincolnshire village of Haxey plays host to the 'Haxey Hood', a village-wide scrummage in which the 'hood' – that is, a long leather pole – is bustled through the town by a scrum of players, known as the 'sway', to any one of four pubs in either Haxey or the neighbouring village of Westwoodside. The pub that wins may then keep the hood for the following year. Perhaps as much as 700 years old, the game is said to commemorate a time when a fourteenth-century local noblewoman, Lady de Mowbray, lost her silk hood whilst out riding in the village.

HEMINGBY, LINCOLNSHIRE
The Hemingby panther

In 2003, a large black cat was reportedly seen in an abandoned caravan in the village of Hemingby in Lincolnshire. Although a subsequent police search for the cat failed to find it, a forensic test on hairs found at the scene later confirmed that the creature indeed belonged to the mammalian genus *Panthera*, the family of animals that includes leopards and jaguars.

HOLKHAM, NORFOLK
Shakespeare in Love film set

Filmed entirely in the UK, *Shakespeare in Love* ends with a memorable shot of Viola (Gwyneth Paltrow) on a vast sandy beach, filmed at Holkham on the Norfolk coast. The film won seven Oscars in 1999, including Best Picture, Best Actress (for Paltrow), and, despite just eight minutes on screen, Best Supporting Actress for Dame Judi Dench's performance as Elizabeth I.

HUNTINGDON, CAMBRIDGESHIRE
Prime Minister John Major's constituency

Prime minister for seven years following Margaret Thatcher's exit in 1990, John Major's term included the signing of the Maastricht Treaty in 1992 and the First Gulf War. He served the constituency of Huntingdon as member of parliament from 1979 to 2001.

IPSWICH, SUFFOLK
Obolensky memorial unveiled

A statue of the Russian-English rugby player Alexander Obolensky was unveiled in Ipswich in 2009. Obolensky, a Russian prince whose family fled to England to escape the revolution in 1917, excelled at rugby whilst studying at Oxford University in the early 1930s, and was subsequently chosen to represent England – he scored two tries on his international debut in 1936, in England's first ever defeat of New Zealand's All Blacks. Tragically, having joined the RAF at the outbreak of World War Two, Obolensky was killed in a plane crash during training at RAF Martlesham Heath near Ipswich in 1940, aged just 24.

LINCOLN, LINCOLNSHIRE
Steep Hill

In November 2011, the British Academy of Urbanism – which aims to recognise and promote the finest examples of urban planning and development – officially named Steep Hill in Lincoln as their 'Best Street in Britain' for 2012, commending its 'strong sense of history and community'. A popular tourist attraction, as its name suggests Steep Hill has a remarkably steep gradient, and connects Lincoln's High Street to the city's nearby castle and cathedral. The street dates back to Roman times and features two Norman-period buildings, one of which – the twelfth-century Jew's House – is believed to be the oldest town house still inhabited today in all of Europe.

'Yellowbellies'

Inhabitants of Lincolnshire are affectionately known as 'yellowbellies', a term whose origin is open to considerable debate – amongst the several potential explanations suggested are: the yellow waistcoats traditionally worn by members of the Royal North Lincolnshire Militia, as well as those worn by drivers of stagecoaches travelling from Lincoln to London; the yellow undersides of the frogs which populate the Lincolnshire Fens; and the familiar yellow carriage of the local Lincolnshire mail train.

'The devil looking over Lincoln'

'The devil looking over Lincoln' is an old phrase describing someone who speaks unfavourably of someone else; the old proverb 'to look as the devil looks over Lincoln' meant to glare or to look at someone in an unpleasant way. If not alluding to a gargoyle at Lincoln Cathedral, the phrase may instead refer to Lincoln College, Oxford, where a stone devil once stood guard over the doorway.

William of Scotland pays homage

Following the succession of King John to the English throne in 1199, the Scottish King William I requested John to restore the kingdom of Northumberland to the Scottish crown. John, however, refused and William responded with a threat of war. The dispute rumbled on inconclusively for several more months, until William met John at Lincoln in November 1200 to 'pay homage', essentially pledging his loyalty to the English crown. After several more years of deteriorating relations between England and Scotland, the dispute was finally settled in 1209 when John forced William to abandon all of his claims to Northumberland.

The Battle of Lincoln

The Battle of Lincoln marked a significant turning point in the events of the First Barons' War, an early thirteenth-century uprising of a group of English barons against the shambolic rule of King John. Wishing to see John ousted from the throne, the barons invited the French prince Louis (later Louis VIII of France) to invade England and seize power, and within months he had indeed proclaimed himself king and taken control of much of southern England. On John's death in 1216, however, it became in the barons' best interest to see John's young son Henry crowned king, and as a result the rebellion promptly turned against Louis' invasion. At the Battle of Lincoln on 20 May the following year, English troops led by Henry III's regent, William Marshal, defeated Louis' French forces and retook the city. The victory proved a heavy blow for Louis' campaign, and within months he relinquished his claim to the throne and returned to France.

Lincoln, Nebraska

Although several of the very largest cities in the United States share their names with places in Britain – notably Boston, Massachusetts and Stockton, California – the largest US city whose British namesake *also* has city status is Lincoln, the state capital of Nebraska. Known as Nebraska's 'Star City', Lincoln was originally called Lancaster (also, coincidentally, a British city) but changed its name in reference to Abraham Lincoln just prior to Nebraska's admission to the Union on 1 March 1867. With a population of more than 250,000, Lincoln is Nebraska's second-largest city after Omaha.

LOWESTOFT, SUFFOLK
England's easternmost point

The second-largest town in Suffolk, Lowestoft is also Britain's easternmost settlement, with the local promontory of Ness Point, or Lowestoft Ness, marking the furthest east it is possible to go in the whole of the British Isles. The town stands almost a full 2 degrees east of the Greenwich Meridian, the same longitude as Paris and Barcelona.

MANTHORPE, LINCOLNSHIRE
The Bowthorpe Oak

The 1,000-year-old Bowthorpe Oak in Manthorpe, near Bourne, Lincolnshire, is certainly amongst the oldest trees in Britain, and is likely the oldest oak tree in England. Despite now being almost completely hollow – indeed, the tree has in the past been used as a storehouse and even as a furnished dining area seating a dozen people – the tree continues to grow, and is in fact one of the largest living oak trees in the whole of the British Isles, with a circumference of nearly 12 metres (40 feet).

NORWICH, NORFOLK
Oscar-winner Stuart Craig

One of the most successful Britons at the Oscars in recent years, Stuart Craig was born in Norwich in 1942. As production designer, Craig has won three Oscars for Best Art Direction – for *Gandhi* (1982), *Dangerous Liaisons* (1988) and *The English Patient* (1996) –

from a total of ten nominations; more recently, he has been involved in the *Harry Potter* film series, for which he received his most recent nomination in 2011.

The Norwich terrier

Both 'Norwich' and 'Norfolk' are the names of two distinct breeds of terrier, with the Norfolk generally considered a 'drop-eared' cousin of the otherwise identical Norwich. Both dogs are amongst the smallest of all terriers and indeed, at a little under 30 centimetres (1 foot) tall, are generally considered the smallest of all 'working' dogs, originally bred in the late nineteenth century to catch vermin. Once known as 'Cantab' terriers (referring to their one-time popularity amongst Cambridge University students) the Norwich was admitted into the English Kennel Club in 1932, with the Norfolk finally classified as a distinct species in 1964.

PETERBOROUGH, CAMBRIDGESHIRE
Sarcolestes discovered

Found in a brick pit near Peterborough in the late nineteenth century, all that has ever been discovered of the dinosaur *Sarcolestes* is a handful of teeth and several fragments of jawbone – such a small amount of evidence, in fact, that this 3-metre (10-foot) Middle Jurassic herbivore was at first mistakenly identified as a meat eater, and ultimately given a name literally meaning 'flesh-thief'. Re-examination of what little exists of this 160-million-year-old species, however, indicates that *Sarcolestes* was in fact one of the earliest types of *Ankylosauria*, a group of bulky herbivorous quadruped dinosaurs with characteristically densely armoured backs.

SANDRINGHAM, NORFOLK
Death of George V

Having succeeded Edward VII to the throne in 1910, much of the latter half of George V's reign was sadly marked by ill health. He suffered from bronchitis and other chronic lung diseases for many years until his death in 1936 at Sandringham House; his son Albert, later George VI, also died at Sandringham in 1952.

First royal Christmas message

In 1932, the first royal Christmas message was broadcast by the BBC from Sandringham House in Norfolk. It was written by the then Poet Laureate Rudyard Kipling, and George V read the message live to more than 20 million people worldwide over the newly launched Empire Service (now the BBC World Service). Since then, every monarch except Edward VIII (who abdicated just weeks beforehand) has since delivered a Christmas message, although it was not established as an annual tradition until 1951; the following year, Elizabeth II gave her first Christmas address, and it was during her reign, in 1957, that the message was televised for the first time.

SOUTHWOLD, SUFFOLK
Iris film set

Jim Broadbent won the Best Supporting Actor Oscar for his role as John Bayley, the husband of authoress Iris Murdoch (played by both Judi Dench and Kate Winslet) in *Iris*, an acclaimed 2001 biopic of the writer's life. One of Murdoch's own favourite holiday destinations, a number of scenes for the film were shot at Southwold Beach in Suffolk.

ST NEOTS, CAMBRIDGESHIRE
The life of St Neot

Thought to have spent much of his life in Cornwall, the ninth-century figure St Neot was once sacristan of Glastonbury Abbey. Following his death in *c.* 870, Neot's remains were supposedly brought to the Cambridgeshire town now bearing his name in the late tenth century, and formed the basis of the monastery there.

SUTTON, SUFFOLK
Hyracotherium discovered

Hyracotherium was a dog-like herbivorous mammal that lived around 45–60 million years ago. First discovered in England in the mid 1800s, numerous specimens of *Hyracotherium* have since been unearthed, with those found at a site in Sutton on the Suffolk coast being amongst the earliest in the world. Despite standing less than 30 centimetres (1 foot) tall at the shoulder, *Hyracotherium* was in fact an ancestor of the modern horse.

SWAFFHAM, NORFOLK
Last known sighting of a great bustard in Britain

At 1.2 metres (4 feet) tall and weighing in at around 14 kilograms (30 pounds), the great bustard is thought to be the heaviest flying bird in the world. Once native to Great Britain, the bustard was hunted into extinction in the mid nineteenth century, with a sighting at Swaffham in 1838 believed to be the last recorded of a native British one. However, a recent scheme to reintroduce the birds to Britain and to re-establish a sustained breeding population here has gone from strength to strength, and in 2009 a pair of birds released in Wiltshire successfully reared the UK's first wild bustard chick since 1832.

THETFORD, NORFOLK
US campaigner Thomas Paine

The pamphleteer and inventor Thomas Paine was born in Thetford in 1737. It was not until 1774 that, after separating from his wife and following a chance meeting with Benjamin Franklin, he emigrated to Philadelphia. Two years later, his pamphlet *Common Sense* was published, which advocated independence for the British colonies in America and quickly became a huge success. After a brief return to Europe, during which time he supported the French Revolution and was even elected to the French National Convention, Paine returned to the US and lived in New York until his death in 1809.

The Great Heathen Army invades

One of the most significant of all Viking invasions of Britain saw the arrival of the so-called 'Great Heathen Army' at the coast of East Anglia in 866. The army had been mustered by the sons of the legendary Viking leader Ragnar Lodbrok, who had earlier been captured and executed by the king of Northumbria, Ælle II, who had supposedly thrown Ragnar into a pit of adders. Having wintered in East Anglia – perhaps in Thetford, to where they would return in 869 – the Great Heathen Army headed north early in 867 and soon met with Ælle and his forces in battle outside York. Whilst most English accounts state that

Ælle was killed in the battle, Viking records claim instead that he was captured by Ragnar's youngest son, Ivar the Boneless, and executed by 'blood-eagle' – a gruesome method in which the victim's ribs were cut from the spine, broken and spread outwards like an eagle's wings.

WARBOYS, CAMBRIDGESHIRE
Witches of Warboys Trial

In 1593, a young woman named Alice Samuel, along with her husband John and daughter Agnes, were all executed for witchcraft in Cambridgeshire. The allegations that brought about their deaths began four years earlier in 1589, when Alice visited her neighbours Robert and Elizabeth Throckmorton in Warboys to see their nine-year-old daughter Jane, who had been ill for some time. Almost as soon as Alice arrived, however, Jane's condition seemed suddenly to worsen and supposedly in some kind of fit the girl began shouting and pointing at Alice, claiming that she was responsible for her illness. The event led to years of local rumours that the Samuels were engaged in witchcraft, and in 1590 even Lady Cromwell, grandmother of Oliver Cromwell and a close friend of the Throckmortons, confronted Alice about her apparent crimes – when Lady Cromwell died some two years later, her 'murder' was added to the list of crimes of which the Samuels were eventually accused. Imprisoned and tried before the bishop of Huntingdon, Alice, John and Agnes Samuel were all found guilty of witchcraft in 1593 and hanged.

WEST RUNTON, NORFOLK
The West Runton Elephant

In December 1990, the hip bone of a steppe mammoth was found entirely by accident at the bottom of cliffs at West Runton on the Norfolk coast. The so-called 'West Runton Elephant', as it is affectionately known, remains the oldest and largest elephant-like skeleton ever found in Britain – indeed, the steppe mammoth itself was probably the largest non-dinosaur ever to have lived on land, standing 4 metres (13 feet) tall and weighing around 10 tonnes – and is perhaps the most complete skeleton of this species ever discovered.

WHITTLESEY, CAMBRIDGESHIRE
The Straw Bear

In 1980, the village of Whittlesey near Peterborough revived a local tradition known as the Whittlesey Straw Bear, in which one of the villagers – the 'Bear' – would be bound head to foot in straw and led through the village by a chain or rope around his neck, stopping off at various points to dance and entertain the crowd, receiving gifts of food or drink in return. Taking place on the Tuesday following so-called 'Plough Monday' (that is, the first Monday after Twelfth Night), the tradition was popular throughout the nineteenth century but died off in the early 1900s.

WISBECH, CAMBRIDGESHIRE
Death of John Alcock

Born in Beverley, East Yorkshire, in *c.* 1430, John Alcock was one of the principal churchmen of the fifteenth century. Appointed bishop of Rochester in 1472, bishop of Worcester in 1476 and bishop of Ely in 1486, Alcock twice held the post of Lord Chancellor. He was also a noted architect, responsible for Jesus College, Cambridge, which he founded in 1496. He died at Wisbech in 1500 and was buried in Ely Cathedral.

WOOLSTHORPE-BY-COLSTERWORTH, LINCOLNSHIRE
Birthplace of Isaac Newton

Often erroneously said to have been born in Grantham, Sir Isaac Newton was in fact born in Woolsthorpe Manor, a farmhouse on the outskirts of the tiny Lincolnshire village of Woolsthorpe-by-Colsterworth, in 1642. Having attended Cambridge University, Newton was made to return to his childhood home in 1665 when the plague forced the university to close. It is said that it was at Woolsthorpe that Newton performed many of his preliminary experiments into optics, and, according to legend, it was here that an apple falling from a tree prompted him to formulate his laws of gravitation.

WYMONDHAM, NORFOLK
Kett's Rebellion

In the summer of 1549, anger over the ever more widespread enclosure of common land in England grew into rebellion in Norfolk, as villagers in Wymondham tore down fences around once publically owned land and, under the leadership of local landowner Robert Kett, marched on to Norwich in protest. As word of the uprising spread, some 15,000 protestors assembled outside the city under Kett's direction, eventually taking the city by force on 22 July; in response, Edward VI ordered John Dudley, Earl of Warwick, to quash the rebellion and retake the city. A bloody battle ensued on nearby Mousehold Heath, ending the rebellion and leading to Kett's capture, and having been found guilty of high treason, he was executed on 7 December 1549.

WHAT'S IN A NAME?

Acre, Norfolk
From Old English *æcer*, meaning 'newly cultivated land'.

Ashley, Cambridgeshire
Derived from *æsc*, the Old English word for an ash tree.

Cotton, Suffolk
Likely derives from the plural of the Old English word *cot*, meaning 'cottage'.

Eagle, Lincolnshire
Means 'oak-tree wood', or 'clearing', derives from a combination of the Scandinavian word *eik* and the Old English words *ac* and *leah*.

Eye, Suffolk
There are several towns named 'Eye' in England, of which this Suffolk market town is just one; the name usually derives from the Old English word *eg*, describing either land surrounded by water, or else a well-drained area surrounded by marshy or boggy land.

Healing, Lincolnshire
Probably derives from the Old English first name Hægel.

Horning, Norfolk
Derives from the Old English word *horn*, here likely referring to a sharp river bend.

Swallow, Lincolnshire
Probably derives from an Old English word for a fast-flowing stream, *swalwe*.

Wendy, Cambridgeshire
Presumably derived from the Old English words *wende* and *eg*, meaning 'island at the river bend'.

Wrangle, Lincolnshire
Perhaps means 'crooked stream', from an obscure English or Scandinavian root.

Yelling, Cambridgeshire
Possibly derives from an Old English first name, Giella.

CENTRAL ENGLAND

Cheshire, Derbyshire, Northamptonshire, Nottinghamshire, Shropshire, Staffordshire, Rutland, Herefordshire, Worcestershire, West Midlands, Warwickshire, Leicestershire

ARELEY KINGS, WORCESTERSHIRE
Layamon's Brut

The first known priest of St Bartholomew's Church in the tiny Worcestershire village of Areley Kings was the thirteenth-century poet and writer Layamon, whose epic 16,000-line poem *Brut* is one of the earliest known written histories of Britain. Estimated to have been written at Areley sometime around 1200, *Brut* deals with the period from the Roman General Brutus' arrival in Britain in the first century BC to the time of the Ancient British King Cædwalla in the mid seventh century, and contains the first known account of the history of King Arthur. Easily amongst the most important early Middle English documents known today, two surviving copies of Layamon's *Brut* are held at the British Museum.

ASHBY-DE-LA-ZOUCH, LEICESTERSHIRE
Ripper suspect Frederick Bailey Deeming

Born in Ashby-de-la-Zouch in 1853, Frederick Bailey Deeming emigrated to Australia with his second wife Emily in 1891. Later that year, he murdered her, burying her body in a cement hearth at their home in Melbourne. When the body was discovered the following year, a police investigation back in England found the bodies of Deeming's first wife and their four children buried in the floor of a house in Rainhill in Lancashire. Whilst in prison in Melbourne, Deeming claimed that he was Jack the Ripper, but it is nevertheless known that he was not in England at the time of the murders. He was executed in Melbourne in 1892.

BAKEWELL, DERBYSHIRE
Bakewell pudding

The Bakewell pudding, a cooked puff pastry dish of jam and ground almonds, takes its name from the Derbyshire town of Bakewell where it is said to have been invented by accident in the nineteenth century. According to the story, a local cook misread a recipe for jam tarts and instead of mixing almonds and egg into the pastry, smeared the mixture on top of a layer of jam, which ultimately rose to the top when cooked. Variations of the pudding include the Bakewell tart, a small, shortcrust pastry tart made with jam and almond sponge, and

the cherry Bakewell, an iced tart topped with a glacé cherry.

BEWDLEY, WORCESTERSHIRE
Prime Minister Stanley Baldwin's constituency

Stanley Baldwin represented his home town of Bewdley as member of parliament from 1908 to 1937, during which time he was personally appointed prime minister by George V following the resignation of Andrew Bonar Law. In all, Baldwin held the position on three separate occasions (1923–24, 1924–29, 1935–37), notably presiding over the General Strike and the abdication of Edward VIII.

BIRMINGHAM
The Birmingham tornado

A tornado that tore through the suburbs of Birmingham at 2.30 p.m. on 28 July 2005 was one of the most powerful recorded in the UK for decades, with maximum wind speeds estimated at 144–210 kilometres per hour (90–130 miles per hour). The storm damaged dozens of buildings, uprooted about 1,000 trees and caused £40 million of damage, making it also the costliest storm in British history.

'Brummies'

Both 'Brummie' and 'Brum', the latter a colloquial name for Birmingham itself, derive from 'Brummagem', an obsolete alternative name for the city. Although today 'Brummie' is used with pride by the people of Birmingham, in the seventeenth century a huge number of counterfeit coins notoriously manufactured in the city led to the use of 'brummagem' or 'brummagem ware' to describe anything poorly made or of little value.

Tony Hancock memorial unveiled

One of Birmingham's most striking statues is that of the comedian Tony Hancock, who was born in the city in 1924. Designed by Bruce Williams and unveiled by Sir Harry Secombe in 1996, the work is positioned in the city's Old Square, appropriately (given the famous 'The Blood Donor' episode of his *Hancock's Half Hour* series) once the site of the city's Blood Transfusion Service.

Holst's The Planets debuts

Following a number of invitation-only performances, one of the first public performances of Gustav Holst's masterpiece *The Planets* took place on 10 October 1920 in Birmingham. Containing, in full, seven movements – one for every planet in the Solar System, excluding Earth and Pluto (not discovered until 1930) – the suite is written for an extensive orchestra including organ, celesta and six timpani; the final movement, 'Neptune, the Mystic', moreover requires two hidden female choruses which, following Holst's instructions, should reside 'in an adjoining room, the door of which is to be left open until the last bar... when it is to be slowly and silently closed', creating what is considered classical music's first fade-out ending.

Discovery of digitalis

Born in Wellington, Shropshire, in 1741, it was whilst employed as a physician at Birmingham General Hospital in the 1770s that the chemist and botanist William Withering noted that a patient suffering from dropsy had made a vast improvement on taking a traditional herbal remedy containing foxgloves. Over several years that followed, Withering carried out a lengthy series of experiments in which he discovered the digitalis the foxgloves contained was effective in treating conditions of the heart. He presented his pioneering findings to the Royal College of Physicians in 1785.

The Birmingham Olympics

Alongside Paris, Brisbane, Belgrade and Amsterdam, Birmingham bid to host the 1992 Olympic Games, losing out to Barcelona. It remains the first and only time the city has bid for the Olympics.

Birmingham, Alabama

Whilst Montgomery is its capital, by far the largest city in Alabama is Birmingham, with a population of over 212,000 (roughly one-tenth that of Birmingham, England). Founded in 1871, by the early twentieth century the city had established itself as a major industrial centre, its remarkably swift growth earning it the nickname of 'The Magic City' – indeed, Birmingham is home to the largest cast-iron statue in the world, a 17-metre (56-foot) model of the Roman god Vulcan, intended to symbolise the city's remarkable industrial heritage.

BISHOP'S CASTLE, SHROPSHIRE
5.1 magnitude British earthquake

In 1990, the Shropshire village of Bishop's Castle near the Welsh border was the epicentre of a 5.1 magnitude earthquake which struck early in the afternoon of 2 April. The tremor could be felt over an immense area, encompassing all of Wales and much of northern England, as well as locations as distant as Tyneside, Cornwall and Kent.

BOSCOBEL, SHROPSHIRE
The Royal Oak

Boscobel House in the tiny village of Boscobel in north Shropshire was once home to the so-called Royal Oak, famed for being the tree in which Charles II hid whilst fleeing from the Roundheads after the Battle of Worcester in 1651. Charles later dictated the story of the Royal Oak to Samuel Pepys in 1680, apparently stating that a parliamentarian soldier passed by directly under the tree as he hid in its branches. As the original oak was sadly destroyed sometime in the seventeenth/ eighteenth century, the tree which stands on the site today is not the original but rather one of its descendants, although even this is thought to be around 200–300 years old.

BRADGATE PARK, LEICESTERSHIRE
The ghost of Lady Jane Grey

Proclaimed queen following the death of her cousin Edward VI, Lady Jane Grey was deposed by Edward's sister, Mary I, after a reign of just nine days and imprisoned in the Tower of London in July 1553. Found guilty of high treason, Jane was sentenced to death and beheaded on Tower Green in London the following February – although her exact birthdate is unknown, she would not have been much more than 17 years old. What remains of her birthplace, Bradgate House in Bradgate Park in north-west Leicestershire, is said to be haunted both by Jane herself and by a phantom royal coach which

has reputedly been seen in the grounds of the house.

BURTON-UPON-TRENT, STAFFORDSHIRE
Founding of Burton Abbey

Burton Abbey in Burton-upon-Trent was founded as a Benedictine abbey by Wulfric Spott, an earl of Mercia likely descended from Alfred the Great, sometime around 1000. The exact date of the abbey's establishment, however, is unclear and depends greatly on the date of Wulfric's death, thought to have been sometime between 1002 (the approximate date of his will) and 1004, with some sources even claiming that he died at the Battle of Ringmere in 1010.

CHESTER, CHESHIRE
Æthelred the Unready attacks Scotland

When Viking raids on the south coast of England temporarily ceased in 1000, the English King Æthelred II took the opportunity to collect his troops together and further his own territorial aspirations. From a temporary base at Chester, Æthelred attacked Cumberland and

Strathclyde with, as is recorded in the *Anglo-Saxon Chronicle*, somewhat significant success. Æthelred's navy, meanwhile, had meant to sail up the Irish Sea to aid his armies on land but were held back by bad weather and instead ravaged the Isle of Man and Anglesey. The following year, Viking raids along the English Channel resumed, and Æthelred's forces returned to defending southern England and harrying the Normandy coast.

The Deva Stadium

The home ground of Chester City FC, the Deva Stadium opened in 1992, replacing the club's previous home ground at Sealand Road. Taking its name from the city's Roman name, the stadium is perhaps the only one in the world to straddle a national boundary – whilst the majority of the ground (including the pitch) stands in Wales, the club gates and, significantly, the main stand are both in England.

Britain's oldest racecourse

Chester Racecourse is generally considered England's oldest course still in frequent use, with the first official race taking place there in 1539. The date is commemorated by a restaurant named 1539 that opened at the course in 2008.

CLAY CROSS, DERBYSHIRE
Nobel Laureate Arthur Henderson

Born in Glasgow in 1863, former Foreign and Home Secretary Arthur Henderson served as member of parliament for Barnard Castle (1903–18), Widnes (1919–22), Newcastle-upon-Tyne (1923) and Burnley (1924–31) before returning to parliament as MP for Clay Cross in Derbyshire in 1933, a position he held until his death in 1935. It was during this time, in 1934, that Henderson was awarded the Nobel Peace Prize for his work in international disarmament following World War One and the increasing tension ahead of World War Two.

COTON IN THE ELMS, DERBYSHIRE
Britain's most landlocked point

The tiny village of Coton in the Elms near Burton-upon-Trent in Derbyshire is considered the furthest point from the sea it is possible to be in the British Isles. As measured by the Ordnance Survey, Church Flatts Farm to the south-east of the village is 113 kilometres (70 miles) from the nearest coastline, standing equidistant from the coast at Lincolnshire, Cheshire, Gloucestershire and Flintshire, north Wales.

COVENTRY, WEST MIDLANDS
Twinned with Belgrade

Coventry has official agreements connecting it with more than twenty different towns and cities worldwide, many of which recognise the fact that it was especially badly affected by Luftwaffe bombings during World War Two – appropriately, its twin cities today include Sarajevo, Volgograd, Arnhem and the village of Lidice in the Czech Republic, whose entire population was murdered by the Nazis in 1942. The connection to Belgrade, also heavily bombed by the Luftwaffe, dates from 1953 when an official gift of Serbian timber was used to construct Coventry's Belgrade Theatre.

'Sent to Coventry'

It is thought that at one time the citizens of Coventry had such a hatred of soldiers that a local woman once seen talking to one was immediately ostracised – to this day 'sending someone to Coventry' means to shun or ignore them.

Frank Whittle and Philip Larkin

World-renowned as the inventor of the jet engine, Sir Frank Whittle was born in the Earlsdon area of Coventry in 1907. One of the most popular and highly acclaimed British poets of the twentieth century, as well as a respected author and critic, Philip Larkin was also born there in 1922.

Britten's War Requiem debuts

Commissioned to compose a piece for the reconsecration of Coventry Cathedral after the original building was destroyed during World War Two, Benjamin Britten combined traditional Latin texts with several works by the war poet Wilfred Owen for his momentous *War Requiem*, which premiered to great acclaim in the rebuilt cathedral on 30 May 1962. The grand one-and-a-half-hour work is scored for three vocal soloists, organ, full chorus and boys' chorus, and two orchestras, including a full chamber orchestra.

DERBY, DERBYSHIRE
Derby County's woeful league performance

Having earlier beaten Newcastle United 1–0 on 17 September 2007, Derby County's home match at Pride Park against Sheffield United on 13 September 2008 saw the club finally end a record-breaking 36 consecutive league games without a win. Just four days short of a full year of no wins, Derby's 3–1 win over Sheffield became the first league victory for their manager Paul Jewell, despite him having taken up the position some ten months earlier.

DERITEND, BIRMINGHAM
Birth of Biblical pioneer John Rogers

John Rogers was born in Deritend, now a suburb of Birmingham, in *c.* 1500. Having left Cambridge University, Rogers was serving as chaplain to English merchants based in Antwerp when he happened to meet William Tyndale in 1534. Following Tyndale's death two years later, Rogers completed his groundbreaking English translation of the Bible for him, publishing it under his own pseudonym Thomas Matthew in 1537. On his return to England, Rogers was arrested for preaching Protestantism under the newly crowned Mary I and was sent to Newgate Prison, becoming the first Protestant martyr executed by Mary when he was burnt at the stake in 1555.

DERNHALL, CHESHIRE
US General Charles Lee

Charles Lee was born in Cheshire on 6 February 1732. First sent to America at the age of 23 to serve in the French and Indian War, Lee returned to Europe for a number of years before his increasing support of the colonists took him back to America in 1773. Having served in numerous campaigns during the American Revolution, Lee was court-martialled by George Washington for disobeying orders in 1778 and released from duty two years later. He lived in Philadelphia until his death on 2 October 1782.

EAST FARNDON, NORTHAMPTONSHIRE

The Northamptonshire 'Black Beast'

In November 1998, a baby alpaca found dead in a field in East Farndon near Market Harborough was thought to have been killed by a big cat. Reports of a large black cat-like creature in and around the Harborough area go back to 1996.

EAST STOKE, NOTTINGHAMSHIRE

The Battle of Stoke Field

Although the defeat of Richard III at the Battle of Bosworth Field in 1485 effectively ended the Wars of the Roses, two years later one final Yorkist rebellion was made by the Earl of Lincoln, John de la Pole, who had been a nephew of the king. Richard had earlier named Lincoln as his heir to the throne, yet on his uncle's defeat the succession slipped from his grasp and Henry VII took the crown instead. Despite apparently accepting the new king, word of another pretender to the throne (in fact an imposter

posing as the earl of Warwick, another of Richard's rightful heirs) gave Lincoln the pretence he needed to challenge Henry's rule himself. Assembling an army of some 8,000 mainly Irish and German mercenaries, Lincoln's troops fought Henry at the Battle of Stoke Field at East Stoke, Nottinghamshire, on 16 June 1487. Lincoln, however, died in the battle and on the death of the real earl of Warwick in 1499 the Plantagenet claim to the throne finally came to an end.

EDALE, DERBYSHIRE

The Pennine Way

In 1965, the Pennine Way was designated Britain's first National Trail. At 429 kilometres (268 miles) it is also one of the longest in Britain, and from its southern starting point at Edale in Derbyshire it passes through a total of eight counties as well as three national parks. As the northernmost National Trail in England, moreover, the Pennine Way is also the only English trail to stray into Scotland, ending at the village of Kirk Yetholm in the Scottish Borders.

EDGBASTON, BIRMINGHAM

Prime Minister Neville Chamberlain's constituency

The son of the mayor of Birmingham, Neville Chamberlain followed his father to the same position in 1915. In parliament, he first represented the Birmingham constituency of Ladywood (1918–29) before becoming MP for his home district of Edgbaston in 1929. He held the seat for 11 years, during which time he was elected prime minister (1937–40) following the third and final term of Stanley Baldwin, and was responsible for declaring war on Germany following the invasion of Poland in 1939. Due to failing health, Chamberlain resigned from office in 1940 and died of stomach cancer just six months later on 9 November.

FOTHERINGHAY, NORTHAMPTONSHIRE

Execution of Mary, Queen of Scots

On 8 February 1587, Mary, Queen of Scots was executed at Fotheringhay Castle in the village of Fotheringhay near Peterborough. Her life was one of the most tumultuous in all British history – a former queen of France, she married three times, was accused of involvement in the murder of her second husband, was forced to abdicate in favour of her one-year-old son, and spent almost all of the final 20 years of her life in prison. It was, however, her supposed involvement in the Babington Plot to assassinate Elizabeth I in 1586 (which she vehemently denied) that saw her finally found guilty of treason and beheaded.

GRAFTON REGIS, NORTHAMPTONSHIRE

Marriage of Edward IV

The fourth child and second son of Richard Plantagenet, 3rd Duke of York, Edward IV secretly married Elizabeth Woodville in her home town of Grafton Regis in 1464. The marriage was Elizabeth's second, following the death of her first husband Sir John Grey at the Second Battle of St Albans in 1461. Ironically, Grey had been a Lancastrian, whilst Edward was the House of York's claimant to the throne. Edward and Elizabeth had ten children, including Elizabeth, the wife of Henry VII, and both

Edward V and Richard, Duke of York, the so-called Princes in the Tower whose right to the throne was suspiciously invalidated by their uncle, Richard III.

HANLEY, STAFFORDSHIRE
Titanic Captain Edward Smith

Edward John Smith, born in Hanley in 1850, was the captain of the *Titanic*. Having started his seafaring career at the age of just 13, Smith joined the White Star Line in 1880 and first served as captain aboard RMS *Majestic* in 1895. His later ships – namely the *Baltic*, *Adriatic*, *Olympic* and then *Titanic* – were each the largest vessel in the world at the time of his captaincy. Reports of Smith's death on the *Titanic* vary, with some claiming that he remained on the bridge as the ship sank, and others that he died in the water, perhaps having jumped overboard to help others onto an upturned raft. His body was never recovered.

HEREFORD, HEREFORDSHIRE
US entertainer Frank Oz

The son of two Holocaust refugees, Richard Frank Oznowicz was born in Hereford in 1944 and emigrated with his family to California when he was just five years old. Despite numerous acting and directing credits, Frank Oz is perhaps best known for his work with Jim Henson's Muppets, working both as voice artist and puppeteer for several memorable characters including Miss Piggy, Fozzie Bear and Animal. Oz is also known for his work with Henson on the fantasy films *Labyrinth* (1986) and *The Dark Crystal* (1982, which he also co-directed), and with George Lucas in the *Star Wars* films, for which he provided the voice and puppetry (until the character became entirely computer-generated) for the diminutive Jedi Master, Yoda.

The Hereford Mappa Mundi

The Hereford Mappa Mundi, one of the largest mediaeval maps of the world known to exist, dates from around 1300. More than 1.5 metres (5 feet) wide, the map is centred on Jerusalem (reflecting the importance of religion in the mediaeval world) and, besides the names of more than 400 towns and cities from across the globe, also features Babylon, Troy, the

Minotaur's Labyrinth on Crete, the Pharos of Alexandria, Noah's Ark, the Garden of Eden and Sodom and Gomorrah, as well as the names and illustrations of a whole host of animals, plants, birds and mythological beings. The map is currently housed in Hereford Cathedral.

IRONBRIDGE, SHROPSHIRE
World Heritage Site

Ironbridge Gorge in the Shropshire town of Ironbridge was made a World Heritage Site in 1986, chosen as one of the most significant symbols of the Industrial Revolution in all of Britain. Located in one of the first truly industrialised areas, the bridge from which the town takes its name was completed in 1779 and is thought to be the first iron bridge anywhere in the world.

KIDDERMINSTER, WORCESTERSHIRE
Walter Nash, twenty-seventh prime minister of New Zealand

Walter Nash was elected prime minister of New Zealand in December 1957, serving for exactly three years. Born in Kidderminster in 1882, he emigrated to New Zealand with his wife in 1909, establishing a successful branch of the New Zealand Labour Party in New Plymouth. After several years with the party, Nash became its national secretary in 1922 and, following the 1935 election, was appointed finance minister of the country's first Labour government. When the party was elected to a second term in office in 1957, Nash became prime minister.

KINGSTANDING, BIRMINGHAM
Charles I

According to local tradition, the district of Kingstanding in Erdington, Birmingham, is named after the English King Charles I, who is said to have addressed his troops there during the Civil War in 1642. The actual mound on which he is said to have stood is today known locally as the 'King's Standing'.

LEICESTER, LEICESTERSHIRE
Black Annis

Black Annis is the name of a witch said to dwell in a cave she carved for herself in the Dane Hills area to the west of Leicester. According to legend, Black Annis snatches children who stray too close to her home and eats them, wearing their dried skins tied around her waist. Although the origins of the legend are unclear, the most likely explanation is that the story developed from that of a nun named Agnes Scott who lived in isolation in the Dane Hills in the fifteenth century.

The Curve Theatre

One of the most striking theatrical venues in the country, Curve in the centre of Leicester opened in 2008 at a cost of more than £60 million. Designed by the internationally acclaimed Uruguayan-born architect Rafael Viñoly (his first project in the UK), the theatre comprises two versatile performance areas, one a remarkable state-of-the-art 800-seater auditorium viewable from street level. Curve was officially opened by the Queen and Prince Philip in 2008, and won a RIBA Regional Award in 2009.

LONGBRIDGE, BIRMINGHAM
Final Longbridge Mini produced

After 41 years of continuous production, the last of over five and a quarter million classic minis rolled off the production line at the MG Rover factory in Longbridge on 4 October 2000. First produced in 1959, over a hundred different models of the car were made over the decades, and in 1995 the Mini was named Car of the Century. With production ceased at the Longbridge plant, manufacture of a new Mini by Rover's parent company BMW began the following year in Cowley on the outskirts of Oxford.

LOUGHBOROUGH, LEICESTERSHIRE
The Hours film set

Scenes set at Richmond Station in 1923 from Stephen Daldry's acclaimed adaptation of the Pulitzer-Prize-winning novel *The Hours* – including a pivotal argument between a fraught Virginia Woolf (an Oscar-winning Nicole Kidman) and her husband – were in fact filmed at

Loughborough Central Station in Leicestershire.

Loughborough FC's farewell season

The 1899–1900 Football League season saw Leicestershire's Loughborough Town win just eight points, conceding 100 goals (including 12 to Arsenal in a single match) and losing 27 of their 34 games (including all away matches) along the way. Understandably, after one of the worst professional performances by a team in British football history, Loughborough failed to be re-elected to the league the following season and the side was disbanded in June 1900.

LUDLOW, SHROPSHIRE
Adolf Hitler autograph auctioned

A signed copy of Adolf Hitler's political manifesto *Mein Kampf* was sold at auction in Ludlow for £21,000 in August 2009. The rare second-edition copy of the book, published eight years before Hitler became German Chancellor in 1933, had been given to a Johann Maurer, who had befriended Hitler whilst both men were in prison in the mid 1920s.

MACCLESFIELD, CHESHIRE
British Olympian Ben Ainslie

As of the 2012 London Games, the sailor Ben Ainslie has won five Olympic medals, one at each of the games since 1996. Born in Macclesfield in 1977, Ainslie was just 19 when he won silver in the mixed one-person dinghy event at Atlanta, before taking gold at each of the games since 2000.

MUCH WENLOCK, SHROPSHIRE
The Wenlock Olympian Games

In the mid 1800s the English scientist William Penny Brookes established a society in his Shropshire home town of Much Wenlock which aimed to revive the Ancient Greek Olympic Games, whilst promoting the 'moral, physical and intellectual improvement' of the townspeople and awarding 'prizes... at public meeting for skill in athletic exercise'. As such, the first so-called Wenlock Olympian Games were held in 1850, featuring an array of pursuits including cricket, football, quoits and athletics. The games soon became a huge success – so much so that in 1890 Baron de Coubertin visited Much Wenlock and met with Brookes to discuss how such a competition could be transferred to a larger scale. De Coubertin went on to found the International Olympic Committee in 1894, which today regulates the entire Olympic Games.

MYDDLE, SHROPSHIRE
Gough's History of Myddle

The *History of Myddle* was written by Richard Gough, a local gentleman and churchwarden, in *c.* 1700. Detailing the lives of almost everyone living in the Shropshire village of Myddle at the turn of the eighteenth century, the book is filled with witty yet scathing descriptions of some of the village's more colourful inhabitants – one woman is described as 'more commendable for her beauty than her chastity' – as well as histories and biographies of the parish's principal families, dozens of local anecdotes and tall tales, and even accounts of the deeds and lives of local thieves and criminals. Today, Gough's work is considered by social historians to be one of the most vivid and significant descriptions of village life in eighteenth-century England.

NEWARK, NOTTINGHAMSHIRE
Death of King John

The youngest son of Henry II, John became king of England in 1199 following the death of his elder brother, Richard I. Throughout his somewhat calamitous reign, John faced rebellion in Wales, Scotland and amongst the barons of England, was personally excommunicated by the Pope, and lost much of England's French territories to both the young Prince Arthur of Brittany, a rival claimant to the English throne, and Philip Augustus, King Philip II of France. A final campaign to recapture the French lands in 1214 failed, as had all others before, and led only to a successful French invasion of the south-east of England two years later by Philip's son Louis. Retreating from the French invasion to fight off a rebellion in the Fenlands, John died of dysentery at Newark Castle in 1216.

Iron Age artefact discovered

An exquisite Iron Age torc (a type of ceremonial necklace) was discovered in a field near Newark in 2005. Comprising several separate gold wires twisted and plaited together, the necklace dates from around 2,000 years ago, and was purchased by Newark and Sherwood District Council for £350,000 in 2005, before going on display at the British Museum in 2010. It remains amongst the most valuable of all ancient treasures discovered in Britain in recent years.

NEWSTEAD, NOTTINGHAMSHIRE

Byron's 'Elegy On Newstead Abbey'

Founded as an Augustine priory by Henry II in *c.* 1170, Newstead Abbey in Nottinghamshire was, from 1540, the ancestral home of the Byron family. Suffering from decades of financial difficulty, however, the abbey was dilapidated and had been practically emptied by the time Lord Byron – George Gordon Byron, 6th Baron Byron – inherited it in 1798 at the age of just ten. As a result, Byron spent considerably little time there, preferring instead to lease the abbey out before eventually being forced to sell it in 1818. His 'Elegy On Newstead Abbey', depicting 'a fast-falling, once resplendent dome', was published in his *Hours of Idleness* anthology in 1807.

NORTHAMPTON, NORTHAMPTONSHIRE

The Holy Sepulchre

The Church of the Holy Sepulchre is the oldest building in Northampton, built around 1100 by Simon de Senlis, a Norman-French nobleman and the 1st Earl of Huntingdon and Northampton. The church is one of only a handful of circular churches remaining in England and is modelled on Jerusalem's own Church of the Sepulchre, which de Senlis would have seen on the First Crusade to the Holy Land in 1099.

NOTTINGHAM, NOTTINGHAMSHIRE

Twinned with Ljubljana

Nottingham and the Slovenian capital of Ljubljana have been officially twinned since 1963. The arrangement was established following an air crash in Slovenia in which several Britons from Nottinghamshire were killed.

Christie's The Mousetrap debuts

Originally a radio play and then a short story (which, at the author's request, should not be printed so long as the play runs in London's West End), Agatha Christie's murder mystery *The Mousetrap* premiered at Nottingham's Theatre Royal on 6 October 1952; following a short national tour, the play went on to debut in London at the Ambassadors Theatre on 25 November. Running continuously at the Ambassadors until 23 March 1974, the play switched immediately to the neighbouring St Martin's Theatre and reopened just two days later, maintaining its status as the longest-running play in theatrical history – having recently celebrated its 24,000th performance, the play marked its sixtieth anniversary in 2012.

THE PEAK DISTRICT
England's first national park

Surrounded by the cities of Manchester, Sheffield and Bradford, as its name suggests much of the Peak District lies over 300 metres (1,000 feet) above sea level, reaching its highest point (636 metres/2,087 feet) at Kinder

Scout near Glossop. The UK's first national park, the Peak District National Park also features the popular spa towns of Buxton and Matlock, and Chatsworth House, the seat of the Dukes of Devonshire. It is also the third most populous national park in Britain; despite a size difference of just 3 square kilometres (1.1 square miles), the Peak District contains 13,000 more people than the North York Moors.

PONTRILAS, HEREFORDSHIRE
Dickens' diamond ring auctioned

A diamond ring given to Charles Dickens by his poet friend Alfred, Lord Tennyson was sold at auction in February 2009. The 0.9-carat ring, inscribed on the inside with the message 'Alfred Tennyson to Charles Dickens, 1854' (the same year Dickens' *Hard Times* was published) fetched £26,000 at the sale in Pontrilas, Herefordshire.

REPTON, DERBYSHIRE
Goodbye Mr Chips film set

Founded in 1557, Repton School in Derbyshire was one of the locations used in filming *Goodbye Mr Chips*, for his performance in which Robert Donat won the Best Actor Oscar in 1939.

RUGBY, WARWICKSHIRE
William Webb Ellis

Although the story is apocryphal, a plaque at Rugby School in Warwickshire commemorates the moment in 1823 that William Webb Ellis, then a pupil at the school, caught the ball during a game of football and ran with it, supposedly inventing the game of rugby as he did so. Indeed, not only is the game itself named after the school, but the Rugby World Cup trophy is now know as the Webb Ellis Cup.

SHERWOOD FOREST, NOTTINGHAMSHIRE
The Major Oak

One of the most well-known trees in the whole of the British Isles, Nottinghamshire's 16-metre (52-foot) Major Oak near the village of Edwinstowe in the heart of Sherwood Forest was supposedly once used as the base of Robin Hood and his men. The tree is estimated to be around 1,000 years old, and likely takes its name from Major Hayman

Rooke, who noted the tree in his 1790 natural history guide, *Description and Sketches of Some Remarkable Oaks*.

SHREWSBURY, SHROPSHIRE
Execution of Dafydd ap Gruffydd

Born in *c.* 1238, Dafydd ap Gruffydd was a prince of Gwynedd and a brother of Llewellyn ap Gruffydd, Prince of Wales. Although for many years violently opposed to his brother's rule (even for a time gaining assistance from Edward I of England to fight against him), eventually Dafydd and Llewellyn were reconciled and collaborated in a fight for Welsh liberation against Edward I in 1282. Llewellyn, however, was soon afterward killed in an ambush, and the following year Dafydd himself was captured by the king's troops and, found guilty of treason, was sentenced to death. He was executed in Shrewsbury in October 1283 – first dragged through the town by a horse, Dafydd became the first prominent figure in recorded history to be hanged, drawn and quartered.

SILVERSTONE, NORTHAMPTONSHIRE
Britain's longest racetrack

Founded in 1948, Silverstone – named after the village of Silverstone in Northamptonshire (although the track actually lies across the Northamptonshire-Buckinghamshire border) – is the longest motor racing circuit in the UK. Like most race circuits, Silverstone's track has several possible layouts or routes, all of varying lengths, of which the 5.13-kilometre (3.2-mile) Grand Prix circuit was for several years the longest; the track was covered by Michael Schumacher in 1997 in a record time of just 1 minute 24.47 seconds. In 2010, however, it was announced that a new configuration of the track, named the 'Arena' layout, would be used for the 2010 British Grand Prix, which added 760 metres (830 yards) to the existing distance.

SOUTHWELL, NOTTINGHAMSHIRE
The Bramley apple

Now the most popular and widely cultivated apple in Britain, the first Bramley apple was grown in Southwell in Nottinghamshire from a seed planted by Mary Ann Brailsford in 1809. Although Brailsford is responsible for the apple's creation, the Bramley actually derives its name from Matthew Bramley, a local merchant who bought the garden containing the tree in 1846 and agreed to the sale of cuttings from it in the 1860s. The bicentennial of the Bramley apple was celebrated in Southwell in 2009.

STAFFORDSHIRE
The Moorlands Pan

The Staffordshire Moorlands Pan, discovered on moorland by two amateur metal detectorists in 2003 and now on permanent display in the British Museum, is perhaps one of the most important antiquarian discoveries of the twenty-first century. Weighing just over 130 grams (4.5 ounces) and less than 10 centimetres (4 inches) in diameter, the shallow bowl or pan, known as a *trulla*, dates from the second century AD and is remarkable not only for its exquisite and colourful decoration but for the enamelled text inscribed just below its rim – MAIS COGGABATA VXELODVNVM CAMMOGLANNA – which names

Bowness-on-Solway, Drumburgh, Stanwix and Castlesteads, the four forts of Hadrian's Wall.

STANTON-IN-PEAK, DERBYSHIRE
The Nine Ladies

The Nine Ladies on Stanton Moor, near the Peak District village of Stanton-in-Peak, comprise a Bronze Age circle of nine stones, all less than 1 metre (3.2 feet) tall, which stand alongside an outer tenth stone known as the King, discovered in 1976. Plans to reopen two quarries barely 200 metres (218 yards) from the site of the Nine Ladies in 1999 met with much opposition from local residents and environmental groups, and led to a High Court ruling in 2005 that the quarries cannot be reopened without the cooperation of the Peak District National Park Authority.

STOURBRIDGE, WORCESTERSHIRE
Ripper suspect William Bury

Born in Stourbridge in 1859, William Bury was convicted of the murder of his wife, Ellen Elliot, in Dundee in 1889, having met her just two years earlier while living in London. Both the nature of his crime and the proximity of his London residence to Whitechapel led to accusations at the time that Bury was Jack the Ripper, but he himself always denied the claims.

STOURTON, STAFFORDSHIRE
Birth of Reginald Pole, Archbishop of Canterbury

In 1500, Reginald Pole was born in Stourton Castle in the village of Stourton near Stourbridge in Staffordshire. A prominent scholar and cleric during the reign of Henry VIII, Pole fell out of favour with the king following his refusal to support his divorce from Catherine of Aragon in 1532. Incensed, Henry had several members of Pole's family executed whilst he was in exile in France, amongst them his mother Margaret, Countess of Salisbury, one of the last Plantagenets. Mary I's accession to the throne in 1553 allowed Pole to return home and soon afterwards he was appointed the last Catholic Archbishop of Canterbury in British history, a position he held until his death in 1558.

STRATFORD-ON-AVON, WARWICKSHIRE
Chapel Street

Standing on the corner of Chapel Street in Stratford, New Place was the final home of William Shakespeare. Built in 1483, the house was purchased by Shakespeare for £60 in 1597, but with much of his later life spent in London, it is believed that he did not move into the house until 1610, remaining there until his death in 1616. Sadly, the house itself has long since been demolished, although its foundations can be seen in the gardens of the neighbouring Nash's House, once owned by and named after the husband of one of Shakespeare's granddaughters, which has since been converted into a museum.

The Gower Memorial

The Gower Memorial in Stratford is one of the most famous statues of Shakespeare in the country. Named after the Victorian writer and sculptor Lord Ronald Gower, the work comprises a statue of Shakespeare surrounded by four of his most memorable characters, namely Lady Macbeth, Hamlet,

Prince Hal and Falstaff, each in turn said to represent philosophy, tragedy, history and comedy. The memorial was completed in 1888, and has been in its current location – Stratford's Bancroft Gardens, in front of the town's Royal Shakespeare Theatre – since 1933.

SUDBURY, DERBYSHIRE
The ghost of Queen Adelaide

Sudbury Hall in the village of Sudbury in south-west Derbyshire was constructed in the late seventeenth century and was the leased home of Queen Adelaide for several years after the death of her husband William IV in 1837. There have been several sightings of her ghost over the years at the hall, including in Sudbury's Queen's Room, which is dedicated to her.

TISSINGTON, DERBYSHIRE
'Well dressing'

The custom of 'well dressing' is common in several rural areas across Britain, and is thought to have developed from the ancient practice of decorating wells and springs with flowers in thanks for their plentiful supply of clean water. And whilst several towns and villages claim to have been the first to revive the tradition, it almost certainly originates in the Peak District area of Derbyshire, where the village of Tissington, near Matlock, claims to have the earliest record of it. Today, though flowers are still used to decorate the wells, elaborate pictures made of individual flower petals pressed into clay are also often used.

WARWICK, WARWICKSHIRE

Prime Minister Anthony Eden's constituency

A three-time Foreign Secretary – including service under Churchill during World War Two, in which his eldest son was killed in action in Burma – Anthony Eden's reputation as prime minister was irreparably damaged by the Suez Crisis of 1956. He served as member of parliament for Warwick and Leamington from 1923 to 1957.

WELBECK, NOTTINGHAMSHIRE

Death of William Cavendish, 1st Duke of Newcastle

Born in 1592, William Cavendish, 1st Duke of Newcastle, died at Welbeck Abbey near the Nottinghamshire village of Welbeck on 25 December 1676. In an extraordinarily varied life, Cavendish made a name for himself across a whole range of different fields, excelling as a statesman, soldier, diplomat, translator, poet, playwright, equestrian and patron to several writers including Jonson, Dryden and Descartes. A staunch Royalist and close friend of Charles I (he was also tutor to Charles' children, including the future Charles II), Cavendish was given command of the northern counties of England during the English Civil War but went into self-imposed exile in Europe after defeat at the Battle of Marston Moor in 1644. Returning to England following the Restoration, Cavendish was made Duke of Newcastle by Charles II in 1665.

WEST BROMWICH, WEST MIDLANDS

Britain's highest football ground

The Hawthorns has been the home ground of West Bromwich Albion since 1900. At 168 metres (551 feet) above sea level, the ground is the highest-altitude league football stadium in Britain.

WHITWELL, RUTLAND
Twinned with Paris

The tiny Rutland village of Whitwell has claimed to be a twin of Paris since the late 1970s when members of the local council wrote to Jacques Chirac, then mayor of Paris, to suggest the agreement, stating that if no response to their suggestion was forthcoming then the agreement would be implied. As no response ever came, Whitwell – albeit somewhat unofficially – can today stand alongside Paris' other partner and twin cities, including Chicago, Buenos Aires, Cairo, San Francisco, Sydney, Tokyo, Washington DC and London.

WINSTER, DERBYSHIRE
Cuddie vs Brittlebank

On 22 May 1821 a duel took place in the Derbyshire village of Winster between William Cuddie, the village doctor, and William Brittlebank, the son of a local landowner. Following an argument in which Brittlebank claimed Cuddie had insulted him in front of his sister, whom Cuddie was courting, Brittlebank challenged Cuddie to a duel. In the resulting standoff, held in the garden of his home in the village, Cuddie was shot and died the next day. Brittlebank, meanwhile, escaped unharmed and, although his eventual fate is unknown, he is though to have fled abroad, never to return to England.

WIRKSWORTH, DERBYSHIRE
Titanic survivor Lawrence Beesley

The Derbyshire-born writer and journalist Lawrence Beesley survived the *Titanic* disaster and went on to write one of its best-known first-hand accounts, *The Loss of the SS Titanic*, just two months later in 1912. During the making of the film *A Night To Remember* in 1958, Beesley was hired as a consultant and famously invaded the set during the sinking scene, attempting to go down with the ship once more.

WOLVERHAMPTON, WEST MIDLANDS
Britain's first automatic traffic lights

Although Britain's first traffic signals had been installed in London almost sixty years earlier, Britain's first set of automatic traffic lights was trialled in

Wolverhampton's Princes Square in 1927 and permanently installed the following year. A blue plaque in the city commemorates the event.

WORCESTER, WORCESTERSHIRE
The Battle of Worcester

The Battle of Worcester on 3 September 1651 is considered the final battle of the English Civil War, marking Charles Stuart's last attempt to regain the throne that he had lost on the execution of his father, Charles I, two years earlier. Worcester proved a decisive victory for Oliver Cromwell's Parliamentarians, whose 30,000-strong New Model Army easily defeated Charles' Royalist supporters, 3,000 of whom were killed, and a further 10,000 – around two-thirds of the entire force – were taken prisoner.

Worcester, Massachusetts

Known as 'The Heart of the Commonwealth' due to its central location in the state, Worcester's population of 181,000 makes it the second-largest city in Massachusetts, and one of the largest cities in the whole of New England. First known by English settlers as Quinsigamond in 1673, Worcester was not successfully established until 1713, eventually gaining city status in 1848. Throughout the nineteenth century, the city earned something of a reputation as an important centre for industrial development and prowess, variously claiming to have witnessed the invention of products as diverse as the monkey wrench, liquid rocket fuel, the oral contraceptive pill, barbed wire, the calliope or 'steam piano', and Shredded Wheat. Worcester was also the location of baseball's first ever 'perfect game', bowled by John Lee Richmond in 1880, as well as Sigmund Freud's only American lectures, given at the city's Clark University in September 1909.

WHAT'S IN A NAME?

Arnold, Nottinghamshire
Means 'the eagles' hook of land', derived from *earn*, the Old English for 'eagle'.

Arrow, Warwickshire
Takes its name from the River Arrow, which is itself derived from a lost Celtic word meaning 'stream'.

Badger, Shropshire
Probably derives from the Old English first name Bæcg.

Bunny, Nottinghamshire
Likely derives from the Old English word for a reed, *bune*.

Clive, Shropshire
Derived from the Old English word for 'cliff'.

Dove, Derbyshire
The Peak District's River Dove has a Celtic-origin name meaning 'dark' or 'black'.

Flagg, Derbyshire
Probably derives from a Scandinavian word, *flag*, describing a place where turf could be cut.

Hope, Derbyshire
Hope is a fairly common place name, usually deriving from the Old English *hop*, meaning 'enclosed plot'.

Kimberley, Nottinghamshire
Actually derives from the Old English first name Cyneburg.

More, Shropshire
From the Old English *mor*, meaning 'marsh'.

Nasty, Hertfordshire
A contraction of the Old English words *east* and *hæg*, meaning 'eastern enclosure'.

Old, Northamptonshire
Old would have originally been Wold (from the Old English word *wald*, meaning 'woodland' or 'forest'), with the initial W slowly lost over time.

Wall, Staffordshire
Literally meaning 'at the wall', referencing a local Roman settlement.

Waterfall, Staffordshire
From the Old English *gefall*, the name literally describes a local location where a stream vanishes into the earth.

Wing, Rutland
Derives from the Scandinavian word *vengl*, 'field'.

WALES

ANGLESEY
Birth of Owen Tudor

Owain ap Maredudd ap Tewdwr – or, more commonly, Owen Tudor – is believed to have been born in 1400, probably on Anglesey in north-west Wales. A courtier in the royal house of Queen Catherine of Valois, widow of Henry V, Owen went on to wed Catherine in *c.* 1428. Although the validity of their marriage was questionable, Owen and Catherine nevertheless had at least six children, including Edmund Tudor, 1st Earl of Richmond, born in 1430 – in turn, Edmund's only child, Henry Tudor, went on to become King Henry VII, and ultimately the Welsh-born Owen is the ancestor of all of the Tudor kings and queens of England. A staunch Lancastrian during the Wars of the Roses, Owen was captured at the Battle of Mortimer's Cross in 1461 and executed.

BANGOR, GWYNEDD
Bangor, Maine

Originally known as Condeskeag, Bangor in Maine was supposedly named by the Reverend Seth Noble after the hymn 'Bangor', written in 1735 by the English hymn-writer William Tans'ur, which was a favourite of the local reverend. The third-largest city in Maine with a population of over 35,000 (almost three times that of the Welsh city of Bangor), its many claims to fame include the home of writer Stephen King, the University of Maine and America's earliest commercially produced chewing gum, which was first manufactured in the city in 1848.

BARRY, VALE OF GLAMORGAN
Julia Gillard, Prime Minister of Australia

On 24 June 2010, Julia Gillard became leader of Australia's Labour Party and, ultimately, the country's first ever female prime minister. Born in Barry in 1961, Gillard moved to Adelaide with her family in 1966, her parents believing the warmer climate would help treat the bronchopneumonia she suffered from as a child. Having trained as a lawyer, Gillard was first elected to the Australian House of Representatives as member for Lalor in Melbourne in 1998, eventually becoming deputy prime minister under Kevin Rudd in 2007, and finally prime minister on Rudd's resignation in 2010.

BEDDGELERT, GWYNEDD
Gelert and Llewellyn the Great

According to local legend, the village of Beddgelert in Snowdonia takes its name from Gelert, a dog once owned by the Welsh leader Llewellyn the

Great. Reputedly, Llewellyn is said to have returned home from a hunting trip to discover his young baby's cradle overturned, the child nowhere to be seen, and Gelert lying nearby with blood around his mouth. Believing the worst, Llewellyn slew the dog only to discover his child unharmed beneath the upturned cradle, lying beside the dead body of a wolf that had seemingly tried to attack the child but had been killed by Gelert. Overcome with remorse, Llewellyn is said never to have smiled again and to have given his most faithful of dogs a grand funeral.

BLAENAVON, TORFAEN
World Heritage Site

As Wales became a world-renowned producer of coal and iron in the nineteenth century, the landscape of the country changed dramatically. At Blaenavon – designated a World Heritage Site in 2000 – much remains of this striking original industrial landscape, characterised by mines, quarries, furnaces, miners' homes and early railway systems.

BRECON, POWYS
The Glyndwr Rising

The last native Welshman to hold the title of Prince of Wales, Owain Glyndwr is one of the most significant figures in all of Welsh history, having led the last true Welsh revolt against England, the Glyndwr Rising, in the early fifteenth century. Although initially the rebellion had been somewhat successful, it soon began to founder and at several decisive battles in the early 1400s Glyndwr's revolt was repeatedly quashed by soldiers of the English King Henry IV. In 1412, when the uprising was almost at an end, Glyndwr and a group of followers ambushed and kidnapped Dafydd Gam, a Welsh supporter of Henry IV, at Brecon. This was the last recorded sighting of Glyndwr, of whom nothing of any certainty is known from this date.

THE BRECON BEACONS
THE PEMBROKESHIRE COAST
SNOWDONIA
The national parks of Wales

Wales' three national parks cover some 20 per cent of the entire country, by far the largest proportion of any constituent country in the British Isles. They are also amongst the earliest of Britain's national parks, with Snowdonia being one of the first four parks established in 1951. Together, they welcome over 12 million visitors a year.

CAERNARFON, GWYNEDD
Birth of Edward II

Edward II was born at Caernarfon Castle in 1284, the fourth surviving son (and sixteenth child overall) of Edward I and his first wife Eleanor of Castile. He came to the throne on his father's death in 1307, but a series of disastrous military defeats against Scotland and a fraught relationship with his queen, Isabella of France, led to Edward's abdication in favour of his eldest son, crowned Edward III in 1327.

Prime Minister David Lloyd George's constituency

David Lloyd George remains the only Welsh mother-tongue speaker to have been prime minister, holding office from 1916 to 1922. Throughout his entire time in parliament (1890–1945) he served as MP for Caernarfon in Gwynedd, becoming the first prime minister ever to represent a Welsh constituency.

CALDEY, PEMBROKESHIRE
Population: 55

The population of Caldey Island, or Ynys Bŷr, off the coast of Pembrokeshire, largely comprises the residents of a Grade II listed Cistercian monastery in use since the early 1900s. As well as the monastery, the island's single village is served by a post office, an ambulance, a fire service – whose single fire engine was airlifted to the island by Chinook helicopter in 2003 – and formerly a primary school, which was forced to close in 2000 when three of its four pupils moved to the mainland. More recently, in 2009 the island's electorate of just 28 successfully fought local government plans that controversially proposed placing the island under the jurisdiction of the nearby Tenby Town Council, allowing Caldey to maintain a semi-independent status originally established in a Royal Charter dating back to the reign of Henry VIII.

CARDIFF
Twinned with Xiamen

Cardiff's association with Xiamen in China dates from 1983 and was the first ever twinning of a British and Chinese city. The Welsh capital is also twinned with Nantes, Stuttgart and Luhansk.

Prime Minister James Callaghan's constituency

Prime Minister for three years from 1976 to 1979, James Callaghan was the last Labour prime minister before Tony Blair and remains the longest-lived former British prime minister, aged 92 on his death in 2005. Throughout his political career, Callaghan represented constituencies in Cardiff from 1945 until his retirement in 1987.

Tasker Watkins statue unveiled

A statue of Sir Tasker Watkins, a former president of Welsh Rugby Union, was unveiled outside of Cardiff's Millennium Stadium in 2009. Watkins, who was knighted in 1971, was also a former deputy chief justice and an eminent war hero, who won

Wales' first Victoria Cross aged just 25 in 1944. He died in 2007 aged 88.

The SWALEC Stadium

Cardiff's SWALEC Stadium – then known as Sophia Gardens – is the only Test cricket ground in Wales, awarded Test match status in 2006. Unusually, the following year Glamorgan cricketer Mike Powell had one of his ribs buried at the stadium, having had it removed during surgery on a blood clot.

The Cardiff Commonwealth Games

Cardiff hosted the Commonwealth Games (then known as the British Empire and Commonwealth Games) in 1958, becoming only the second British city to do so after London. Although the city had never bid to host the Olympics, in 2012 Cardiff's Millennium Stadium staged football matches as part of London's 2012 Olympics.

Welsh Olympian Paul Radmilovic

The swimmer Paul (or Paulo) Radmilovic won four Olympic medals in his career, all of which were gold – following his debut at the 1906 Athens Games, at London in 1908 he took gold as part of both the men's 4 × 200 metres freestyle relay and Britain's water polo team, before winning gold again in water polo at both Stockholm in 1912 and Antwerp in 1920. Born in Cardiff in 1886, he remains Wales' most successful Olympian.

CHEPSTOW, MONMOUTHSHIRE
British Olympian Richard Meade

As well as being the most successful equestrian in British Olympic history, Richard Meade's tally of three gold medals – one from the Mexico City Games of 1968 and two from Munich in 1972 – rank him amongst the most successful of all British Olympians. Born in Chepstow in 1936, Meade made his Olympic debut in Tokyo in 1964. His gold medal in the individual three-day event at Munich in 1972 was the first individual gold won by any British equestrian competitor.

CORWEN, DENBIGHSHIRE
Statue of Owain Glyndwr unveiled

In 2007, a statue of the Welsh hero Owain Glyndwr, who led the so-called Glyndwr Rising against English rule in the fifteenth century, was unveiled in his home town of Corwen in north-east Wales. Intended to commemorate the day Glyndwr was proclaimed the first Prince of Wales on 16 September 1400, the statue stands an imposing 4.5 metres (14.5 feet) tall in the town square and depicts Glyndwr, sword in hand, astride his horse.

DINAS HEAD, PEMBROKESHIRE
Vagrant bird spotted

A thrush-like member of the flycatcher family, Moussier's redstart is usually native to the Atlas Mountains of North Africa. A single bird spotted on the Pembrokeshire coast at Dinas Head in spring 1988 remains Britain's only recorded sighting of this species.

EWENNY, VALE OF GLAMORGAN
Morganucodon discovered

In 1947, the German palaeontologist Walter Georg Kühne discovered teeth and tiny fragments of bone belonging to an unknown creature in a fissure in rocks at Duchy Quarry near the village of Ewenny, south of Bridgend. The creature, named *Morganucodon* ('Glamorgan tooth'), would have lived in the Late Triassic period around 200 million years ago, making it one of the earliest known mammals. Indeed, whilst it would probably have appeared similar to a modern-day shrew or mouse, *Morganucodon* dates from such an early point in the development of mammals that it is likely that it would have still exhibited some of the reptilian characteristics of the animals from which it had only relatively recently evolved.

FISHGUARD, PEMBROKESHIRE
The last invasion of Britain

In 1797, a fleet of French ships landed at Carregwastad Head near Fishguard on the Welsh coast in what is generally considered the last invasion of mainland Britain by a foreign force. The brainchild of the French General Lazare Hoche, the invasion was originally planned as a three-pronged attack with troops due to land in Wales, the north-east of England, and in Ireland to aid the Irish Republican cause. However, inclement weather kept two of the invading fleets at bay so that only the Welsh invasion eventually – and unsuccessfully – went ahead.

FOEL, POWYS
The Welsh Panther

In 2004 a tourist in mid north Wales reported seeing a black cat stalking through undergrowth near the village of Foel in Powys, managing to catch the creature on film. A subsequent investigation, however, concluded that the sighting was probably nothing more than a large domestic cat. Nonetheless, in 2011 a report released by Dyfed-Powys Police showed that between 2000 and 2005 some 32 sightings of a mysterious big cat were reported in the area.

GLAMORGAN
Morgan ab Owain

The Welsh county of Glamorgan came into being as the kingdom of Morgannwg in 942, formed by the temporary union of the ancient kingdoms of Glywysing and Gwent under the leadership of the Welsh prince Morgan ab Owain, known as Morgan Hen or Morgan the Old. The prince gave his name to his new united kingdom (Morgannwg means 'Morgan's shore') although the union dissolved soon after his death in 974, and the region eventually came under control of the Normans as the Lordship of Glamorgan in about 1091.

GLYNDYFRDWY, DENBIGHSHIRE
Owain Glyndwr proclaimed Prince of Wales

The year 1400 saw the beginning of the 14-year Glyndwr Rising, a bloody but eventually unsuccessful revolt against English rule in Wales. The uprising was spearheaded by the Welsh leader Owain Glyndwr, whose manor at Glyndyfrdwy near Wrexham is thought to be the place where, on 16 September 1400, he was proclaimed Prince of Wales by his followers, making him the last Welsh-born holder of the title.

HARLECH, GWYNEDD
Ffordd Penllech

A contender for the steepest road in the whole of the British Isles, Ffordd Penllech in Harlech is a remarkably precipitous lane leading down from Harlech Castle in Gwynedd. So steep that it has been signposted 'unsuitable for motors', the one-way street (that is, downward only) has a gradient of around 18 degrees, almost 1:3.

KENFIG, BRIDGEND
The village lost to the sands

The Welsh mediaeval settlement of Kenfig is thought to have once been one of the largest towns in Glamorgan, a port on the Bristol Channel with its own Norman castle and a population perhaps as much as 1,000 at its peak in the mid 1300s. Gradually, however, the town was deserted as vast amounts of sand from nearby dunes slowly encroached on it, choking fields and engulfing whole buildings and roads. Finally, with the loss of the village church to the sands in the late fifteenth century, Kenfig was abandoned, with many of its inhabitants moving further inland to the nearby village of Pyle to rebuild their lives. Today, the only part of the original village still visible above the sands is the ruined topmost point of what was once Kenfig Castle.

KNIGHTON, POWYS
The Offa's Dyke Path

The Offa's Dyke Path is the only National Trail walkway to lie partly in both England and Wales, roughly following a route formed by the remains of Offa's Dyke itself and the English-Welsh border. The path is 285 kilometres (177 miles) in length and stretches from Sedbury in Gloucestershire to Prestatyn, and passes through the Brecon Beacons National Park. At Knighton in Powys, the path meets with the shortest and newest of Wales' other National Trails, Glyndwr's Way.

LADY PARK WOOD, MONMOUTHSHIRE
Wales's easternmost point

Whilst the town of Chepstow may lay claim to being the easternmost town in Wales, the actual easternmost point is found in Lady Park Wood, a nature reserve in the Wye Valley straddling the English-Welsh border. Indeed, such is the layout of the border between the two nations that the wood's Welsh stretches all lie further east than the English cities of Liverpool, Chester and Shrewsbury.

LAWRENNY, PEMBROKESHIRE
Grand National winner Kirkland

When Kirkland, trained by a Mr E. Thomas at the village of Lawrenny in south-west Wales, won the Grand National in 1905, it became the first and only Welsh-trained horse to win the race. Ridden by Liverpool-born jockey Frank Mason, nine-year-old Kirkland won by three lengths at odds of 6/1 in the third consecutive year that both Mason and Kirkland had finished in the first four.

LLANDAFF, CARDIFF
US statesman Francis Lewis

Francis Lewis was the only Welsh-born signatory of the US Declaration of Independence. Born in Llandaff in 1713, he originally emigrated to New York in 1734 but was caught helping British troops during the French and Indian War and sent back to Europe to be imprisoned in France. Nevertheless, he returned to America on his release and became a successful businessman in New York, representing the state in Continental Congress from 1775 to 1779. He retired two years later and died in 1802 aged 89.

LLANGADOG, CARMARTHENSHIRE
The Carmarthenshire Cat

In January 2003, a supposed big cat was sighted attacking and killing a whippet on farmland in the village of Llangadog in Carmarthenshire. This was followed two weeks later by an apparent sighting of a large black cat crossing the nearby A40. Whilst the later sighting remains unexplained, an investigation into the attack on the dog found no big cat DNA, concluding that either another dog or even a badger may have been responsible.

LLANGERNYW, CONWY
St Digain's Yew

The yew tree standing in the churchyard of St Digain's Church in Llangernyw is the oldest tree in Wales, thought to be around 4,000 years old. The churchyard also contains two ancient standing stones and pillars, inscribed with crosses.

LLYN PENINSULA
The Llyn Earthquake

On 19 July 1984, the Llyn Peninsula in north-west Wales was struck by an earthquake measuring 5.4 on the Richter scale, enough to cause local landslides and to damage walls and chimneys as far away as Liverpool. The earthquake, which fortunately centred on a fairly remote area south of Caernarfon, remains the largest onshore quake ever recorded in Britain, and led to an unprecedented three-month-long series of aftershocks, the strongest of which was even powerful enough to be felt in Dublin.

MERTHYR DYFAN, VALE OF GLAMORGAN
MERTHYR TYDFIL, MERTHYR
The lives of St Dyfan and St Tydfil

The Welsh word *merthyr* is related to the English word 'martyr', and hence both of these towns in the south of Wales are named after early Christian saints. Although little is known of St Dyfan, it is understood that he was a missionary sent to Britain by Pope Eleutherius in the late second century. If, as it is alleged, St Dyfan is buried in the town that today bears his name, then Merthyr Dyfan would potentially be the earliest Christian site in Wales. Merthyr Tydfil, meanwhile, is named after St Tydfil, who is thought to have been one of the many daughters of the Welsh King Brychan (after whom Brecon is named), and who was murdered by pagans in Merthyr in *c.* 480.

MONMOUTH, MONMOUTHSHIRE
Birthplace of Henry V

Henry V was born in Monmouth Castle in about 1387. King of England for nine years following the death of Henry IV in 1413, Henry is renowned for his series of military victories in France during the Hundred Years' War, including the decisive Battle of Agincourt in 1415. Whilst on a third campaign in France, however, Henry died of dysentery in 1422. He was succeeded by his only child, who became Henry VI.

NEATH, NEATH PORT TALBOT
Oscar-winner Ray Milland

The Welsh actor Ray Milland, born in Neath in 1907, became the first Welsh Oscar winner in 1945 for his role in *The Lost Weekend*, beating off competition from Bing Crosby, Gene Kelly and Gregory Peck. Never again nominated for an Oscar, Milland nevertheless holds the record for the shortest acceptance speech by any actor – on receiving the statuette he simply bowed silently and left the stage.

NEWTOWN, POWYS
Mail order shopping devised

The Welsh entrepreneur Sir Pryce Pryce-Jones, born in the Powys village of Llanllwchaearn in 1834, is considered the inventor of what we now know as mail order shopping. He began his career as an apprentice to a draper's shop in Newtown at the age of 12, and later started his own business selling Welsh flannel in the town in 1855. When it began to thrive, he took advantage of improvements in the postal service to deliver leaflets advertising his products throughout the surrounding area, uniquely allowing customers to both purchase and receive their goods by mail. This method proved immensely successful and, as time went on, Pryce-Jones' business expanded alongside the flourishing transport service on which it relied – eventually, he found himself selling his produce across Europe and on to America and Australia, and even added Queen Victoria and Florence Nightingale to his list of customers.

PEMBROKE, PEMBROKESHIRE
Birthplace of Henry VII

Born at Pembroke Castle in 1457, Henry VII remains the last British monarch to have been born in Wales and the last to take the throne by force, defeating his predecessor Richard III at the Battle of Bosworth Field in 1485. Henry held the throne for 23 years until his death in 1509 and was succeeded by his second son, who became Henry VIII.

THE PEMBROKESHIRE COAST
see under The Brecon Beacons

PONTCYSYLLTE AQUEDUCT, WREXHAM

World Heritage Site

The Pontcysyllte Aqueduct is the highest and longest aqueduct in Britain, as well as being a Grade I listed construction and the most recent of Britain's World Heritage Sites. One of the greatest engineering feats of its time, the aqueduct was completed in 1805 to a design by the architect and civil engineer Thomas Telford and carries water some 307 metres (1,007 feet) between the Wrexham villages of Trevor and Froncysyllte. The aqueduct, and the 18-kilometre (11-mile) Llangollen Canal of which it forms a significant part, were together appointed World Heritage status in June 2009.

PONTYPRIDD, RHONDDA CYNON TAFF

'Land of My Fathers'

'Hen Wlad Fy Nhadau', 'Land of My Fathers', is traditionally considered the national anthem of Wales. Written in 1856 by a weaver and poet from Pontypridd in Rhondda Cynon Taff named

Evan James, and set to music by his son James James, the song was originally known as 'Glan Rhondda', 'The Banks of the Rhondda', until it appeared in print under its present name in a popular 1860 anthology, *Gems of Welsh Melody*. Although never officially adopted as the Welsh anthem, at official events the song is nevertheless often used alongside or in place of 'God Save the Queen'.

SEALYHAM, PEMBROKESHIRE

The Sealyham terrier

Developed in the nineteenth century by crossing several breeds (including basset hounds, West Highlands and Dandie Dinmonts), the Sealyham is a small, well-tempered, instantly recognisable terrier that was once one of the most popular of Welsh dogs but today is listed as one of the most vulnerable of all British breeds. It is named after an area of Haverfordwest in south-west Wales. Alfred Hitchcock can be seen walking two of his own Sealyham terriers in a cameo appearance in his 1963 film *The Birds*.

THE SEVERN
Britain's longest river

The River Severn is the longest river in Great Britain. Rising at Plynlimon in Wales' Cambrian Mountains, the Severn flows for 354 kilometres (220 miles) through Shrewsbury, Ironbridge, Worcester, Tewkesbury and Gloucester before emptying into the Bristol Channel. It also boasts what is believed to be the second-largest tidal range of any waterway in the world, with the difference between high and low tide measured at an astonishing 15 metres (49 feet). Due to the funnel-like shape of the Bristol Channel, the huge surge of incoming water forced up the river channel between low and high tides creates an eagre, a noticeable and powerful wave of incoming water known as the 'Severn bore', which travels upstream at around 16 kilometres per hour (10 miles per hour) and can typically reach a height of 2 metres (6.5 feet) or more.

SNOWDON, GWYNEDD
Wales' highest peak

The summit of Mount Snowdon, Yr Wyddfa, stands at 1,085 metres (3,560 feet) above Snowdonia National Park, making it roughly equivalent in height to South Africa's Table Mountain. The highest mountain in Wales – one of only four Welsh peaks over 1,000 metres – and the highest mountain in Britain outside of Scotland, Snowdon was famously used by Sir Edmund Hillary and his team in training for their successful ascent of Everest in 1953.

SNOWDONIA
see under The Brecon Beacons

ST ASAPH, DENBIGHSHIRE
Ancient Roman coin discovered

A 2,000-year-old Roman coin was found on a path near St Asaph by a metal-detecting enthusiast in early 2008. The coin, which is thought to date from sometime around the second century BC if not earlier, is embossed with an image of a chariot pulled by two horses. It is thought to be the oldest coin ever unearthed in Wales.

SWANSEA, WEST GLAMORGAN
Dylan Thomas and Princess Lilian

Arguably the most famous son of the city of Swansea is Dylan Thomas, the poet and author of *Under Milk Wood*, who was born there in 1914. Perhaps the city's most illustrious former citizen, however, is Lillian May Davies – born in Swansea in 1915, Davies married Prince Bertil of Sweden, the uncle of King Carl XVI Gustaf, to become Princess Lilian of Sweden, Duchess of Halland, in 1976.

The fuel cell invented

Partly basing his work on observations on the reaction of hydrogen and oxygen by the German scientist Christian Schönbein, Swansea's William Robert Grove constructed and successfully demonstrated the first hydrogen fuel cell in 1842. Essentially, Grove's fuel cell – which he called the 'gas voltaic battery' – performed the process of electrolysis in reverse: instead of dividing water and molecules into hydrogen and oxygen by administering an electrical current, Grove combined hydrogen and oxygen to produce water and electricity.

TRAPP, CARMARTHENSHIRE
Carreg Cennen Castle completed

Amongst the most spectacular of all Welsh castles, situated atop a 250-metre (820-foot) limestone crag above the River Cennen, work began on Carreg Cennen near the tiny hamlet of Trapp in the late twelfth century. In 1283, the castle was gifted to John Giffard, an English nobleman and close friend of Edward I, who went on to remodel and extend the castle to its current outline in 1300. Although only ruins of it exist today, Carreg Cennen never sustained any extensive damage in battle but was instead dismantled during the Wars of the Roses by Yorkists who had captured the castle from the Lancastrians in 1462.

TREGARON, CEREDIGION
Tregaron broth

The Ceredigion village of Tregaron gives its name to *cawl tregaron*, a traditional Welsh broth made of beef, cabbage, and root vegetables.

TRELLECH, MONMOUTHSHIRE
Remarkable big cat attack

In 2000, an 11-year-old boy was attacked by a big cat in a field near his home in Trellech in south Wales. He needed stitches to his face and head following the attack in which the creature, thought to be a panther or juvenile leopard, lashed out at him before running away.

TREMADOG, GWYNEDD
Birthplace of Lawrence of Arabia

Thomas Edward Lawrence, better known as Lawrence of Arabia, was born in the small village of Tremadog on the outskirts of Porthmadog in 1888. At the outbreak of World War One, Lawrence was in the Middle East where he had been working as an archaeologist for several years. His knowledge of the area proved invaluable to the British cause, enabling him to coerce the Arab forces into an effective revolt against Turkey. Tragically, he died in a motorcycle accident in 1935 aged just 46.

WHAT'S IN A NAME?

Angle, Pembrokeshire
Probably from the Old English word *angel*, used of a bend or hook.

Barry, South Glamorgan
Known as Y Barri, from the Welsh word for 'hill'.

Broadway, Carmarthenshire
Literally means 'broad road'.

Cardigan, Ceredigion
Means 'the land of Ceredig', as in the regional name Ceredigion.

Hope, Flintshire
A relatively common place name, derived from the Old English *hop*, 'valley'.

Mold, Flintshire
Means 'high hill', originally from the French *mont* and *hault*.

Trapp, Carmarthenshire
Thought to literally mean 'trap', either in the sense of a good hunting ground, or a lucrative ambush point for robbers.

NORTH-WEST ENGLAND AND THE ISLE OF MAN

Cumbria, Lancashire, Merseyside,
Greater Manchester, Isle of Man

ASHTON-UNDER-LYNE, GREATER MANCHESTER
The Black Knight Pageant

The traditional Black Knight Pageant held each year in Ashton-under-Lyne in Manchester is thought to derive from a despised fifteenth-century local tyrant named Sir Ralph Assheton who, according to legend, would ride around the town on a black horse tormenting the local people. To commemorate Sir Ralph's death, many years later in the mid 1700s the town began a tradition of parading an effigy of the black knight through the streets, at the end of which it was customarily

hung up and burnt or even shot at. Today, however, the recently revived tradition is happily a much more sedate affair, and sees a rider dressed in black armour parade through the town as part of a pageant raising funds for local causes.

BACUP, LANCASHIRE
The Nutters Dance

On Easter Saturday in the Lancashire village of Bacup the annual 'Nutters Dance' takes place, in which a troupe of dancers dressed and painted in black, save for a red and white striped kilt and white socks and

189

sash, make their way across town performing various traditional folk dances en route. Whilst it has been suggested that the dances themselves were brought to the area by Cornish miners in the eighteenth century – and that the participants' blackened faces are thought to symbolise those of the local coal miners – on the whole, the history and meaning of this somewhat unusual custom remains unclear.

BLACKPOOL, LANCASHIRE
US actor John Mahoney

Born in Blackpool in 1940, the American actor John Mahoney is best known for his role as Martin Crane, the farther of Frasier Crane in the long-running US sitcom *Frasier*. A US citizen since 1959, Mahoney served in the US Army, worked as an English teacher and edited a medical journal before turning to acting in the late 1970s. He made his film debut in 1980, won the 1986 Tony Award for Best Featured Actor in a Play, and appeared in *Moonstruck* (1987), Roman Polanski's *Frantic* (1988) and the Coen brothers' *Barton Fink* (1991) before making his first

appearance in *Frasier* in 1993 playing one of only three regular characters to appear in all 264 episodes. He received two Golden Globe and Emmy Award nominations before the show's finale in 2004.

Britain's first monorail

Blackpool Pleasure Beach opened Britain's first commercial monorail system in 1966. One mile long and with two stations, the system had four trains – one of which was completely open to allow for maximum views of the park – each capable of transporting 60 passengers. It is still in operation today.

BRANTWOOD, CUMBRIA
Death of scholar John Ruskin

From 1872, Brantwood House overlooking Coniston Water in Cumbria was the home of the writer and scholar John Ruskin. A controversial Victorian art critic renowned for championing the works of artists including Turner and Millais, Ruskin was also an accomplished poet and a prolific essayist, publishing works on subjects as diverse as architecture, economics, politics and religion. He died at Brantwood on 20 January 1900, aged 80.

BURGH-BY-SANDS, CUMBRIA
Death of Edward I

Although more successful in ending a Welsh rebellion at the end of the thirteenth century, it is as the 'Hammer of the Scots' that Edward I is best remembered today in recognition of his lengthy battle against William Wallace's violent uprising in Scotland. Despite his nickname, however, Edward never managed to entirely end the rebellion and on a final campaign against Scotland in 1307 died of dysentery at Burgh-by-Sands on the Cumbrian coast.

THE CALF OF MAN
Population: two

Aside from the Isle of Man itself, which has a population of over 80,000, today the only other inhabited island in the Man group is Yn Cholloo, or Calf of Man, a 2.5-square-kilometre (0.9-square-mile) islet situated off the southernmost tip of the main island. An interim census in 2006 recorded a population here of just two, namely the wardens of a bird observatory established there in 1959.

Vagrant bird spotted

Also known as the Carolina pigeon, Western Europe's first recorded mourning dove was spotted on the Calf of Man in October 1989. Since data from the Isle of Man is excluded from official British ornithological records, Britain's first officially recorded mourning dove was spotted in the village of Carinish on North Uist in the Outer Hebrides in November 1999.

CARLISLE, CUMBRIA
Adam Bell

Alongside his companions William of Cloudesley and Clym of the Clough, the story of the English outlaw and archer Adam Bell dates from well before the sixteenth century, although the earliest full written version dates from 1565. In it, Bell and his men are said to reside in Inglewood Forest near Carlisle and, having fought against the mayor of the city and his men, are taken before the king and made to prove their archery skills in order to save their lives. Understandably, the story has several parallels to both that of Robin Hood – indeed it is thought to have influenced several later adaptations of the Robin Hood story – and the legendary Swiss hero William Tell, as the ballad even features a scene in which Cloudesley shoots an apple from his son's head.

CARTMEL, CUMBRIA
Britain's shortest racecourse

Although the course itself is, at a little over a mile in length, the shortest National Hunt course in Britain, Cartmel Racecourse's run-in – that is, the distance from the final fence to the finish line – is Britain's longest, at a little over four furlongs (804 metres).

CASTLERIGG, CUMBRIA
Castlerigg Stone Circle

The stone circle at Castlerigg near Keswick is thought to date from *c.* 3000 BC, placing it amongst the oldest in the whole of the British Isles. Perhaps an ancient trading post or meeting place, the monument comprises more than thirty stones in total, arranged in an oval roughly 30 metres (100 feet) across with a gap in its northern edge presumed to have been some sort of entrance. Within the circle itself, a further ten stones are arranged in a vague rectangle, the exact purpose of which is unclear.

CHORLEY, LANCASHIRE
Chorley cakes

Chorley cakes are small, round, flattened pastries filled with a mixture of raisins or currants. Although many different versions exist, traditionally the cakes are made with unsweetened shortcrust pastry. The similar Lancastrian Eccles cakes are made with puff pastry and are usually served with a light dusting of sugar.

Titanic Officer Charles Lightoller

Commander Charles Herbert Lightoller was second officer on board the *Titanic*. Born in Chorley in 1874, he began his naval career as a ship's apprentice aged just 13, before joining the White Star Line in 1900. Initially appointed first officer, Lightoller assisted in the evacuation of the portside lifeboats as the *Titanic* went down, until he was eventually forced to jump overboard. Managing to climb onto a nearby upturned lifeboat along with several other survivors, Lightoller was eventually rescued by the *Carpathia*. He was the highest-ranking officer to survive the disaster.

COCKERMOUTH, CUMBRIA
Birth of Dorothy Wordsworth

Dorothy Wordsworth, the younger sister of the former Poet Laureate William Wordsworth, was born on Christmas Day 1771 in Cockermouth. A prolific writer in her own right, Dorothy's output includes letters, diaries, travelogues and poetry (her poem 'To A Child' appeared in her brother's 1815 collection *Poems*), whilst the *Grasmere Journal* she first published in 1897 offers a fascinating insight into both life in nineteenth-century Lakeland and into the lives of her brother and his contemporaries – including Robert Southey, Samuel Taylor Coleridge and Sir Walter Scott – who frequently visited the family at Grasmere. Outliving her brother by almost five years, Dorothy died aged 83 in 1855.

COLNE, LANCASHIRE
Titanic band leader Wallace Hartley

Wallace Hartley was a violinist and leader of the orchestra onboard the *Titanic*. Having earlier worked as a musician aboard Cunard's flagship *Mauretania*, Hartley joined the crew of the *Titanic* shortly after proposing to his fiancée in 1912. Neither he nor any other member of the ship's band survived the disaster, having continued to play whilst other passengers boarded the lifeboats around them; they are popularly said to have finally played the hymn 'Nearer, My God, to Thee'. Hartley's body was not recovered until two weeks after the ship sank, and it was not until May 1912 that it was returned to England. His funeral in his home town of Colne near Burnley was attended by thousands of mourners, and in 1915 the town erected a statue in his memory.

CROSS FELL, CUMBRIA
The peak of the Pennines

At 893 metres (2,930 feet), Cross Fell is the highest peak in the Pennines, and is England's highest mountain outside of the Lake District.

DOUGLAS, ISLE OF MAN
'Arrane Ashoonagh'

Although its title literally translated from Manx is simply 'National Anthem', 'Arrane Ashoonagh' is better known in English by the title 'O Land of Our Birth' and has been the official national anthem of the Isle of Man since 2003. The eight-verse song dates from the early 1900s, when it was written by the London-based scholar William Henry Gill, translated into the Manx language by Douglas-born linguist John Kneen, and set to a local traditional melody known as 'Mylecharaine's March'. As a self-governing crown dependency of the UK, however, the Isle of Man still retains 'God Save the Queen' as its official royal anthem, used at events when the monarch or a member of the royal family are present.

Statue of George Formby unveiled

A bronze statue of the entertainer George Formby stands, appropriately, leaning on a lamppost at the corner of Ridgeway Street in Douglas on the Isle of Man. Designed by Manx artist Amanda Barton, the statue depicts Formby in full racing leathers in reference to *No Limit* (1935), one of his most popular and successful films, in which he plays a racing driver who enters the Isle of Man TT competition.

Commonwealth Games success

Unlike in the Olympics, the Commonwealth Games not only allow all individual constituent countries of the UK to enter separately, but also permit all British dependencies and territories to field their own teams. As such, besides England, Scotland, Wales and Northern Ireland, the Commonwealth Games includes entrants from such locations as Gibraltar, the British Virgin Islands, Montserrat and St Helena. Of all the British dependencies, however, the Isle of Man is by far the most successful, having garnered eight medals (including three gold) since it first took part in 1958, whilst the Isle of Man's Peter Buckley has held a Commonwealth record for road-race cycling since 1966; the island won its last gold medal in 2006, when Douglas-born cyclist Mark Cavendish won the scratch-race event at the Melbourne Games. Of similar success are Guernsey (six medals from all 11 games since 1970); Bermuda (five medals from 15 games); and Jersey (four medals, including one gold for shooting in 1990). Amongst the least successful British territories are Gibraltar, who have yet to take home a single medal despite taking part in every games since 1958, and the Falkland Islands, who have won no medals from all eight games since 1982.

DUDDON, CUMBRIA

Wordsworth's 'River Duddon' sonnets

Cumbria's River Duddon rises in Wrynose Pass in the Lake District and flows for around 24 kilometres (15 miles) before emptying into the Irish Sea at Broughton-in-Furness. Perhaps the most famous of the so-called Lake Poets, William Wordsworth wrote extensively of the Duddon, publishing a series of 34 sonnets dedicated to the river – 'Pure flow

the verse, pure, vigorous, free, and bright, / For Duddon, long-loved Duddon, is my theme!' – in 1820.

ECCLESTON, MERSEYSIDE

Richard Seddon, fifteenth prime minister of New Zealand

New Zealand's longest-serving prime minister, Richard Seddon was born in Eccleston in 1845. At 18, he moved to Australia where he lived in Melbourne before trying his luck at the Bendigo gold rush in Victoria. In 1866, he moved to New Zealand and began his political career on the council for New Zealand's Westland Province, before becoming mayor of Kumara and eventually member of parliament for Hokitika in 1879. In the early 1890s, Seddon was serving in New Zealand's first Liberal government when Prime Minister John Ballance suddenly took ill and died. Despite several other contenders, he became Ballance's replacement and went on to serve as prime minister of New Zealand for an unsurpassed 13 years. He died at sea, returning from a trip to Australia, in 1906 and was buried in Wellington.

FLEETWOOD, LANCASHIRE

Created by Peter Hesketh-Fleetwood

Born in Lancaster in 1801, Peter Hesketh-Fleetwood inherited his family's extensive estate on the Lancashire coast after the death of his father in 1824. Two years after being elected to parliament as MP for Preston, in 1835 Hesketh-Fleetwood masterminded a plan to construct a coastal resort from scratch on his land which would link London, via the west-coast railways of England, to Scotland, which at the time could only be reached from the English west coast by sea. The town of Fleetwood, as it became known, was designed in 1836 by the noted architect Decimus Burton (responsible for the layout of London's Hyde Park) and took over eight years to build.

FORMBY, MERSEYSIDE

Stronghold of the red squirrel

The red squirrel is the only species of squirrel native to the British Isles. Since the introduction of the larger and more gregarious grey squirrel from North America, Britain's population of reds has decreased dramatically, partly owning to competition for food and habitat as well as a fatal virus carried solely by the greys. Currently, the British Isles has a population of around 180,000 red squirrels (roughly two-thirds of which is confined to Scotland and one-fifth to Ireland) compared to a flourishing population of over 2.5 million greys; a 2011 report meanwhile claimed that the reds' population has dropped by 50 per cent in the last fifty years. Besides other increasingly isolated strongholds in the Isle of Wight, Brownsea Island, Norfolk, Anglesey, and the northernmost counties of England, Sefton Coast Woods in Formby is today home to almost one-tenth of the red squirrel's entire English population.

GRANGE, CUMBRIA

Southey's 'Cataract of Lodore'

Robert Southey was Poet Laureate from 1813 until his death in 1843. His poem 'The Cataract of Lodore', describing Lodore Falls near the village of Grange at the southern end of

Cumbria's Derwent Water, stands amongst his most remarkable works as a brilliant example of onomatopoeia, wherein words are used evocatively to express sounds. Opening with the line 'How does the water come down at Lodore?', Southey goes on to use more than fifty sets of rhyming words to describe the water, including 'glittering and frittering', 'guggling and struggling', 'sprinkling and crinkling and twinkling', 'thumping and bumping and flumping and jumping'.

HUYTON, LANCASHIRE
Prime Minister Harold Wilson's constituency

Having first represented Ormskirk (1945–50), Harold Wilson was elected member of parliament for the newly created constituency of Huyton in Lancashire in 1950, serving until the seat was abolished in 1983. Twice prime minister (1964–70, 1974–76), Wilson won an unprecedented four general elections, contesting a total of five throughout his leadership, and is the last British prime minister to have served two non-consecutive terms in office.

KENDAL, CUMBRIA
Kendal mint cake

Kendal is world-famous for its mint cake, a small sugary confection flavoured with peppermint that originated in the nineteenth century. Made from sugar, glucose syrup, water and peppermint oil, Kendal mint cake is renowned for being a high-energy food and has long been used as such by local climbers and fell walkers, and even explorers – the cakes were famously used as a quick source of energy by Ernest Shackleton on his expedition attempting to cross the Antarctic in 1914, and by Sir Edmund Hillary in his scaling of Mount Everest in 1953.

THE LAKE DISTRICT
England's largest national park

At 2,292 square kilometres (885 square miles), the Lake District is England's largest national park and the second largest in the whole of the British Isles. It also features England's highest mountain, Scafell Pike, England's largest natural lake, Windermere, and claims to be the wettest place in England – the tiny village of Seathwaite near Coniston Water endures 3.15 metres (10.3 feet) of rain a year. The Lake District is thought to be the most visited of all British national parks, welcoming more than 15 million people every year, who together spend almost £1 billion in the local area.

LANGWATHBY, CUMBRIA
Long Meg and Her Daughters

Long Meg and Her Daughters north of the Cumbrian village of Langwathby is the largest stone circle in the north of England and the third largest in the whole of the UK. The site's somewhat unusual name alludes to its layout, comprising fifty or so stones (the 'daughters') set out in a roughly circular shape 100 metres (330 feet) in diameter, presided over by a much larger sandstone monolith, namely Long Meg herself. Of the many legends which surround Meg and her Daughters, one claims that they were in fact once a coven of witches turned to stone by a powerful Scottish wizard, whose spell will only be broken if the exact number of stones in the group is ever counted correctly.

LIVERPOOL, MERSEYSIDE
Penny Lane

Along with London's Abbey Road, Liverpool's Penny Lane has become one of the most famous addresses in the world thanks to The Beatles, who released their single 'Penny Lane' as part of a double A-side with 'Strawberry Fields Forever' in 1967. The actual Penny Lane from which the song takes its name runs from Greenbank Road to Allerton Road in the south-east of the city, where both John Lennon and Paul McCartney once lived.

Scousers

The term 'Scouser' derives from 'lobscouse', a Scandinavian meat stew thought to have been brought to the Liverpool area by sailors in the nineteenth century. Even today, 'scouse' is a traditional Merseyside stew, similar to Irish stew, made of lamb or beef with potatoes, carrots and onions.

Execution of Peter Anthony Allen

In 1964, Peter Anthony Allen and Gwynne Owen Evans were found guilty of the murder of John West, a van driver from Workington in

Cumbria, whom they killed during a robbery early on the morning of 7 April. Charged with what was then known as 'capital murder' (as opposed to non-capital murder), both men were sentenced to death, and at 8 a.m. on 13 August 1964, Allen was hanged at Liverpool's Walton Prison whilst Evans was hanged simultaneously at Strangeways in Manchester. Theirs were the last executions in British history.

Nobel Laureate Ronald Ross

The first Briton ever to win a Nobel Prize, Ronald Ross was born in Almora in Uttarakhand, India, in 1857. Educated in England, Ross returned to India in the late nineteenth century and there began studying malaria, by the late 1890s discovering that the disease – which he himself caught in 1897 – was spread by the bite of the anopheles mosquito via a malarial parasite in its saliva. Returning to Britain in 1899, Ross became a professor at the Liverpool School of Tropical Medicine, now affiliated to the University of Liverpool, during which time his earlier pioneering research earned him the 1902

Nobel Prize for Medicine. A blue plaque commemorating his work at the school was unveiled in 1998.

US statesman Robert Morris

Born in Liverpool in 1734, Robert Morris emigrated to America with his father when he was 13; by 18 he was already partner of a major shipping firm in Philadelphia. In 1775, he was elected to both Pennsylvania's Provincial Assembly and the Continental Congress, and from 1781 to 1784 served as superintendent of finance, essentially acting as treasurer to the newly formed United States. In this role, Morris is credited with having popularised the use of the dollar sign ($), becoming the first senior public figure to use the sign in official documents. He died in Philadelphia in 1806.

Elgar's Pomp and Circumstance Marches debut

Edward Elgar completed five *Pomp and Circumstance Marches* in his lifetime. Although the final three all premiered in London, the first two received their debut performances in Liverpool in 1901. The first, *March No. 1 in*

D, is by far the most popular and most recognisable today as its *Trio* section was later adapted into the anthem 'Land Of Hope And Glory', and is now played annually at the Last Night of the Proms. The *Marches*' somewhat unusual name is in fact a quotation from Act III of Shakespeare's *Othello* – 'Farewell the neighing steed… the spirit-stirring drum, the ear-piercing fife, the Royal banner, and all quality, pride, pomp and circumstance of glorious war'.

Blood Brothers and Shirley Valentine premieres

Both Willy Russell's Olivier Award-winning musical *Blood Brothers* and his monologue *Shirley Valentine* premiered in Liverpool before transferring to London in 1983 and 1986 respectively. After a short opening run, *Blood Brothers* reopened at London's Albery Theatre in 1988 before transferring to the Phoenix Theatre in 1991, where it continues to be shown, making it the Phoenix's longest-running production. *Shirley Valentine*, meanwhile, was commissioned by Liverpool's Everyman Theatre before it transferred to the Vaudeville in

London where it won the Olivier Award for Best New Comedy. Pauline Collins, who also won the Olivier and Tony Awards for her performance in the play's London and Broadway productions, also won a BAFTA for her role in the 1989 film adaptation.

LOW MILL, CUMBRIA
Early studies of platinum

Although the discovery of chemical element number 78, platinum, is credited to the eighteenth-century Spanish explorer Antonio de Ulloa, the first true investigative experiments performed on the metal were carried out at a forge at Low Mill in Cumbria owned by the English metallurgist Charles Wood. Wood had previously been in charge of a lead mine in Jamaica, and on his return to England in 1749 brought with him some smuggled platinum on which principal experiments were carried out by him and his fellow scientist William Brownrigg.

MANCHESTER
Sir Matt Busby Way

Sir Matt Busby Way in Manchester is the location of Old Trafford,

Manchester United's home ground. Originally named Warwick Road North, the street was renamed in honour of the team's longest-serving manager in 1993, just a year before his death in January 1994.

Manchester, New Hampshire

There are places named Manchester in over half of all of the states of the USA, including at least two in New York and three in both Texas and Wisconsin. By far the largest – and the only American Manchester with a population over 100,000 – is found in New Hampshire, where it is almost three times larger than the state capital, Concord. Previously known as Amoskeag, Tyngstown and then Derryfield, the city adopted its current name from its English namesake in 1810 and continued to flourish throughout the nineteenth century thanks to a prosperous local cotton industry that saw the city's population increase by more than 1,200 per cent between 1840 and 1890 alone.

Twinned with St Petersburg

Manchester's association with the former Russian capital St Petersburg is one of the longest standing in the whole of Britain; a renewal of the agreement in 2007 ensured that it would continue until at least its fiftieth anniversary in 2012.

The Manchester Ship Canal

Construction began on the Manchester Ship Canal in November 1887, overseen by engineer Edward Leader Williams, who was knighted by Queen Victoria at the official opening ceremony on 21 May 1894. The 58-kilometre (36-mile) canal opened the otherwise landlocked city of Manchester to sea traffic via the Mersey and Irwell rivers.

Prime Minister Arthur Balfour's constituency

Arthur Balfour became prime minister on the resignation of the Marquess of Salisbury in 1902; he went on to resign himself in 1905. Nevertheless, he spent almost fifty years in parliament, during which time he represented three different constituencies, of which the second was the newly created seat of Manchester East (1885–1906).

Birth of John Byrom

The English writer John Byrom was born in Manchester on 29 February 1692. After studying in Chester and London, Byrom attended Trinity College, Cambridge, in the early eighteenth century, where he developed an early form of shorthand. Today, however, he is best remembered as a poet, most notably for 'My Spirit Longeth for Thee', published posthumously in 1773, and his 'Hymn for Christmas Day', written for his daughter Dolly in 1745 and later set to music as the hymn 'Christians Awake, Salute The Happy Morn'.

The B of the Bang

Manchester's *B of the Bang* sculpture was commissioned in 2003 to commemorate the city's hosting of the Commonwealth Games the previous year. Its extraordinary design comprised 180 tapered spikes, each emanating from a single central point and reaching up to a height of 56 metres (184 feet), taller than the Statue of Liberty, with the whole 165-tonne steel structure positioned at an angle of 30 degrees, more than seven times that of the Leaning Tower of Pisa. Designed by Thomas Heatherwick, *The B of the Bang* – named after a quote by Olympic sprinter Linford Christie, who claimed to start running not at the bang of the starter's pistol, but at the 'B of the bang' – soon proved somewhat controversial, with Manchester City Council taking legal action against the company responsible for its construction in 2007 after several of its six-foot spikes broke off. It was finally dismantled in 2009.

The Civil Justice Centre

Manchester's Civil Justice Centre was completed in 2007 at a cost of £160 million. Designed by the Melbourne-based architectural firm Denton Corker Marshall, the building is one of the largest courts in the country and, as well as being the first court building of its kind built in Britain for 150 years, at 80 metres (260 feet) in height it is also one of the tallest structures in Manchester. Its striking design, featuring the largest suspended glass wall in Europe, saw it shortlisted for the Stirling Prize and earned it a RIBA regional award in 2008.

Bax's November Woods premieres

One of a number of 'tone poems' written by the English composer Sir Arnold Bax, *November Woods* was completed in 1917 and was first performed on 18 November 1920 by Manchester's famed Hallé Orchestra. The evocative piece remains one of Bax's most famous and popular works.

Du Maurier's The Years Between debuts

The first of only two original plays written by the English novelist Daphne du Maurier, *The Years Between* premiered at Manchester's Opera House in 1944 before transferring to London's Wyndham Theatre early in 1945. Set during World War Two, the play concerns the homecoming of an English colonel thought to have been killed in a plane crash in 1942.

The Manchester terrier

The Manchester terrier is probably originally descended from the whippet, and whilst so-called 'black-and-tan' terriers – from which Manchesters and several other breeds are thought to have developed – have been known since before the 1600s, the breed as it is today essentially developed around the Manchester area in the early 1800s as a means of controlling vermin. Typically standing around 40 centimetres (16 inches) tall, the Manchester is one of the larger British terriers, although the Chihuahua-like toy variety, also known as the English toy terrier, stands little more than half its size.

The Manchester Commonwealth Games

Manchester has bid to host the Olympic Games on two occasions – it lost the 1996 games to Atlanta, and having made it down to the final three contenders in 2000, eventually lost out to Sydney. Nevertheless, the city hosted the Commonwealth Games in 2002, becoming the fourth city in Britain (and the second in England) to do so.

MARDALE GREEN, CUMBRIA
The drowned village of Mardale Green

The old Lake District village of Mardale Green in Cumbria is one of several across the country that have been 'drowned' by the construction of reservoirs or dams. Mardale itself was lost in 1935 with the opening of Haweswater Reservoir, formed by the construction of a dam that flooded the valley in which the village once stood. Although most of its buildings were simply demolished in the process, Mardale's local church was instead painstakingly dismantled brick by brick, with the stone being used to create a short pier on the reservoir shore. What little remains of the rest of the village can still occasionally be seen when water levels in the reservoir are at their lowest.

MORECAMBE, LANCASHIRE
Eric Morecambe memorial unveiled

Perhaps the most popular landmark in Morecambe is a bronze statue of the entertainer Eric Morecambe, who was born in the town in 1926 – originally named John Eric Bartholomew, he later adopted the name of his home town as his stage name. The statue, which also features the names of over one hundred famous faces who appeared on *The Morecambe & Wise Show*, stands on Morecambe promenade and was unveiled by Queen Elizabeth II in July 1999.

OLDHAM, GREATER MANCHESTER
Churchill's parliamentary debut

The 1900 UK general election saw the Conservatives under Lord Salisbury win just over 50 per cent of all votes cast, taking a considerable majority over Henry Campbell-Bannerman's Liberal Party, admittedly thanks to victories in scores of uncontested seats. The election, as well as being the first to feature what would become the Labour Party, also saw a 25-year-old Winston Churchill elected to parliament for the first time, winning one of the two seats returned by the Manchester borough of Oldham in October. He would hold a seat in parliament for all but one of the next 64 years.

World's first 'test tube baby' born

Born on 25 July 1978 at Oldham and District General Hospital, Louise Brown was the first baby in the world to have been successfully conceived by *in vitro* ('in glass') fertilisation, or IVF. A commonplace fertility treatment today, the IVF procedure involves the controlled fertilisation of an egg cell outside of the womb, with the successfully fertilised egg then transferred back into the patient's uterus.

British Olympian Henry Taylor

The legendary Olympic swimmer Henry Taylor was born in Oldham in 1885. He won his first medals at the 1906 Athens Games, including silver in the men's 400-metre freestyle and gold in the men's 1-mile freestyle. Over a 14-year Olympic career, Taylor went on to win a record eight medals, more than any other British swimmer, and uniquely won medals in the same event – the men's 4 × 200-metre freestyle relay – at three consecutive Olympics.

PATTERDALE, CUMBRIA
The Patterdale terrier

Although not officially recognised by the UK Kennel Club, the little-known Patterdale terrier, a medium-sized working dog named

after a small village in the Lake District, is nevertheless listed by the American Rare Breed Association as one of the most vulnerable terrier breeds. Formerly used for hunting, Patterdales are lively and mischievous dogs related to the Welsh terrier and, like several other breeds, are probably also descended from the earlier black-and-tan terrier.

PENDLE HILL, LANCASHIRE
The Pendle Witch Trials

The Pendle Witch Trials of 1612 are amongst the most famous in British history, partly because their events are so well documented and partly because so many individuals were executed – in all, ten men and women were hanged as a result of the trial, whilst only one of the accused was found not guilty. The trials began when Alizon Device, a young woman from Pendle, was accused of cursing a local merchant who soon afterwards had suffered a stroke. When news of this reached the authorities, an investigation began which eventually led to the arrest and trial of several members of Alizon's family (including her grandmother, a notorious local practitioner of witchcraft who was known as Demdike), who in turn went on to implicate just as many members of another local family, the Redfernes, with whom they had reportedly had a long-standing feud. Many of the families' friends and supporters were also implicated in the trial and ultimately executed.

PIEL ISLAND, CUMBRIA
Population: five

A Site of Special Scientific Interest and the location of a remarkable fourteenth-century castle built by Edward III, Piel is the smallest of the four inhabited Islands of Furness situated in the Irish Sea off the coast of Cumbria's Furness Peninsula. Whilst the largest of the islands, Walney, is the eighth largest in England and has a population of over 10,000, Piel by contrast is just 20 hectares in size (50 acres, 0.78 square miles) and has a permanent population solely comprising the landlord – known as the 'King of Piel' – of the island's Grade II listed eighteenth-century Ship Inn and his family.

PRESTON, LANCASHIRE
Trial of murderer Harold Shipman

At Preston Crown Court on 31 January 2000, Harold Shipman was sentenced to life imprisonment for the murders of 15 of his patients. Shipman, a GP then working in Hyde, Greater Manchester, was found to have administered lethal doses of morphine to his victims in a series of killings from 1995 to 1998. However, a report published in 2002 concluded that he may in fact have been responsible for the deaths of at least 250 patients, perhaps stretching back as far as 1975. Shipman hanged himself in Wakefield Prison in 2004.

Oscar-winner Nick Park

Renowned for his popular animated characters Wallace and Gromit, the Preston-born filmmaker Nick Park remains one of Britain's most successful Oscar winners, having won a total of four awards – Best Animated Short Film for *Creature Comforts* (1989), *Wallace & Gromit: The Wrong Trousers* (1993) and *Wallace & Gromit: A Close Shave*

(1995), and Best Animated Feature for *Wallace & Gromit: The Curse of the Were-Rabbit* (2005) – from a total of six nominations.

RAAD NY FOILLAN, ISLE OF MAN
Isle of Man National Trail

Established in 1986, Raad ny Foillan ('the road of the gulls') is a National Trail walking route roughly following the entire coastline of the Isle of Man. It is 153 kilometres (95 miles) in length and starts and finishes in the island's capital, Douglas, taking in the towns of Peel, Ramsey and Castletown, as well as several nature reserves and beauty spots along the way.

RAMSBOTTOM, GREATER MANCHESTER
The Black Pudding Throwing Championship

The World Black Pudding Throwing Championship takes place each year at Ramsbottom near Bury in Greater Manchester. In the contest, competitors have three attempts in which to throw a 6-ounce black pudding underarm at a pile of Yorkshire puddings

perched on a ledge some 6 metres (20 feet) off the ground. The winner, simply, is the competitor who knocks the most puddings off the shelf.

RAMSEY, ISLE OF MAN
Solway Harvester disaster

Amidst force 9 gales on the afternoon of 11 January 2000, the scallop dredger *Solway Harvester* was lost in the Irish Sea, along with all seven of its crew. The boat had been heading for shelter at Ramsey on the Isle of Man as conditions worsened, but sank roughly 18 kilometres (11 miles) off the south-east coast of the island. The incident was Britain's worst fishing tragedy for 26 years.

RAVENGLASS, CUMBRIA
Death of notorious trickster Tom Skelton

Often cited as being the last court jester in English history, Tom Skelton, known as 'Tom Fool', was jester to the Pennington family of Muncaster Castle near Ravenglass in Cumbria in the late 1500s. Although little is known of his life, Tom appears to have been a much crueller and more twisted character than the stereotypical mischievous fool – for a macabre joke, he would often deliberately lead travellers asking for directions into a deadly bog near the castle, and is even believed to have murdered a local carpenter on his master's orders, decapitating him as punishment for falling in love with Sir Francis Pennington's daughter. Tom died in 1600, and his ghost is still said to haunt Muncaster Castle to this day.

SADDLEWORTH, GREATER MANCHESTER
see under Urswick, Cumbria

SALFORD, GREATER MANCHESTER
James Prescott Joule and Peter Maxwell Davies

One of the most significant British scientists of the nineteenth century, James Prescott Joule was born in Salford in 1818. His groundbreaking experiments into the relationship between work and heat remain some of the most important ever carried out in physics, and accordingly his name today is used for the SI base unit of energy. Peter Maxwell Davies,

meanwhile, was born in Salford in 1934. The current Master of the Queen's Music, he remains one of the most popular and acclaimed British composers and conductors of the twentieth century.

Notorious Midland Bank robbery

Four armed robbers ambushed a Securicor van outside a Midland Bank Clearing Centre in Salford at 8 a.m. on 3 July 1995. Holding the driver at gunpoint, the men commandeered the van and made off with over £6.5 million. The driver, Graham Huckerby, was later accused of being involved in the robbery and sentenced to 14 years in prison in 2002, but in 2004 had his sentence overturned by the Court of Appeal. The theft remains unsolved, and none of the money has ever been recovered.

SAMLESBURY, LANCASHIRE
The Samlesbury Witch Trial

The trials of the Samlesbury Witches – Jane Southworth and Jennet and Ellen Brierly – took place during the same court assizes as the more familiar Pendle Witches in 1612. The three women were accused both of 'bewitching' a young girl, Grace Sowerbutts, and of killing and cannibalising a young boy. Incredibly, it appears that the whole story was concocted by a local cleric who had, for whatever reason, apparently coerced the girl into testifying against them. All three of the women were acquitted.

SCAFELL PIKE, CUMBRIA
The peak of England

England's highest mountain, Scafell Pike (978 metres/3,209 feet) in the Cumbrian Mountains stands in the heart of the Lake District National Park, roughly 45 kilometres (28 miles) south of Carlisle. In 1919 the mountain was gifted to the National Trust by Charles Henry Wyndham, 3rd Lord Leconfield, as a memorial to those who lost their lives in World War One.

SKELTON, CUMBRIA
Britain's tallest structure

The tallest structure in Britain – and indeed the whole of the European Union – was formerly the steel mast of the Belmont transmitting station in Lincolnshire, until it was shortened by 36 metres (118 feet) to its present height of 351.5 metres (1,153 feet) in April 2010. Now Britain's tallest structure is the Skelton transmitting station mast in Cumbria which, completed in 2001, stands at a height of 365 metres (1,197 feet) – more than 40 metres (131 feet) taller than the Eiffel Tower.

STANHILL, LANCASHIRE
Invention of the spinning jenny

Originally known as the 'spinning jennifer', the spinning jenny was invented by James Hargreaves in 1764. At the time, Hargreaves was working as a carpenter and weaver at his home in the Lancashire village of Stanhill near Accrington. It was here that he conceived of a yarn-making machine that, rather than using a single spinning wheel to produce one spool of thread, comprised a row of several spindles all of which could be run from a single wheel. By dramatically increasing the amount of yarn produced by a single weaver, the jenny not only revolutionised the textile industry but today is also considered one of the earliest catalysts of the Industrial Revolution.

ST BEES, CUMBRIA

The life of St Bega

The name of St Bees in Cumbria is thought to be a corruption of the name of St Bega, a seventh-century Irish saint (and, if legend is believed, princess) who fled across the Irish Sea to the Celtic kingdom of Rheged on the eve of her marriage to a Viking prince of Norway. Whilst in England, Bega is believed to have met with both St Oswald and St Aidan, and went on to found a nunnery at St Bees, where she served as abbess until her death.

STOCKPORT, GREATER MANCHESTER

Oscar-winner Wendy Hiller

Born in the Stockport suburb of Bramhall in 1912, the English actress Dame Wendy Hiller became the first British-born actress to be nominated for an Oscar in 1938 for her lead role in *Pygmalion*, before becoming the first British Oscar-winning actress for *Separate Tables* in 1958. She was nominated a third and final time in 1966 for *A Man For All Seasons*.

STONYHURST, LANCASHIRE

Conan Doyle's Hound of the Baskervilles

One of the most well known and most adapted of all Sherlock Holmes stories, *The Hound of the Baskervilles* is set predominantly on Dartmoor, where a hellish black dog is said to be at large, targeting and killing members of the great Baskerville dynasty. Arthur Conan Doyle's former school, Stonyhurst College near Clitheroe in Lancashire, is generally considered to have been the basis of Baskerville Hall, the grand manor that is home to the eponymous family.

URSWICK, CUMBRIA
SADDLEWORTH, GREATER MANCHESTER

'Rushbearing'

The tradition of 'rushbearing' observed in many towns and villages across Britain historically derives from the custom of renewing the dried rushes and reeds once used to cover the earthen floors of churches and other buildings. Traditionally, the event was often associated with the feast day of the saint to which the church was dedicated, as is the case at St Mary and St Michael's Church in Urswick, Cumbria, where a procession of 'rushbearers' works it way through the town on the Sunday nearest to St Michael's Day, 29 September. The procession is all the more elaborate in Saddleworth, Manchester, where one of the local morris dancers is each year chosen to ride atop a vast 'rush cart' as it is pulled through the streets of the local villages.

WINDERMERE, CUMBRIA
England's largest lake

At 14.6 square kilometres (5.6 square miles), Lake Windermere in Cumbria's Lake District is the largest natural lake in England, and also one of the deepest, reaching a maximum depth of –66.7 metres (–219 feet). Of comparable size is Rutland Water (12.5 square kilometres/4.8 square miles), the largest artificial lake in the British Isles, although Northumberland's Kielder Water reservoir has a greater capacity and is capable of holding 200 billion litres of water.

WHAT'S IN A NAME?

Douglas, Isle of Man
Means 'black stream'.

Liza, Cumbria
The 'shining river', from the Norse *ljós á*.

Peel, Isle of Man
Comes from a Middle English word for a palisade, *pel*.

Sprint, Cumbria
The name of a river, probably derived from the Old Norse *spretta*, meaning 'gushing'.

Waver, Cumbria
A river name, perhaps meaning 'restless', derived from the Old English *wæfre*, 'wave'.

NORTH-EAST ENGLAND AND YORKSHIRE

Northumberland, Tyne and Wear, County Durham, North Yorkshire, East Yorkshire, West Yorkshire, South Yorkshire

AIREDALE, WEST YORKSHIRE
Airedale terrier

The Airedale is the largest British terrier, standing around 60 centimetres (2 feet) tall with a characteristically narrow body, thick light-brown and black fur, and long, sturdy legs. Originally bred in the mid 1800s to hunt vermin and other mammals – including even otters, hence the breed's earlier alternative name of 'waterside terrier' – Airedales were amongst the first dogs used by the police force and were even used to deliver medical supplies and messages during World War One. The breed has twice been awarded Best in Show at Crufts.

ALLENDALE, NORTHUMBERLAND
Tar barrelling

On New Year's Eve night each year, dozens of men in Allendale gather in fancy dress in the town square, where each is given a tub containing a mixture of tar and wood shavings to carry on their heads. The tub is then set alight and the men carry the barrels through the town. The ceremony continues until the stroke of midnight when, with a shout of 'be damned he who throws last', the tubs are thrown onto a pile of fir-tree branches to set them alight. Thought to have originally been Viking or Pagan in origin, the Allendale tar-barrelling ceremony as it is today probably dates from the mid 1800s.

ASHINGTON, NORTHUMBERLAND
Statue of Jackie Milburn unveiled

Following the death of the former Newcastle United and England centre forward Jackie Milburn in 1988, an appeal was started to erect a statue in his honour in his home town of Ashington. After four years of campaigning, the statue was finally unveiled by both Milburn's wife and Jack Charlton, one of his former teammates, on 5 October 1995. Designed by the renowned sculptor John W. Mills, the 2.5-metre (8-foot) bronze statue shows Milburn kicking a football and wearing the familiar stripes of Newcastle United, the club for which he made over 350 league appearances over 14 years.

AYSGARTH, NORTH YORKSHIRE
Stronghold of the dormouse

Taking its name from the French word for 'sleep', the common or hazel dormouse has suffered a 50 per cent reduction in its distribution in recent years, with the national population now estimated to be around 45,000 individuals. The decline in the creature's numbers is likely due to increased predation and the destruction of its habitat, including the removal of the hedgerows in which it lives. Besides the release of 35 individual dormice into Freeholders' Wood near Aysgarth in North Yorkshire in June 2008 – now perhaps the most northerly population in the UK – further schemes to reintroduce the species in recent years have seen it return to locations in Suffolk, Cheshire, Lincolnshire and Cambridgeshire.

BAMBURGH, NORTHUMBERLAND
Becket film set

Much of Peter Glenville's acclaimed 1964 biopic of Thomas à Becket – which won just one of the record 12 Oscars for which it was nominated – was filmed on location at Bamburgh Castle in Northumberland, which also provided locations for the 1998 Best Picture nominee *Elizabeth*, starring Oscar-nominated Cate Blanchett as Elizabeth I.

BEDLINGTON, NORTHUMBERLAND
Bedlington terrier

Once also known as the Rothbury terrier, the Bedlington is a hardy, medium-sized terrier standing around 40 centimetres (16 inches) tall and named after the town of Bedlington in south-east Northumberland. Originally bred in the late eighteenth century to catch rats and other vermin, today the breed is somewhat rare, yet is nonetheless easily identifiable owing to a characteristically pale, dense, curly coat and a somewhat square-shaped head.

BERWICK-UPON-TWEED, NORTHUMBERLAND
The Royal Border Bridge

A 660-metre (720-yard) arched rail bridge spanning the Tweed from Berwick to Tweedmouth, the Royal Border Bridge was opened by Queen Victoria in 1850. Designed by Robert Stephenson, son of the engineer George Stephenson, the bridge took three years to build and today still forms an integral part of the East Coast Mainline linking Edinburgh and London.

BEVERLEY, EAST YORKSHIRE
Grand National winner Peter Simple

It was at Beverley that the nineteenth-century Grand National winner Peter Simple – the oldest horse ever to win the National – was trained by Tom Oliver. Running in its fifth National, the horse was a remarkable 15 years old when it won the race in 1853, following an earlier victory in 1849.

BILLINGHAM, DURHAM
Vagrant bird spotted

Widespread throughout North America, Britain's first recorded double-crested cormorant was spotted on the Cleveland coast near Billingham in 1989. The bird, which is similar to but smaller than the common cormorant native to the British Isles, derives its name from the white feather crests adult birds grow in breeding season above each eye.

BOROUGHBRIDGE, NORTH YORKSHIRE
The Devil's Arrows

The Devil's Arrows near the village of Boroughbridge is the name given to three large standing stones or 'menhirs', amongst the tallest of all such stones in the whole of England. The precise date, origin and purpose of the stones – measuring roughly 5.5 metres (18 feet), 6.7 metres (22 feet) and 7 metres (23 feet) in height respectively – are all unknown, but it is likely that they are relics of the Bronze Age, dating from *c.* 2000 BC.

BRADFORD, WEST YORKSHIRE
Twinned with Skopje

When a 6.9 magnitude earthquake struck the now Macedonian capital of Skopje on 26 July 1963, more than three-quarters of the city was destroyed and well over 200,000 of its inhabitants were left homeless. As part of the international aid effort that followed, a team of students from the Bradford Institute of Technology (now Bradford University) aided the reconstruction of Skopje, and the two cities have been twinned ever since.

The Yorkshire terrier

The Yorkshire terrier is one of the smallest of all terriers, generally weighing only 2.5 kilograms (6 pounds), but is nevertheless the most intelligent. Originally bred to catch rats and other vermin in nineteenth-century industrial Yorkshire, 'Yorkies' are of unclear ancestry but are likely descended from crossbreeds of Skye, Clydesdale and Airedale terriers, with their distinctive colouring possibly linked to the black-and-tan terriers from which several other breeds have developed. Yorkshire terriers are a popular breed and are known for their friendly and playful demeanour.

BROTHERTON, NORTH YORKSHIRE
Birth of Thomas Brotherton

Thomas Brotherton, the first child of the English King Edward I and his second wife Margaret of France, was born in Brotherton near Castleford on the border of North and West Yorkshire on 1 June 1300. On Edward's death in 1307, Thomas' half-brother – the eldest son from Edward's first marriage to Eleanor of Castile – became Edward II, inferring on Thomas the title of 1st Earl of Norfolk, and in 1316 Thomas was furthermore made Lord Marshal of England. He died in 1338 and was buried in Bury St Edmunds.

CAWOOD, NORTH YORKSHIRE

Death of Thomas Rotherham, Archbishop of York

Thomas Rotherham was born in the South Yorkshire town that shares his name in 1423. Appointed Archbishop of York in 1480, Rotherham held several other significant clerical posts under King Edward IV, including Keeper of the Privy Seal and Lord Chancellor, a title he held twice in his lifetime. On the accession of Richard III in 1483, however, Rotherham remained loyal to Edward's widow, Elizabeth Woodville, and was consequently imprisoned by the new king in the Tower of London. Removed from many of his offices by Henry

VII on his release following the death of Richard III, Rotherham nonetheless remained Archbishop of York until his death from the plague at Cawood near Selby in 1500. He was buried in York Minster.

THE CHEVIOT, NORTHUMBERLAND

The peak of the Cheviot Hills

Situated close to the border with Scotland, The Cheviot (816 metres/2,677 feet) is the tallest peak of northern England's Cheviot Hills, and as such is England's highest peak outside of Cumbria.

DRURIDGE BAY, NORTHUMBERLAND

Vagrant bird spotted

Although considerable debate still surrounds the exact identity of a juvenile bird spotted at Druridge Bay on the north Northumberland coast in May 1998, the bird is officially recorded as a slender-billed curlew. If correct, this would not only be the first record of this species in the British Isles, but also a significant sighting of one of the rarest birds in the world

– it is likely that fewer than fifty individuals remain in the wild.

DURHAM, COUNTY DURHAM

Durham Cathedral, World Heritage Site

Stood atop a steep-sided promontory on a bend of the River Wear, Durham Cathedral was built to accommodate the remains of St Cuthbert in the late eleventh century. Perhaps the largest Norman-style structure still standing in the British Isles, together with nearby Durham Castle it was appointed a World Heritage Site in 1986.

THE FARNE ISLANDS, NORTHUMBERLAND

The House of Farne

Although uninhabited today, for many hundreds of years the Farne Islands off the coast of Northumberland had a resident population comprising the various monks, clerics and hermits who came to the islands seeking solitude. In 1255, the House of Farne, a small Benedictine monastery, was built on Inner Farne, which was followed by the Chapel of St Cuthbert, completed in 1300. The chapel still stands today.

Vagrant bird spotted

The only Aleutian tern ever recorded in Europe was spotted on the Farne Islands in May 1979. The species takes its name from the Aleutian Islands, a chain of volcanic islands forming the westernmost point of Alaska, and is ordinarily restricted to the northernmost and westernmost stretches of the Pacific Ocean.

FERRYBRIDGE, WEST YORKSHIRE

Ancient burial sight unearthed

In March 2005, an ancient British burial ground was accidentally unearthed during construction work to upgrade the A1 near Ferrybridge in Yorkshire. The site, dating from around 2,400 years ago, held the remains of a 5-foot-9-inch, 30–40-year-old man as well as hundreds of cattle, suggesting that the grave was that of a somewhat significant figure. If so, it is likely that the site would have remained important to ancient Britons until long after his death.

FLAMBOROUGH HEAD, EAST YORKSHIRE
Vagrant birds spotted

Usually native to central and northern Asia, two taiga flycatchers were spotted in Britain in 2003, the first in April at Flamborough Head on the Yorkshire coast, and the second in Shetland, six months later.

GATESHEAD, TYNE AND WEAR
The Angel of the North

Standing at 20 metres (65 feet) tall, weighing in at 208 tonnes and with a 54-metre (175-foot) wingspan, Antony Gormley's *Angel of the North* beside the A1(M) motorway in Gateshead is one of the largest sculptures in Europe. It was completed in 1998.

The Sage Gateshead

Gateshead's prestigious performance and arts centre The Sage Gateshead was one of several developments completed as part of a multimillion pound scheme to regenerate the town's quayside on the Tyne, which also included the groundbreaking RIBA Award-winning Millennium Bridge completed in 2001. Designed by Sir Norman Foster, The Sage features two state-of-the-art music halls – one a three-level concert hall able to be acoustically modified to suit different performances, the other a smaller performance area thought to be the only ten-sided music venue in the world – and is home to the acclaimed Northern Sinfonia orchestra. Since opening in 2004, the building has won several significant architectural and design awards, including two RIBA Awards in 2005.

GAWTHORPE, WEST YORKSHIRE
The Coal Carrying Championships

The World Coal Carrying Championships have traditionally taken place every Easter Monday since the 1960s in the tiny Yorkshire village of Gawthorpe near Wakefield. Competitors race from the village pub to a maypole on the village green, almost a mile away, carrying with them a hundredweight of coal. A record time of 4 minutes 6 seconds was set in 1991.

HARROGATE, NORTH YORKSHIRE
Twinned with Wellington

The sister-city agreement between Harrogate and Wellington, New Zealand, officially dates from 1978 yet has its origins in World War Two when 23 New Zealand aircraftmen were killed near Harrogate and were buried in the town. In 2010, a Maori elder travelled to Harrogate to confer a traditional Maori blessing on the town's newly restored New Zealand Gardens, erected in the 1950s to commemorate the airmen who had lost their lives.

HARTLEPOOL, DURHAM
'Monkey hangers'

Inhabitants of Hartlepool are affectionately known as 'monkey hangers' due to an unusual tale from local folklore – according to the story, during the Napoleonic Wars a French ship was wrecked off the coast of the town with the loss of all of the crew except for a monkey found washed up on the shore. Mistaken for a French spy, the monkey was reportedly promptly put on trial by the townspeople and, found

guilty, was hanged on a makeshift gallows erected on the beach. Once considered somewhat derogatory, in more recent years the term 'monkey hanger' has been embraced by the people of Hartlepool, so much so that the mascot of the local football team is quirkily named H'Angus the Monkey.

JARROW, TYNE AND WEAR
The Jarrow March

When the shipbuilding industry on Tyneside declined during the Great Depression, unemployment in Jarrow rose to almost 70 per cent as 8,000 men in the area were made redundant. Consequently, in an attempt to bring the issue to the attention of parliament, two hundred men marched for 25 days from Jarrow to London's Hyde Park in October 1936, joined for much of the way by 'Red Ellen', their local MP, Ellen Wilkinson. The marchers took with them an 11,000-name petition to present to the House of Commons, yet on their arrival in London Prime Minister Stanley Baldwin refused to meet with any of the men, leaving Wilkinson to present the petition herself on 4 November.

Despite the marchers' huge effort, it took a further two years for industry on Tyneside to begin to show any kind of recovery.

KINGSTON-UPON-HULL, EAST YORKSHIRE

Twinned with Freetown

Hull has been officially twinned the Sierra Leonean capital of Freetown since 1980. The agreement was proposed by Dr June Holst-Roness, a former mayor of Freetown, whose colleague, High Commissioner Dr S. T. Matturi, was a graduate of the University of Hull.

William Wilberforce and Amy Johnson

Born in Hull in 1759, William Wilberforce is known today as a philanthropist, a politician (MP of his home town from 1780 to 1784) and, perhaps most importantly, as a leading abolitionist, introducing the first of his parliamentary bills calling for an end to Britain's involvement in the slave trade in 1791. Amy Johnson, meanwhile, was born in Hull in 1903. In her tragically short life she became the first woman to fly solo from England to Australia (1930), the first to cross the Atlantic east to west (1932) and the first to fly to Moscow (1931), Tokyo (1931) and India (1934). In 1932, moreover, she broke her husband Jim Mollison's record for a non-stop flight from London to Cape Town by ten hours. She died during World War Two aged just 37.

England's first penalty shoot-out

When half an hour of extra time failed to resolve a match between Hull and Manchester United on 5 August 1970, Britain's first ever penalty shoot-out took place at Boothferry Park, the former home ground of Hull City. The first player to score in a penalty shoot-out was United's George Best; the first to miss was Denis Law.

KNARESBOROUGH, NORTH YORKSHIRE

Mother Shipton

The prophetess Mother Shipton was born Ursula Southeil in 1488 in, according to some accounts of her life, the cave in Knaresborough which bears her name today. From a young age,

Southeil had allegedly been at the centre of several supernatural incidents and had a striking gift for being able to tell the future. In 1512, she married Toby Shipton, a local carpenter, becoming known as 'Mother Shipton' as her astonishing abilities and notoriety spread throughout the country. She died in 1561, having reportedly predicted the date of her death. Although Mother Shipton has since become something of a legendary figure with dozens of the different stories associated with her likely concocted over the centuries since her death, she is nevertheless said to have foreseen the English Civil War, the Great Fire of London, the invasion of the Spanish Armada and Henry VIII's dissolution of the monasteries.

LEEDS, WEST YORKSHIRE
Titanic victim Father Thomas Byles

Born in Leeds in 1870, the Catholic priest Father Thomas Roussel Byles was travelling to America on the *Titanic* to officiate the wedding of his brother, William, in New York. Originally scheduled to travel on another liner, Byles switched to the *Titanic* at the last minute. As the ship went down, he is reported to have given up several offers of places in lifeboats to other passengers and instead remained on board reciting prayers and hearing passengers' confessions. His body was never recovered.

Town Hall

Designed by architect Cuthbert Brodrick, who also designed Scarborough's Grand Hotel and Leeds' Corn Exchange, the Grade I listed Leeds Town Hall was opened by Queen Victoria in 1858. At 69 metres (225 feet), the building was the city's tallest for a century until the opening of the Park Plaza Hotel in 1966.

Vaughan Williams' A Sea Symphony

The first and, at over an hour, the longest of Vaughan Williams' nine symphonies, *A Sea Symphony* was written between 1903 and 1909 and was conducted by the composer himself at its premiere at the Leeds Triennial Festival on 12 October 1910, Vaughan Williams' thirty-eighth birthday.

Written for soprano and baritone soloists, chorus, full orchestra and organ, the text of all four movements is adapted from poems by the American writer Walt Whitman.

LINDISFARNE, NORTHUMBERLAND
Early Viking invasion

In 793, the island of Lindisfarne off the coast of Northumberland was attacked by Viking invaders, 'heathen men', as recorded in the *Anglo-Saxon Chronicle*, who wrought 'havoc in the Church of God' in a raid widely considered to be the first recorded Viking incursion on the English coast. Whilst perhaps not as rampageous nor as bloodthirsty as many other attacks appear to have been, it was no less effective, leaving much of the island's seventh-century priory desecrated and causing great consternation amongst the English Christian community at the time. The Lindisfarne raid, however, was to prove only the beginning, as Viking raids on the east coast of England soon escalated and would continue for more than two centuries.

MARSHALL MEADOWS, NORTHUMBERLAND
England's northernmost point

The cliffs overlooking Marshall Meadows Bay, a small picturesque inlet on the North Sea coast of Northumberland, mark the northernmost point in England, standing just a stone's throw away from the Scottish border. The nearby Georgian mansion of Marshall Meadows House and its adjacent farm in turn comprise England's northernmost settlement, standing roughly 2 kilometres (1.2 miles) further north than Berwick-upon-Tweed, and barely 500 metres (546 yards) from the Scottish border.

MARTON, NORTH YORKSHIRE
Birthplace of Captain Cook

Captain James Cook was born in a cottage in the tiny North Yorkshire village of Marton, now a suburb of Middlesbrough, in 1728. One of Britain's foremost explorers and navigators, Cook joined the navy in 1755 and quickly excelled as a navigator, before going on to captain the HMS *Endeavour* on her research trip to the South Pacific in 1766. On this epic voyage, and the two that followed, Cook charted the coast of New Zealand, completed the southernmost circumnavigation of the globe yet attempted and discovered what he then called the Sandwich Islands, including Hawaii, where he was killed in 1779.

MYTHOLMROYD, WEST YORKSHIRE
Birthplace of Ted Hughes

One of the most respected and celebrated poets of the twentieth century, Ted Hughes was born in Mytholmroyd near Halifax in 1930. Hughes was Poet Laureate from 1984 until his death in 1998, the same year that his final collection of work, *Birthday Letters*, exploring his troubled marriage to the American poet and author Sylvia Plath, won the Whitbread Prize for British Book of the Year.

NEWCASTLE-UPON-TYNE, TYNE AND WEAR
Grey Street

Dating from the 1830s, Newcastle-upon-Tyne's Grey Street was voted the Best Street in the UK by BBC Radio 4 listeners in 2002, commended for exhibiting 'design, maintenance and activity in perfect harmony'. Home to superb Georgian and Victoria architecture, including the city's Grade I listed Theatre Royal completed in 1837, Grey Street is named after the former British Whig Prime Minister Charles Grey, 2nd Earl Grey, a monument dedicated to whom stands at the top of the street in the heart of Newcastle's city centre.

Twinned with Bergen

Newcastle's links with Norway were reinforced in 1968 when the Norwegian King Olav V officially opened the city's new Civic Centre. In a tradition dating from World War Two, its twin city of Bergen also supplies Newcastle with a Christmas tree each December.

'Geordies'

Whilst certainly a pet form of the first name George, quite which 'George' is the origin of the term 'Geordie', the name for an inhabitant of Newcastle or Tyneside, is debateable. Amongst numerous suggestions are that the renowned local inventor

George Stephenson may be the source, or else, more likely, George II, as Newcastle was a known stronghold of support for the Hanoverian kings during the Jacobite Rebellion of the eighteenth century.

'Carrying coals to Newcastle'

'To carry coals to Newcastle' means to do something that is clearly unnecessary or redundant, the phrase implying that taking coal to the north-east of England is futile as there is already so much there.

Newcastle county corporate formed

Despite their name, the 'counties corporate' of the Middle Ages were in fact a collection of major cities, so named because they were officially granted rights separate to those of the counties in which they stood. Scattered across England, Wales, Scotland and Ireland, the counties corporate were essentially mediaeval local authorities, allotted their own sheriffs and permitted to hold their own distinct court sessions. The first, appointed in 1132, was the City of London, and over the years that followed more than a dozen more British cities followed suit, of which the fifth was Newcastle in 1400.

The High Level Bridge

A remarkable dual-level combined road and rail bridge, Newcastle's Grade I listed High Level Bridge was designed by Robert Stephenson and constructed between 1847 and 1849. At over 400 metres (440 yards) in length, it is the second-longest bridge over the Tyne and, as its name suggests, stands some 25 metres (80 feet) above the water. Officially opened on 27 September 1849 (shortly after Stephenson turned down a knighthood from Queen Victoria), the bridge recently underwent three years' significant renovation and was finally reopened to pedestrians and restricted traffic in 2008.

Shaw's Caesar and Cleopatra debuts

One of George Bernard Shaw's earliest plays, the extravagant historical drama Caesar and Cleopatra was written in 1898 and premiered at Newcastle's Theatre Royal in March the following year, starring the renowned British stage actress Mrs Patrick Campbell and her company. It was not until 1907 that the play debuted in London, opening at the Savoy theatre on 25 November.

Unique football hat-trick

In April 1986, West Ham's Alvin Martin uniquely scored a hat-trick against three different goalkeepers in a First Division home game against Newcastle United – when original Newcastle keeper Martin Thomas was taken off injured, Martin went on to complete his hat-trick by scoring against both of Thomas' replacements, namely Chris Hedworth and then, after Hedworth got injured, fellow England player Peter Beardsley. West Ham went on to a decisive 8–1 victory.

NORTHUMBERLAND

England's northernmost national park

The Northumberland National Park was established in 1956. It is the northernmost national park in England, and is the only park in Britain to contain a World Heritage Site, namely Hadrian's Wall, which crosses the park's southern stretches near the village of Haltwhistle. Northumberland is also the least populated UK national park with a resident population of just over 2,000 people.

THE NORTH YORK MOORS

National park

The North York Moors were designated a national park in 1952. As well as being home to Rievaulx Abbey and both the Cleveland Way and Lyke Wake walking routes, the Moors also include almost 50 kilometres (30 miles) of Heritage Coastline, including the 200-metre (655-foot) cliffs at Boulby near Whitby, which are the highest cliffs on England's east coast.

PONTEFRACT, WEST YORKSHIRE

Pontefract cakes

Pontefract cakes are small, round sweets made of liquorice, traditionally embossed with an image of Pontefract Castle. Also known as 'Pomfret' cakes, the confectionaries have been made in the town for centuries and today Pontefract holds an annual Liquorice Festival in celebration of the town's liquorice industry.

Richard III (III.iii)

Pontefract Castle dates from the eleventh century, and was once considered one of the strongest castles in the country. Recognising its notorious history (James I of Scotland was imprisoned there, Richard II killed there in 1400), in the third act of Shakespeare's *Richard III*, Earl Rivers exclaims, 'O Pomfret, Pomfret! O thou bloody prison / Within the guilty closure of thy walls, Richard II here was hacked to death', before going on to describe Pontefract as 'fatal and ominous to noble peers' as he is taken there to be executed on the orders of the king.

REDCAR, NORTH YORKSHIRE
Atonement film set

One of the most highly acclaimed films of 2007, Joe Wright's adaptation of Ian McEwan's World War Two novel *Atonement* was partly filmed on the seafront at Redcar on the Yorkshire coast – for three days in August 2006, Redcar beach and its nearby high street were transformed into the war-ravaged beaches of Dunkirk. The film was nominated for seven Oscars, including Best Picture, and a record 14 BAFTAs.

Pontefract Racecourse

Originally horseshoe-shaped, an extension to Pontefract Racecourse opened in 1983 expanded the course to its present oval shape and to a length of 2 miles and 125 yards (1.8 kilometres), making it Britain's longest continuous flat circuit.

RICCALL, NORTH YORKSHIRE
Norse invasion of Britain

Ahead of the Norman Conquest, in September 1066 the Norwegian King Harald Hardrada sailed across the North Sea to the north-east coast of England, aiming to seize the throne from the English King Harold Godwinson. Harald's ships – which were joined from the Tyne by those of his English ally, the king's estranged brother Tostig Godwinson, Earl of Northumbria – soon reached the mouth of the River Ouse and from there he set up camp at Riccall near York. On

20 September, Harald's forces met those of the northern earls still loyal to the English king and won a decisive victory at the ensuing Battle of Fulford. Just five days later, however, King Harold marched his own troops north and defeated the Norwegian invaders at Stamford Bridge to maintain – albeit briefly – his place on the English throne.

SALTAIRE, WEST YORKSHIRE
Sir Titus Salt

Built by the Victorian industrialist Sir Titus Salt for his workforce in 1853, the village of Saltaire outside Bradford was appointed a World Heritage Site in 2001. It is an outstanding example of both a nineteenth-century industrial town and of Victorian philanthropy. Salt built houses, schools, a hospital, allotments and bathhouses for his workers, as well as providing them with a library, a concert hall and a gymnasium.

SCARBOROUGH, NORTH YORKSHIRE
Scarborough chapel

An early Christian chapel was built in Scarborough in 1000, yet was destroyed in 1066 in a raid on the town by the invading Harald Hardrada, King Harald III of Norway, who was intent on claiming the English throne. At the Battle of Stamford Bridge in September 1066, however, Harald's invasion was defeated by the English King Harold Godwinson, and Harald was slain on the battlefield having been struck in the throat with an arrow.

Titanic Officer James Paul Moody

Sixth Officer James Paul Moody was the only junior officer on board the *Titanic* to die in the disaster. Born in Scarborough in 1887, he joined the White Star Line in 1911 and was appointed to the crew of the *Titanic* at the age of 24. On watch at the time of the ship's collision, it was Moody who answered the telephone call from the lookout Frederick Fleet warning of an 'iceberg, right ahead'. Having helped dozens of passengers into lifeboats, Moody went down with the ship having given up his own place in a raft to Fifth Officer Harold Lowe.

Ayckbourn's Relatively Speaking debuts

One of the earliest and most popular plays written by Alan Ayckbourn, *Relatively Speaking* premiered as *Meet My Father* at Scarborough's Library Theatre on 8 July 1965. Two years later, the play debuted in London at the Duke of York's Theatre, starring Celia Johnson, Michael Hordern and Richard Briers.

Oscar-winner Charles Laughton

The actor Charles Laughton was born in Scarborough in 1899. Appearing in films from the late 1920s, Laughton won the 1933 Best Actor Oscar for his lead role in *The Private Life of Henry VIII*, becoming the first British-born Oscar winner. Nominated again in 1936 for *Mutiny On the Bounty*, Laughton became an American citizen in 1950 prior to his third and final nomination for *Witness for the Prosecution* in 1958. He died in California in 1962. Scarborough gave Britain another great cinema star in Ben Kingsley. Born in Stainton on the outskirts of the town in 1943, he took the Best Actor Oscar for *Gandhi* in 1982.

Scarborough, Tobago

Scarborough is the capital and largest town on Tobago, one of the southernmost of the islands of the Caribbean and the smaller of the two main constituent islands of the Commonwealth Republic of Trinidad and Tobago. Scarborough stands on the south coast of the island and has a population of 17,000, almost one-third that of the entire island. It is home to an eighteenth-century fort, Fort King George, named in honour of George III.

SEAHAM, COUNTY DURHAM
Prime Minister Ramsay MacDonald's constituency

Both the first Labour prime minister and the first to appoint a female Cabinet minister, Ramsay MacDonald held three terms as prime minister and was remarkably always preceded *and* succeeded by Stanley Baldwin. He represented four constituencies during his career, serving as member of parliament for Seaham in County Durham throughout his longest term as prime minister (1929–35).

SEATON CAREW, COUNTY DURHAM
'Disappearance' of John Darwin

One of the most notorious missing person cases of recent years is that of John Darwin, who 'disappeared' whilst canoeing off the North Sea coast at Seaton Carew in Cleveland in March 2002. When a search returned only the wreckage of his boat, a death certificate was issued which subsequently allowed Darwin's wife to claim a vast sum of money from his life insurance, money that she apparently used to emigrate to Panama. Her husband's disappearance, however, was eventually found to have been a hoax, yet it was not until late 2007 that the extent of the couple's scheme came to light – on 1 December, Darwin walked into a police station in London claiming to have no memory of the previous five years, but when the story of the missing canoeist who had seemingly 'returned from the dead' became a national news story, a photograph dated 2006 showing Darwin and his wife looking for properties in Panama was discovered which proved that the whole disappearance had been faked.

SEDGEFIELD, COUNTY DURHAM
Prime Minister Tony Blair's constituency

Born in Edinburgh in 1953, Anthony Charles Lynton Blair became leader of the Labour Party in 1994 following the sudden death of John Smith. He went on to lead the party to victory at an unprecedented three general elections, and remains the longest serving Labour prime minister. He was member of parliament for Sedgefield throughout his entire political career (1983–2007).

Sedgefield Racecourse

A 2008 survey by the animal welfare charity Animal Aid notoriously named Sedgefield Racecourse, which hosts 19 National Hunt fixtures throughout the year, as Britain's most lethal racecourse after its ten-furlong (2-kilometre) course claimed the lives of 11 horses in as many months.

SELBY, NORTH YORKSHIRE
Birthplace of Henry I

Henry I, the fourth son of William the Conqueror, is believed to have been born in Selby in *c.* 1068. The first king since the Norman Conquest to have been born in England (and the last for another hundred years), Henry came to the throne on the death of William II in 1100. In his 35-year reign, Henry fathered three children with his consort Matilda of Scotland and none with his second wife, Adeliza of Louvain, yet it is thought that he had as many as 25 illegitimate children, if not more. He died in 1135.

SHEFFIELD, SOUTH YORKSHIRE
Sheffield Town Hall

The design of Sheffield's impressive town hall building was originally open to a competition, and from almost two hundred entries a design by E. W. Mountford – who also designed London's Old Bailey and Liverpool's Technical College – was chosen. Mountford's somewhat extravagant design, however, not only proved expensive but took seven years to complete. The building was finally opened by Queen Victoria on 21 May 1897.

The Full Monty film set

Both set in and filmed on location in Sheffield, Peter Cattaneo's hugely popular comedy *The Full Monty* gained a total of four Oscar nominations – including Best Director and Best Picture – and won one. It also memorably beat *Titanic* and *L.A. Confidential* to win Best Picture at the BAFTAs in 1998.

Unique football ground records

Sheffield's Bramall Lane Stadium was founded in 1855. Having hosted its first football match in 1862, the ground saw its first international game (an England-Scotland friendly) in 1883; in 1902, it played host to an international Test cricket match between England and Australia; and in 1912, Barnsley beat West Bromwich Albion there in the final of the FA Cup. As such, Bramall Lane remains (alongside the Oval in London) one of only two venues in England to have hosted an international cricket match and an FA Cup final.

SNAPE, NORTH YORKSHIRE
Ghost of Catherine Parr

Snape Castle in North Yorkshire dates from the mid fifteenth century and is said to be haunted by a young, fair-haired girl in a blue Tudor-period dress, typically identified as Catherine Parr. Catherine's time at Snape predates her marriage to Henry VIII in 1543, and instead relates to her earlier marriage to John Neville, 3rd Baron Latymer. Snape had long been the ancestral home of the Neville family, and it is likely that much of Catherine's marriage to John Neville, from 1534 to 1543, was spent there caring for her two stepchildren; indeed, Catherine and the children were held hostage at the castle by rebels during the so-called Pilgrimage of Grace, the northern uprising against Henry VIII's closure of the monasteries in 1536.

SOUTH SHIELDS, TYNE AND WEAR
William Fox, second premier of New Zealand

Sir William Fox was born in Westoe in South Shields in 1812. He emigrated to New Zealand in the 1840s, where he found work with the New Zealand Company promoting British colonisation of the islands. On becoming the company's senior officer, Fox returned to England in 1851 to meet with several influential business and political figures to discuss the future of the colony, recommending the establishment of a New Zealand constitution and an elected parliament. On his return, the new constitution was in effect and Fox was elected MP for Wanganui in 1855. The following year he served the first (and shortest) of his four periods in office as premier of New Zealand.

The Great North Run

South Shields on the North Sea coast is the finishing line of the annual Great North Run, thought to be the largest half-marathon race in the world. First held in 1981, when around 12,000 runners took part in the race, by 2011 some 54,000 runners participated, raising millions of pounds for good causes and making it the largest running event in the UK.

SPURN, EAST YORKSHIRE
Vagrant bird spotted

The first of only three British sightings of the black lark was at Spurn on the East Yorkshire coast in April 1984. One of the largest species of lark, the bird is usually native to central Russia and Kazakhstan.

STAINDROP, COUNTY DURHAM
Birth of Richard Neville

Raby Castle near the Durham village of Staindrop was, in 1400, the birthplace of Richard Neville, later the 5th Earl of Salisbury. The eldest son of the earl and countess of Westmoreland, Neville's control of a vast area of the north of England led to years of bitter feuding with Northumberland's Percy family which flared up into several bloody battles in the mid fifteenth century. As the conflict rumbled on, Neville allied himself with his brother-in-law Richard Plantagenet, Duke of York, eventually joining with the Yorkists at the Battle of St Albans, the first battle of the Wars of the Roses, in 1455. At the Battle of Wakefield just five years later, however, Neville was captured and executed the following day, on 31 December 1460.

STOCKTON-ON-TEES, COUNTY DURHAM
The Infinity Bridge

Stockton's 120-metre (393-foot) Infinity Bridge was completed in 2008, and opened the following year. A pedestrian footbridge crossing the Tees at Durham University's Queen's Campus, the bridge's extraordinary design comprises a 32-metre (104-feet) tall continuous double archway which, when reflected in the water below, forms the mathematical symbol for infinity, ∞, giving the bridge its name. Shortlisted for a RIBA regional award in 2010, the bridge won the prestigious Institution of Structural Engineers' Supreme Award for Structural Excellence in 2009.

STUDLEY ROYAL PARK, NORTH YORKSHIRE
World Heritage Site

The British politician John Aislabie inherited the estate at Studley Royal Park near Ripon in 1699. He was Chancellor of the Exchequer under Prime Minister Charles Spencer, 3rd Earl of Sunderland, and when his political career ended in 1720, Aislabie turned his attentions to the estate, transforming and landscaping its gardens into some of the most impressive eighteenth-century water gardens in all of Europe. After his death in 1742, Aislabie's work was carried on by his son, who went on to purchase the nearby remains of Fountains Abbey. Studley Royal Park, including the abbey and nearby Fountain Hall, was appointed a World Heritage Site in 1986.

SUNDERLAND, TYNE AND WEAR
'Mackems'

A colloquial name for an inhabitant of Sunderland, 'Mackem' is thought to derive from the local slogan *mak'em an' tak'em* (that is, 'make them and take them'), which is itself thought to refer to the ships which were made on the Wear during World War Two before being transferred to the nearby Tyne for fitting out – and so, the Wearside workers would 'make them', and the Tyneside workers would 'take them'.

HMS Investigator

Under the captaincy of cartographer Matthew Flinders, in the early 1800s HMS *Investigator* became the first ship to circumnavigate Australia. Launched on the River Wear at Sunderland as the *Fram* in 1795, the ship was bought by the navy three years later and served as an escort vessel named *Xenophon* until being selected to map the coastline of Australia in 1801. Renovated and renamed *Investigator*, Flinders took command of the ship in January, left Britain in July and reached Australia the following December. The circumnavigation took over 18 months to complete, at the end of which the *Investigator* was deemed unseaworthy and Flinders was left to return home by other means. After extensive repairs, however, *Investigator* sailed back to Britain in 1805.

Extraordinary goalkeeper's goal

In a football match between Sunderland and Manchester City on 14 April 1900, Manchester's goalkeeper Charlie Williams became the first league goalkeeper ever to score a goal in a professional match, when a clearance kick he made ended up in the back of Sunderland's net at their former home ground of

Roker Park. Williams also went on to make football history in Denmark, becoming the national team's first manager in 1908.

TANFIELD, COUNTY DURHAM
The world's oldest rail bridge

Causey Arch near the former colliery village of Tanfield in the north of County Durham is Britain's – and indeed the world's – oldest surviving railway bridge. Built in 1725–26, the bridge spans the Causey Burn, a distant tributary of the Tyne, and carries two train tracks, one originally used to transport coal northwards towards Newcastle and the other to return the empty wagons.

THIRSK, NORTH YORKSHIRE
Thirsk Castle

Built in 1100, the castle at Thirsk in North Yorkshire was destroyed in 1176 on the orders of Henry II, as its owner at the time, Roger de Mowbray, had been a supporter of an ill-fated revolt against the king by his eldest son, Prince Henry, who was angry that his father had failed to give him sufficient funds and influence following his coronation as 'Junior King' in

1170. The revolt effectively led to a short-lived civil war, ending in September 1174 with the reconcilement of Henry and his sons.

TOP WITHENS, NORTH YORKSHIRE
Emily Brontë's Wuthering Heights

Published under the pseudonym Ellis Bell in 1847, Emily Brontë's only novel *Wuthering Heights* takes its name from the moorland house owned by the Earnshaw family in which much of the story is set. Although there is considerable debate as to which – if any – real-life location inspired Brontë's description of Wuthering Heights, local tradition holds that it was Top Withens, a now derelict farmhouse near the village of Haworth in the North Yorkshire Pennines.

TOWTON, NORTH YORKSHIRE
The Battle of Towton

The Battle of Towton was fought during a blinding snowstorm on Palm Sunday, 29 March 1461. One of the most significant conflicts of the Wars of the Roses, Towton involved some 75,000 – mainly Lancastrian – soldiers, of whom more than 25,000 are thought to have been killed. If this is the case, this one battle would have instantly wiped out almost one per cent of the entire population of England at the time, making Towton the largest and bloodiest battle ever fought on British soil.

WALLSEND, TYNE AND WEAR
RMS Carpathia

One of the first of Cunard's great passenger liners completed in the twentieth century, the RMS *Carpathia* was built at Wallsend on the Tyne and launched in 1902. She made her maiden voyage from Liverpool to Boston the following year, and was en route from New York to Fiume (now Rijeka, Croatia) on the night of 15 April 1912 when ship's captain Sir Arthur Rostron heard that the RMS *Titanic* had struck an iceberg – the *Carpathia* arrived at the scene at around 4 a.m. and was able to rescue more than 700 survivors from the water. Unfortunately, the *Carpathia* herself was lost in 1918, torpedoed by a German U-boat off the coast of Ireland.

WHARRAM PERCY, NORTH YORKSHIRE
Extraordinary abandoned mediaeval village

One of the most well-preserved deserted mediaeval villages in the country, Wharram Percy in North Yorkshire is also one of the most thoroughly investigated – the subject of a 40-year archaeological study, it is believed that the village flourished in the twelfth to fourteenth centuries but was abandoned in the early 1500s when the land was turned over to pasture by the local lord of the manor.

WHITBY, NORTH YORKSHIRE
Twinned with Nuku'alofa

In, at first glance, perhaps one of the most unusual pairings of twin towns, Whitby is twinned with the Tongan capital of Nuku'alofa in recognition of Yorkshire-born Captain Cook's two successful visits to the country, which he named the Friendly Islands, in the early 1770s. Whitby is also twinned with Anchorage in Alaska and Port Stanley in the Falklands, both of which have similar associations with Cook's voyages.

HMS Endeavour

One of the most important exploratory ships in British history, Captain Cook's HMS *Endeavour* began life as a collier named *Earl of Pembroke* built at Whitby in 1764. Four years later, the *Pembroke* was bought by the Royal Navy for use in a research expedition to the Pacific Ocean, with Cook in command and the ship refitted and renamed the *Endeavour*. The expedition set off westward from Plymouth on 26 August 1768, and eventually reached the Pacific via Madeira, Rio de Janeiro and Cape Horn early the following year. She returned home via Tahiti, Australia, Cape Town and St Helena to reach Plymouth once more on 13 July 1771.

Bram Stoker's Dracula

Of several English towns mentioned in Bram Stoker's *Dracula*, the North Sea port of Whitby is perhaps the most renowned, as it is here that the eponymous Count first arrives in England stowed aboard the *Demeter*, a Russian ship which had run aground during a storm in Whitby harbour: 'The waves rose in growing fury, each over-topping its fellow, till in the very few minutes the lately glassy sea was like a roaring and devouring monster. White-crested waves... broke over the piers, and with their spume swept the lanthorns of the lighthouses which rise from the end of either pier of Whitby Harbour.'

WILLIMOTESWICK, NORTHUMBERLAND
Birth of Nicholas Ridley

It is thought that Nicholas Ridley was born at Willimoteswick Castle in Northumberland in *c*. 1500. Ordained soon after leaving Cambridge University in 1525, Ridley served as chaplain to Thomas Cranmer, Archbishop of Canterbury, before being promoted to bishop of London in 1550. A supporter of Edward IV's church reforms, when the king died in 1553 Ridley's explicit support for Lady Jane Grey led to his imprisonment under Mary Tudor and his eventual execution in 1555.

WINSTON, COUNTY DURHAM
The Durham Puma

In July 2009, a series of 9-centimetre (3.5-inch) paw prints were found in a muddy field by the River Tees in Winston near Darlington. The sighting was the latest in a long line of reports of the so-called 'Durham puma', captured on film in 1995 carrying a dead rabbit in its mouth.

WYLAM, NORTHUMBERLAND
Birthplace of George Stephenson

The so-called 'Father of the Railways', George Stephenson was born in the Northumberland village of Wylam in 1781. Having taught himself to read and write, at 17 Stephenson took a job at a local coal pit as a brakeman; within little more than a decade, he was responsible for the maintenance of all of the colliery engines in the local area. Inspired by Richard Trevithick's steam locomotive, Stephenson designed his first locomotive, the *Blücher*, in 1814, going on to complete the world's first railway entirely used by such engines in 1822.

YORK, NORTH YORKSHIRE
The Shambles

Several towns and cities across the UK and Ireland have streets or areas known as 'Shambles', the name deriving from a now obsolete

term for an open-air butchers' market or slaughterhouse. The Shambles in York is amongst the most popular and well known in Britain – built more than 900 years ago, the narrow, inward-leaning buildings comprise the oldest street in the city, voted Britain's most picturesque in a 2010 survey.

Guy Fawkes and W. H. Auden

Amongst the many famous former citizens of the city of York are one of the twentieth century's greatest poets and one of the most infamous figures in all British history – W. H. Auden was born in York in 1907 and wrote more than four hundred poems throughout his career, whilst Guy Fawkes was born in Stonegate in York in 1570 and is known the world over as one of the principal conspirators in the Gunpowder Plot of 1605.

Execution of Dick Turpin

Born in Essex in 1705, the highwayman Dick Turpin was originally a butcher before turning to poaching, robbery and housebreaking with the 'Gregory Gang', a group of bandits active throughout Essex and south

London in the early 1700s. When one of the robbers was captured in 1735, the gang disbanded and Turpin turned to highway robbery. He eventually fled London in 1737, but was soon afterwards captured in Yorkshire posing as 'John Palmer' (the alias that appears on his gravestone) and was imprisoned in York Castle. Charged with theft of a horse – which at the time was a capital offence – Turpin was hanged at Knavesmire in the south of the city of York on 7 April 1739.

Death of Thomas of Bayeux

One of the earliest Archbishops of York, Thomas of Bayeux died at York Minster in November 1100. Thomas was the first foreign-born Archbishop of York, having been personally chosen by William the Conqueror to succeed the previous archbishop on his death in 1070. He held the post for 30 years, during which time he arranged for extensive reconstruction of the Minster, wrote the epitaph for William's grave at Abbaye-aux-Hommes in Caen, and oversaw the Accord of Winchester, which sought to establish once and for all the precise relationship between the rivalling ecclesiastical sees of York and Canterbury.

Birth of astronomer William Parsons

On 17 June 1800, the astronomer William Parsons was born in York. Educated at Trinity College, Dublin, and Magdalen College, Oxford, on the death of his father in 1841 Parsons inherited the title of Earl of Rosse and took over his family's estate at Birr Castle in Offaly, Ireland. It was here, in the 1840s, that he constructed what was to become the largest telescope of the nineteenth century, a huge 1.8-metre (6-foot) aperture reflecting telescope nicknamed the Leviathan, which over the next two decades Parsons used to discover and describe hundreds of galaxies and nebulae, becoming the first astronomer to discern the characteristic spiral shape of certain celestial objects which had until then been too distant to be viewed in any great detail. After his death in 1867, Parsons' son Lawrence continued his groundbreaking research, publishing all of their work in 1878.

Marriage of Edward III

King of England from 1327 to 1377, Edward III married Philippa of Hainault at York Minster in January 1328, just under a year after his accession to the throne. Both great-grandchildren of Philip III of France, Edward and Philippa were also teenagers at the time of the marriage – born in Valenciennes in 1311, even at just 16 Philippa was still over a year older than her husband. Nevertheless, the marriage lasted over forty years until Philippa's death in 1369 and she and Edward had 14 children, including John of Gaunt, Thomas of Woodstock, and Edward, the 'Black Prince', father of Richard II. The intense rivalry and disagreement which developed between Edward and Philippa's children, however, would eventually lead to the Wars of the Roses.

The Pilgrimage of Grace

Led by Robert Aske, a local landowner and lawyer, in October 1536 thousands of armed insurgents entered the centre of York in protest against new taxes levied by Henry VIII, as well as Archbishop Thomas Cranmer's suppression of Catholicism and the ongoing dissolution of the monasteries. In response, Henry sent the Duke of Norfolk north with word that the king would pardon the insurgents so long as they agreed to disband. Believing the king's word, Aske ended the revolt and, having met with the king in London, even went on to help quash further rebellions in Scarborough and Hull. Henry, however, soon reneged on his word and had Aske executed in York in 1537.

Statue of Emperor Constantine unveiled

Designed by the sculptor and artist Philip Jackson, outside of York Minster stands a 1.8-metre (6-foot) bronze statue of the Roman Emperor Constantine the Great, close to the site where he was proclaimed emperor following the death of his father and predecessor Constantinus in AD 306. The statue was erected in 1998 eight years ahead of the 1,700th anniversary of Constantine's accession.

Oscar-winner John Barry

Perhaps best known for his theme tune to the James Bond films, the composer John Barry, born in York in 1933, is the most successful British-born musician at the Oscars, having won four awards for Best Score (for *Born Free*, *The Lion in Winter*, *Out of Africa* and *Dances with Wolves*) and one for Best Original Song (*Born Free*, shared with lyricist Don Black), alongside two further nominations (for *Mary, Queen of Scots* and *Chaplin*). He died in New York in January 2011.

THE YORKSHIRE DALES

England's second-largest national park

Established in 1954, the Yorkshire Dales is the largest landlocked national park in England. Amongst its many notable features are the famous Aysgarth Falls featured in the film *Robin Hood, Prince of Thieves*, the extensive cave systems at Ingleborough and Gaping Gill, the beauty spot of Malham Cove, and the extraordinary Grade II listed Ribblehead Viaduct built in the 1870s.

WHAT'S IN A NAME?

Beverley, East Yorkshire
Perhaps a Celtic-origin name, meaning 'beaver's lodge'.

Brandon, Northumberland
Meaning 'hill where broom grows', from the Old English word *brom*.

Cargo, Cumbria
Derives from *carreg*, a Celtic word for 'rock', and *haugr*, a Scandinavian word meaning 'hill'.

Clint, North Yorkshire
From an Old Scandinavian word, *klint*, used of a steep, rocky bank.

Crackpot, North Yorkshire
The Moorland village of Crackpot derives its name from the Scandinavian word for 'crow', *krákr*.

Idle, West Yorkshire
From Old English *idel*, meaning 'empty', probably in the sense of unused or uncultivated land.

Ogle, Northumberland
Derives from the Old English first name, Ocga.

Settle, North Yorkshire
Comes from the Old English word *setl*, meaning 'dwelling' or 'house'.

Stanley, Durham
A 'stony woodland clearing', from the Old English words *stan* and *leah*.

Stella, Gateshead
From the Old English words *stelling* and *leah*, roughly meaning 'clearing by the place for catching fish'.

Swine, East Yorkshire
Likely comes from the Old English word *swin*, denoting a creek or channel of water.

Whale, Cumbria
Derives from a Scandinavian word for a round hill, *hváll*.

SOUTHERN SCOTLAND

Scottish Borders, Dumfries and Galloway,
East Lothian, Midlothian, Edinburgh, West Lothian,
Falkirk, North Lanarkshire, South Lanarkshire,
East Dunbartonshire, West Dunbartonshire, Glasgow,
Inverclyde, Renfrewshire, East Renfrewshire,
North Ayrshire, South Ayrshire, East Ayrshire,
Argyll and Bute, Stirling, Clackmannanshire, Fife

ABINGTON, SOUTH LANARKSHIRE
Death of Cuilén of Scotland

Cuilén became king of the Scots following the death of his predecessor, Dubh, who was slain in battle at Forres in 967. Cuilén himself was killed in 971, burnt to death in a fire at Abington started by Riderch, a prince of Strathclyde, whose daughter is believed to have been abducted and raped by the king.

ALEXANDRIA, WEST DUNBARTONSHIRE
Alexander Smollett

Although Alexander Smollett is the name of the captain of the *Hispaniola* in Robert Louis Stevenson's *Treasure Island*, the namesake of Alexandria is Lieutenant-Colonel Alexander Smollett MP, who was born there in the mid eighteenth century. A member of the Coldstream Guards, Smollett was killed at the Battle of Alkmaar in the Netherlands in 1799.

ALLOWAY, SOUTH AYRSHIRE
Tam o'Shanter

The legendary character Tam o'Shanter (after whom the traditional flat Scottish hat is named) was created by the poet Robert Burns in a work first published in 1791. In the poem, which is one of Burns' longest, Tam is said to be riding home one night on his horse when he passes the old haunted kirk at Alloway, and witnesses a diabolical ritual and dancing witches and warlocks, presided over by the Devil, 'auld Nick, in shape o' beast'. Just as the dancing becomes wilder and bawdier, Tam is discovered and flees, pursued by the 'hellish legion'. He manages to escape unharmed over a nearby bridge, yet one of the witches manages to tear off his horse's tail.

ARDNAVE, ARGYLL AND BUTE
Vagrant bird spotted

Usually found in central North America and the southern USA, a male brown-headed cowbird was spotted at Ardnave on the island of Islay in the Inner Hebrides in April 1988. It remains the only

sighting of this finch-like bird on record for the British Isles.

LOCH AWE, ARGYLL AND BUTE
Britain's longest lake

At 39 square kilometres (14.8 square miles), Loch Awe is the third-largest freshwater loch in Scotland, and the fifth-largest lake in the whole of the UK. Measuring 41 kilometres (25.5 miles) from end to end, yet never more than 1 kilometre (1,009 yards) wide at any point, Awe is also the longest lake in Britain. The loch's northernmost stretches contain a handful of islands, amongst them Fraoch Eilean, the site of a mediaeval castle and former royal residence once home to the Scottish King Alexander III.

AYR, SOUTH AYRSHIRE
Ayr Racecourse

Run every April over 27 fences and a distance of a little over 4 miles, Ayr Racecourse has been home to the Scottish Grand National since the closure of Bogside Racecourse near Irvine in 1966. Scotland's largest racecourse, Ayr also hosts the annual Ayr Gold Cup, and was, until its termination in 2005, home of the Scottish Derby.

BENNANE HEAD, SOUTH AYRSHIRE
Sawney Bean

Whether it is true or not, the story of Alexander 'Sawney' Bean is amongst the most gruesome in all of Scottish folklore. Allegedly, Bean was born in East Lothian sometime during the reign of James VI, and he and his wife are supposed to have lived in a cave on Bennane Head near Girvan in Ayrshire with their inbred family of 14 children and over 30 grandchildren. The whole clan were robbers and murderous cannibals who would set traps to ambush and kill passers-by, then take their bodies back down into the caves to be dismembered and eaten. Eventually, when one of their ambushes failed, the monstrous family were discovered and fled Bennane only to be captured in a manhunt ordered by the king himself, and executed without trial.

BORTHWICK, MIDLOTHIAN
Ghost of Mary, Queen of Scots

Borthwick Castle was built in 1430 and was where Mary I of Scotland fled when rebels planned to capture her and her third husband, the Earl of Bothwell, in 1567. Mary escaped the castle by disguising herself as a pageboy but was later captured, imprisoned and eventually executed for treason in 1587. Her ghost, still wearing the disguise that had saved her, has allegedly been spotted at Borthwick on several occasions since.

BOTHWELLHAUGH, NORTH LANARKSHIRE
Abandoned colliery village

The village of Bothwellhaugh near Glasgow developed rapidly from a tiny farming community in the late 1880s after extensive coal seams were discovered in the area. As a result, several collieries were founded nearby, with rows of new houses built in the village as homes for the pit workers and their families – a report of 1910 found that Bothwellhaugh's 458 houses were home to some 965 colliery staff and their families. However, the community steadily declined throughout the mid 1900s, as far more efficient machinery meant fewer miners were needed on site. Finally abandoned in the 1960s, nothing remains of Bothwellhaugh today.

CAERLAVEROCK, DUMFRIES AND GALLOWAY
Edward I takes Caerlaverock Castle

Following his first campaign in 1296, throughout his reign Edward I of England launched several attacks on Scotland in an attempt to maintain control of the country. In July 1300, he mustered his troops at Carlisle and marched along the Solway Coast, headed for Caerlaverock Castle. The castle was besieged and Edward, accompanied by more than eighty knights, three thousand troops and a host of impressive siege engines from across the North Country, quickly took control. Caerlaverock remained in English hands until 1312.

CERES, FIFE
US statesman James Wilson

Born in 1742 in the hamlet of Ceres in Fife, James Wilson emigrated to America aged 24, where he taught literature at the College of Philadelphia and opened a successful legal practice. Considered a foremost opponent to British rule in America, Wilson published one of the earliest pamphlets in support of independence in 1774 and became an important member of the Continental Congress on his election two years later. He died in North Carolina in 1798.

CLYDEBANK, WEST DUNBARTONSHIRE
RMS Lusitania

Built at Clydebank in less than two years, at the time of its maiden voyage in 1907 the RMS *Lusitania* was the largest passenger ship in the world. Eight years into its service with Cunard, however, on 7 May 1915 she was torpedoed by a German U-boat and sank in just 18 minutes off the south coast of Ireland, taking with her nearly 1,200 lives.

COYLTON, SOUTH AYRSHIRE
The Galloway Puma

In July 2009, a horse in Coylton near Ayr was thought to have been attacked by a big cat, having suffered several serious bite and claw marks to its back and hindquarters. The attack followed an earlier sighting in May of a large, sandy-coloured cat prowling the grounds of nearby Sundrum Castle. Such sightings of a puma-like cat have been reported numerous times in and around Scotland's Machars Peninsula since the early 1990s, leading to the local legend of the so-called 'Galloway puma'. The creature's existence, however, remains unproven.

CROSSHOUSE, EAST AYRSHIRE
Andrew Fisher, fifth prime minister of Australia

Born in Crosshouse in 1862, Andrew Fisher emigrated to Queensland in 1885. As he had done in Scotland, Fisher first worked as a miner in Burrum and then Gympie, where he was elected the first president of the local branch of the Australian Labour Party in 1891. Two years later, he entered the Queensland Legislative Assembly, quickly becoming deputy leader, and following the federation and establishment of the Commonwealth of Australia in 1901, won the Queensland

electorate (constituency) of Wide Bay and entered parliament. He became leader of the Labour Party in 1907, and the following year became Australia's fifth prime minister, serving the first of his three terms in office from November 1908 to June 1909. Later serving as Australian high commissioner to the UK, Fisher died in London in 1928.

DUMBARTON, WEST DUNBARTONSHIRE
The Cutty Sark

The last tea-clipper ever built in Britain, the *Cutty Sark* was launched from Dumbarton on the Clyde on 22 November 1869. Initially serving the Chinese tea trade in the 1870s, as faster steamships began to replace the slower and less reliable tea-clippers, the *Cutty Sark* was sold to Portugal in 1895 and did not return to Britain until 1922. She was moved to the Thames in 1938 for use as a cadet training ship and eventually, after extensive renovation, was placed in a specially built dry dock at Greenwich and opened to the public in 1954.

DUNBAR, EAST LOTHIAN
The Battle of Dunbar

At the Battle of Dunbar on 3 September 1650, Oliver Cromwell's Parliamentarian forces met with a Scottish army loyal to Charles II under the leadership of the Scottish general David Leslie. The battle was amongst the last in the English Civil War to be fought on Scottish soil and proved to be yet another decisive victory for the Parliamentarians, who ultimately all but obliterated Charles' Scottish support. In the aftermath, Cromwell was able to take control of Edinburgh and much of southern Scotland, whilst at Worcester exactly one year later, Charles' Royalist forces would be finally defeated altogether.

DUNFERMLINE, FIFE
Birth of Charles I

On 19 November 1600, Charles Stuart, the second son of James VI of Scotland, was born at Dunfermline Palace in Fife. On the death of his elder brother Henry in 1612, Charles became heir to the throne and succeeded his father as King Charles I in 1625. His reign lasted 24 years, during which time

he saw England collapse into a bloody civil war fought between his Royalist supporters and the Parliamentarians, who were outraged at his repeated disregard for parliamentary authority as well as his somewhat dubious actions as head of the Church of England. Captured in 1647, Charles was eventually found guilty of treason and executed at Whitehall on 28 January 1649. His eldest son became Charles II following the restoration of the monarchy in 1660, the same year that Charles himself was canonised by the Anglican Church. He remains the last British monarch to have been made a saint.

Birthplace of Scottish kings

Although little is known of the lives of many of Scotland's earliest leaders, at least four kings are believed to have been born at Dunfermline, and consequently the town can claim to be the birthplace of more monarchs than any other place in Scotland. Alexander I, fifth son of Malcolm III of Scotland, is though to have been born in Dunfermline in *c.* 1077, around the time that his mother, St Margaret, founded a

Benedictine friary in the town. As Dunfermline grew in importance, the friary was raised to an abbey and its residential quarters were extended into what would eventually become Dunfermline Palace, the birthplace of both David II and James I of Scotland in 1324 and 1394 respectively.

Former royal residence
Dunfermline Palace

Once one of the most significant royal palaces in Scotland, Dunfermline Palace fell into disrepair following the relocation of the Scottish court to London on James VI's accession to the English throne in 1603. Last used as a royal residence by Charles II in 1650, Dunfermline was abandoned soon afterwards and is now in ruins.

EAST FIFE
Prime Minister H. H. Asquith's constituency

Herbert Henry Asquith became prime minister following the resignation of Henry Campbell-Bannerman in 1908. Asquith himself went on to serve until 1916, following an eventful premiership that saw Britain declare war on Germany following the invasion of Belgium in 1914. Throughout most of his career, Asquith served as member of parliament for East Fife (1886–1918), although he later represented Paisley (1920–24) shortly before his death in 1928.

EAST KILBRIDE, SOUTH LANARKSHIRE
WEST KILBRIDE, NORTH AYRSHIRE
The life of St Brigid

Supposedly born in Ireland's County Louth, St Brigid – often known as Brigid of Kildare, having founded the abbey there in 470 – is one of the most important saints in Irish history. After her death in *c.* 525, Irish missionaries took word of Brigid to Scotland, where she is commemorated in (amongst many others) the names of both East and West Kilbride.

EDINBURGH
The Royal Mile

Directly linking Edinburgh Castle to the Palace of Holyrood House, as its name suggests Edinburgh's Royal Mile covers a distance of approximately one old Scots mile (1,980 yards, a little more than a standard mile of 1,760 yards), and is though to date back to the reign of King David I in the twelfth century, when it was known as Via Regis, 'the king's way'. Today, Edinburgh's St Giles Cathedral, Parliament House, City Chambers and the new Scottish Parliament building all stand on the Royal Mile.

Edinburgh rock

Very much different from traditional rock, Edinburgh – or Edinburgh castle – rock is made from sugar, water and cream of tartar, the latter preventing the sugar from crystallising and ultimately giving the rock its characteristic cloudy appearance and softer, crumblier texture.

'Flower of Scotland'

Scotland has no official anthem of its own, although several songs have been suggested and used as such in various national contexts over the years. Amongst the most well known of these contenders is 'Flower of Scotland', written in 1967 by Edinburgh-born musician Roy Williamson, of the Scottish folk group The Corries. The song, whose lyrics make reference to Scotland's victory over Edward II of England at the Battle of Bannockburn in 1314, has long been used as the entrance anthem of the Scottish national rugby union and football teams, and in 2010 replaced 'Scotland The Brave' as the official Scottish victory anthem at the Commonwealth Games. 'Flower of Scotland' was also chosen by more than two-fifths of respondents in a 2006 poll by the Scottish National Orchestra to choose Scotland's favourite anthem.

Execution of William Burke

William Burke and William Hare were both born in Ireland in 1792, moving to Scotland in the early 1800s. Both men eventually settled in Edinburgh, becoming close friends when Burke moved into the same street as a guesthouse run by Hare's wife. It was here, over the 12 months from November 1827 to October 1828 that the pair murdered 17 people, delivering their bodies to Dr Robert Knox, a nearby private anatomy lecturer, who paid anything up to £10 for the corpses; contrary to popular belief, Burke and Hare were murderers, not grave-robbers. After a year, the duo's horrific crime spree finally came to light and they were imprisoned. Hare, however, was offered immunity from prosecution if he agreed to testify against his accomplice, and so whilst Burke was executed at Edinburgh's Lawnmarket on 28 January 1829, Hare was released from jail the following month. Nothing else of any certainty is known of the rest of his life.

Birth of John Ogilby

Although his exact birthplace is unknown, the prominent seventeenth-century scholar John Ogilby is believed to have been born in or near to Edinburgh in 1600. A successful translator (producing English versions of Virgil, Aesop and Homer whilst at Cambridge University in the 1640s) and poet (he was commissioned to write verse commemorating the coronation of Charles II in 1661), it is nevertheless as a cartographer that Ogilby is most celebrated today, having published his pioneering *Britannia* atlas in 1675. An astonishing undertaking for

its time, the *Britannia* comprised a collection of one hundred maps showing all of the major contemporary road routes of England and Wales drawn to the now-standard scale of one inch to one statute mile. As such, the *Britannia* is considered Britain's first detailed road atlas, and indeed the first of any country in Western Europe.

Edward Stafford and Thomas Mackenzie, premiers of New Zealand

Both Sir Edward William Stafford and Sir Thomas Mackenzie were born in Edinburgh, in 1819 and 1854 respectively. Stafford served three terms as the third premier of New Zealand and holds the record for the longest time in office for any leader not affiliated to any particular party. Although he was initially reluctant to take a political office in the New Zealand Parliament, when former leader William Fox's premiership ended after less than two weeks it was decided that Stafford was best suited to be his replacement. As the eighteenth prime minister of New Zealand, meanwhile, Thomas Mackenzie held office just once, for a little over three months, in 1912. Having lived in New Zealand since the age of four, prior to his political career Mackenzie was also a keen explorer and led several investigative expeditions into rural areas of New Zealand in the early twentieth century.

Assassination of Lord Darnley

Henry Stuart, better known as Lord Darnley, the consort of Mary, Queen of Scots, was assassinated on the night of 9–10 February 1567 in Kirk o'Field in central Edinburgh. That night, the house in which Darnley had been staying was partially destroyed by an explosion, and the following day the bodies of Darnley and his servant were found in a nearby orchard. Unusually, both appeared unharmed by the explosion and had instead apparently been strangled. Whether the explosion was intended to kill Darnley, who had consequently fled the house only to be killed outside, or whether the explosion was intended to cover up the murders remains unclear. However, suspicion soon fell on Mary and her companion

James Hepburn, Earl of Bothwell, whom she married just three months later.

Stoppard's Rosencrantz and Guildenstern Are Dead debuts

Originally a one-act piece written in 1964, the world premiere of Tom Stoppard's *Rosencrantz and Guildenstern Are Dead* took place at Edinburgh's Fringe Festival in August 1966 before debuting in London the following year. The play, which focuses almost entirely on its two title characters whilst the events of Shakespeare's *Hamlet* (from which Rosencrantz and Guildenstern are taken) take place in the background, was Stoppard's first and remains a masterpiece of twentieth-century comic theatre. Stoppard himself directed a 1990 film adaptation starring Gary Oldman and Tim Roth.

Oscar-winner Sean Connery

Born in Edinburgh in 1930, Sir Sean Connery became the first Scot ever to win an Oscar when, in 1998, he won the award for Best Supporting Actor for *The Untouchables*. It was his first – and remains his only – Oscar nomination.

The Scottish Parliament Building

The Scottish Parliament in Holyrood, Edinburgh, was officially opened by the Queen in 2004. Designed by the Catalan architect Enric Miralles, the building was designed as if to appear to be rising out of the ground rather than sitting upon it and, partly due to this ambitious concept, over the five years of its construction the overall cost of the project rose from an original estimate of £10–40 million to a total of more than £400 million. Nevertheless, it has since won numerous international architectural prizes, including the RIBA's 2005 Stirling Prize. Sadly, Miralles died during construction and never saw the project completed.

The discovery of nitrogen

Following on from earlier experiments with carbon dioxide carried out by Joseph Black, the Scottish scientist Daniel Rutherford isolated nitrogen – which he called 'noxious air' – whilst still a student at Edinburgh University in 1772. Both Black and Rutherford (who was also the uncle of the writer Sir Walter Scott) now have buildings named after them at the university.

Anaesthesia pioneered

The acclaimed Scottish obstetrician Sir James Young Simpson was one of the earliest pioneers of anaesthesia. Whilst professor of midwifery at Edinburgh University in the mid nineteenth century, Simpson experimented with the use of chloroform as a way of causing unconsciousness, first administering it to women during childbirth in 1847. The practice soon became widespread – popularised by Queen Victoria's use of chloroform during the birth of Prince Leopold, her eighth child, in 1853 – until the potential toxicity of the drug became known in the early twentieth century.

The Edinburgh Commonwealth Games

Edinburgh, alongside Auckland, is one of only two cities to have hosted the Commonwealth Games twice, namely in 1970 and 1986. The 1970 games were the first to use photo-finish technology, the first to be known as the

British Commonwealth Games, and the first to comprehensively use the metric system. The 1986 games, meanwhile, proved more notorious than remarkable as over thirty nations chose to boycott the event in response to British sport's attitude toward the ongoing apartheid in South Africa.

Scottish Olympian Chris Hoy

Sir Chris Hoy is Scotland's (and Britain's), most successful Olympian, having won a total of seven medals since taking silver in the team sprint cycling event at Sydney in 2000. His gold in the time trial at the 2004 Athens Games was followed by a further three gold medals at the Beijing Games. His remarkable success was recognised by a knighthood in the 2009 New Year Honours and he has since added a further two golds at the London 2012 Games.

Edinburgh, Tristan da Cunha

The 207-square-kilometre (80-square-mile) volcanic island group Tristan da Cunha in the South Atlantic claims to be the most remote inhabited archipelago in the world, lying some 2,816

kilometres (1,750 miles) from the nearest mainland in South Africa. Part of a British overseas territory which also includes St Helena and Ascension Island, Tristan da Cunha's only town is Edinburgh of the Seven Seas, named to commemorate Prince Alfred, Duke of Edinburgh and second son of Queen Victoria, who visited the island in 1867 as part of a round-the-world trip. The current Duke of Edinburgh, Prince Philip, also visited the island in 1957.

THE FORTH BRIDGE
'Painting the Forth Bridge'

Any task that is said to be like 'painting the Forth Bridge' is unending, alluding to the erroneous belief that the Forth Bridge is so large that once painting it is complete it is time to start all over again.

GIFFORD, EAST LOTHIAN
US statesman John Witherspoon

Born in Gifford in 1723, John Witherspoon (an ancestor of the Oscar-winning actress Reese Witherspoon) served over twenty years as a minister before emigrating to New Jersey in 1768, where he took up a professorship at the small Presbyterian college which would eventually become Princeton University. He served in Continental Congress from 1776 to 1782, becoming the only clergyman to sign the Declaration of Independence in 1776.

GLASGOW

Ripper suspect Thomas Neill Cream

Born in Glasgow in 1850, Dr Thomas Neill Cream was convicted of the murder by strychnine poisoning of a London prostitute named Matilda Clover and was hanged at Newgate in 1892. Cream was subsequently blamed for the deaths of several more women, including some that he had killed whilst in Canada and the USA. Although tellingly none of Jack the Ripper's victims were poisoned, Cream's unfinished last words are nevertheless reputed to have been, 'I am Jack the–'.

The Glasgow Police Act

On 30 June 1800, the British government officially passed the Glasgow Police Act, creating the first professional police force in the country, predating London's

Metropolitan Police by almost thirty years. The following September, a local merchant named John Stenhouse was appointed the city's first master of police, soon recruiting an initial staff of three sergeants and six officers. Despite these somewhat humble beginnings, however, the Glasgow Police Force went on to last for 175 years until it was merged with Strathclyde Police in 1975.

Glasgow City Chambers

Situated on Glasgow's George Square, the City Chambers were designed by the Scottish architect William Young and have been the seat of local government in the city since Queen Victoria's official opening ceremony in 1888. Young's impressive design – including an entrance inspired by Rome's Arch of Constantine – took several years to build and, after work began in 1882, it was not until 1889 that the first regular council meetings were held there.

Prime Minister Andrew Bonar Law's constituency

Born in New Brunswick, Canada, in 1858, Andrew Bonar Law

remains the only British prime minister to have been born outside of the British Isles. He represented four different constituencies during his 23 years in parliament, of which Glasgow Central (1918–23) was the last. He served as prime minister for just one day short of seven months, from 23 October 1922 until 22 May 1923, when he retired due to failing health.

John Alexander Macdonald, first prime minister of Canada

John Alexander Macdonald was born in Glasgow in 1815. He and his family emigrated to Kingston, now in Ontario, when Macdonald was just five years old and on leaving school there he trained as a lawyer. His political career began in 1843 when he was elected alderman of Kingston and in the years that followed, he served as receiver general, attorney general, and finally joint premier of the Province of Canada before the British North America Act of 1867 created the new Dominion of Canada, of which the now knighted Sir John Macdonald became the first prime minister. He held office intermittently until 1891.

Extraordinary Opus Clavicembalisticum debuts

Considered by some to be one of the most difficult pieces of music ever written and, at the time, easily the longest known work for piano, the little-known British-Parsi composer Kaikhosru Shapurji Sorabji's 260-page solo piano work *Opus Clavicembalisticum* was first performed in its entirety by the composer himself at Glasgow's Stevenson Hall on 1 December 1930. The piece, which contains 12 movements made up of fugues, interludes, cadenzas and a passacaglia with some 81 variations, takes roughly four hours to perform in full and as such remains something of a musical enigma, largely only recognised today for its remarkable length and notorious musical complexity.

Oscar-winner Peter Capaldi

The Scottish actor and filmmaker Peter Capaldi was born in Glasgow in 1958. Perhaps best known for his BAFTA-winning role as the foul-mouthed spin doctor Malcolm Tucker in the acclaimed BBC comedy *The Thick of It*, in 1995 Capaldi won the Oscar for

Best Live Action Short for his film *Franz Kafka's It's a Wonderful Life*, which he wrote and directed. He was only the second Scot ever to win an Oscar.

Bud Neill memorial unveiled

One of Glasgow's most unusual sculptures is that of Lobey Dosser and Rank Bajin, sat astride the two-legged horse El Fideldo – all of whom are characters created by Glaswegian cartoonist Bud Neill. Born in Partick, Neill provided cartoons for *The* (Glasgow) *Herald* and *Sunday Mail* from the mid 1940s, with the characters of his *Sheriff Lobey Dosser of Calton Creek* strip, his most famous creations, first appearing in 1949. *The Lobey Dosser* statue was erected in 1992, following an appeal for public donations in *The Herald*, and is meant as a memorial to Neill, who died in 1970.

Rare whisky auctioned

One of the most expensive bottles of whisky ever sold in Britain was bought for £11,750 at an auction in Glasgow in August 2009. The bottle, a 50-year-old Macallan malt whisky distilled in the mid

1920s, was bought by an unnamed Californian collector.

Lister's early antisepsis measures

Joseph Lister was born at Upton in Essex in 1827. Having studied medicine at both University College London and the University of Edinburgh, Lister became professor of surgery at Glasgow University in 1860. It was here that he pioneered the use of antiseptics by swabbing wounds with a solution of carbolic acid, which vastly reduced the occurrence of gangrene in his patients. He outlined his revolutionary findings in a paper published in the *British Medical Journal* in 1867.

The Glasgow Commonwealth Games

In 2004, Glasgow defeated Edinburgh to become Scotland's official bid to host the 2014 Commonwealth Games, and three years later, in November 2007, it was announced that the bid had been successful. Having beaten the Canadian city of Halifax and the Nigerian capital Abuja, Glasgow will indeed host the games from 23 July to 3 August 2014, making

Glasgow the second Scottish city (and the UK's fifth overall) to host the event, and also marking the third hosting of the games in Scotland – only Canada and Australia have hosted them more often.

HAMILTON, SOUTH LANARKSHIRE

Former royal residence Cadzow Castle

What remains today of Cadzow Castle on the outskirts of Hamilton was built in the early 1500s, likely on the site of a much earlier royal castle thought to date from the reign of David I in the twelfth century. Cadzow remained the property of the Scottish crown until Robert the Bruce granted it to the local nobleman Sir Walter Fitzgilbert in the fourteenth century. Rebuilt in the 1500s, the castle was soon afterwards destroyed and has stood in ruin ever since.

HAWICK, SCOTTISH BORDERS

Memorial to James Thomson unveiled

A statue designed by the local artist Bill Landles commemorating the Scottish poet James Thomson was unveiled in Hawick in October 2006. Thomson, who penned the traditional Burns' Night ode 'The Star o' Rabbie Burns', was born in Bowden in 1827 but lived most of his life in Hawick. A nearby footbridge over the River Teviot opened in the same year has also been named after him.

HELENSBURGH, ARGYLL AND BUTE

The Helensburgh Panther

On 29 July 2009, a big cat sighting was reported in the Argyll town of Helensburgh. Significantly, the creature – roughly the size of a dog, with jet black fur and a long tail – was caught on film walking alongside a railway track, yet expert opinion of the footage suggested that it was probably nothing more than a large domestic cat.

INCHCOLM, FIFE

Macbeth (I.ii)

In the opening act of *Macbeth*, Ross states '... Nor would we deign him burial of his men till he disbursed, at St Colm's Inch, ten thousand dollars to our general use', informing King Duncan that following Macbeth's victory over King Sweno of Denmark, the Danish king has been charged for the right to bury his dead on the island of 'St Colm's Inch'. Inchcolm, as it is now known, is a tiny islet in the Firth of Forth just off the mainland from Aberdour. Taking its name from St Columba, it was frequently used as a burial site in the Middle Ages.

IONA, ARGYLL AND BUTE
Macbeth (II.iv)

Colmekill, now known as the island of Iona, was once the ancient burial place of the kings of Scotland, mentioned as such in the second act of Shakespeare's *Macbeth*, as the place where the body of King Duncan has been taken – 'Carried to Colmekill, the sacred storehouse of his predecessors'; indeed, besides Duncan, the real-life Scottish kings Malcolm, Kenneth and Macbeth are all buried there. Its name is Gaelic in origin, and refers to St Columba who lived there in the late sixth century.

JEDBURGH, SCOTTISH BORDERS
'Jedburgh justice'

The phrase 'Jedburgh justice' describes the hasty 'hang first, try later' approach to justice, in which the accused would be executed before a fair trial had been carried out. Similar phrases exist across Britain, including 'Abingdon law' named after Abingdon in Oxfordshire, 'Lydford Law' from Lydford in Devon, and 'Cupar justice', named after the town of Coupar Angus in Perth and Kinross.

JURA, ARGYLL AND BUTE
Jura, France

The island of Jura in the Inner Hebrides lies between Islay and the Scottish mainland in Argyll and Bute, and is the thirteenth-largest island in the British Isles. Its continental namesake is the Jura mountain range on the French-Swiss-German border near Lake Geneva, which gives its name to both a department of France and a north-western canton of Switzerland. The Jurassic period of geological history, the second of the three

Mesozoic periods in which dinosaurs existed, is also named after the mountains.

KILRENNY, FIFE
Vagrant bird spotted

Usually native to the south-east Mediterranean and north Africa, Britain's first ever masked shrike was spotted on Kilrenny Common to the north of the village of Kilrenny in Fife in 2004. A second bird was sighted two years later in the Scilly Isles.

KIRKCALDY, FIFE
Landale vs Morgan

The last duel in Scottish history took place at a farm on the outskirts of Kirkcaldy on 23 August 1826, between David Landale, a local linen merchant, and George Morgan, a banker. Landale is thought to have challenged Morgan to the duel after details of his financial situation were made public, for which Morgan refused to apologise. In the subsequent confrontation, Morgan was shot in the chest and killed, whilst Landale escaped unharmed. He was later tried for murder but acquitted.

KIRKCUDBRIGHT, DUMFRIES AND GALLOWAY
The life of St Cuthbert

Kirkcudbright takes its name from St Cuthbert, a seventh-century cleric and one of the earliest bishops of Lindisfarne. After his retirement in 686, Cuthbert returned to a life of solitude on Inner Farne in Northumberland's Farne Islands and died there the following year. Although buried on Lindisfarne, after an attack by Danish invaders in 875 Cuthbert's remains were exhumed and taken by monks to several locations, including Kirkcudbright, before being returned to the north-east and eventually reinterred at Durham Cathedral.

LEITH, EDINBURGH
Base of pirate Thomas Green

On 11 April 1705, the English captain Thomas Green was found guilty of piracy and hanged, along with two of his crewmen, on the beach at Leith in Edinburgh. According to reports, Green's ship, the *Worcester*, had been seized by Scottish authorities on entering the Firth of Forth, whereupon Green and his crew were accused of having forcibly boarded a ship off India's Malabar Coast, killing those on board and stealing its cargo. Today, however, the trumped-up charges that were brought against the men appear to have been nothing more than hearsay, more likely rooted in the prevalent anti-English sentiment widespread throughout Scotland at the turn of the eighteenth century, and understandably Green's cursory trial and swift execution were met with much anger and condemnation throughout England at the time.

The Darien Scheme

The brainchild of William Paterson, a Scottish-born banker and co-founder of the Bank of England, the Darien Scheme of the late seventeenth century was an audacious yet disastrous attempt by Scotland to establish what could otherwise have been a potentially lucrative trade colony in Panama. Led by an initial fleet of ships which left Leith in July 1698 and sailed to the gulf of Darien, the ill-fated scheme was plagued with problems from its outset, with the colonists decimated by disease, famine and skirmishes with nearby

Spanish colonies, and the native people little interested in the bizarre assortment of goods – including combs, mirrors and wigs – that the expedition had brought with them for trade. Even after the arrival of a second expedition the following year, the colony of New Caledonia was finally abandoned in 1700.

Irvine Welsh's Trainspotting

One of the most significant books of the late twentieth century, *Trainspotting* is set in the mid 1980s in Leith, an area of Edinburgh, the home town of its author Irvine Welsh.

LINLITHGOW, WEST LOTHIAN
Former royal residence
Linlithgow Palace

Although the site is thought to have been inhabited since Roman times, the first royal residence at Linlithgow was built by David I in the twelfth century. Following a fire in 1424, the castle was rebuilt by James I of Scotland and greatly extended by his descendants to become one of the most important royal residences of its time. Long since abandoned, Linlithgow was devastated by a second fire in

1745 and, whilst still impressive, remains in ruins today.

LOCH LOMOND
Britain's largest lake

At 71 square kilometres (27 square miles), Loch Lomond is both the largest loch in Scotland and the largest lake in Great Britain, and moreover contains Inchmurrin, the largest freshwater island in the British Isles. Other islands in the loch include Inchlonaig, whose trees were supposedly planted by Robert the Bruce to provide bows for his archers, and Inchconnachan, home to a flourishing population of Australian wallabies. Historically marking the boundary between Dunbartonshire and Stirlingshire, the loch area is now divided between the council areas of Argyll and Bute, Stirling, and West Dunbartonshire.

LOCH LOMOND AND THE TROSSACHS
Scotland's first national park

Officially opened in 2002, Loch Lomond and the Trossachs was the first of Scotland's two national parks. Less than half the size of the Cairngorms National Park, Lomond is nevertheless the fourth-largest national park in the whole of the British Isles, covering some 1,865 square kilometres (720 square miles) of Stirling, West Dunbartonshire, Perth and Kinross and Argyll and Bute.

MOTHERWELL, NORTH LANARKSHIRE
Football's fastest hat-trick

Motherwell's Ian St John scored British football's fastest ever hat-trick during a game at Fir Park against Hibernian in August 1959, scoring all three goals within two and a half minutes, an average of one every 50 seconds. Motherwell went on to win 4–2.

THE MULL OF GALLOWAY, DUMFRIES AND GALLOWAY
Scotland's southernmost point

The Mull of Galloway is the southernmost tip of Scotland, oddly standing some 90 kilometres (55 miles) further south than the northernmost point of England. Comprising a 1,000-metre (1,093-yard) headland at the southernmost tip of The Rhins – the noticeably two-pronged peninsula lying to the west of Stranraer – today the Mull of Galloway is an RSPB reserve and the site of a lighthouse built there in 1830. The nearby hamlet of Cairngaan, meanwhile, is Scotland's southernmost settlement and lies even further south than Newcastle, Sunderland and Carlisle.

MUSSELBURGH, EAST LOTHIAN
Musselburgh Links Golf Course

The nine-hole golf course at Musselburgh Links in Lothian is thought to be the oldest surviving golf course in Britain, if not anywhere in the world. Although officially recorded as dating from 1672, Mary, Queen of Scots, is thought to have played golf there more than a century earlier in 1567. Musselburgh also assured its place in golf history in 1893 when its 4.5-inch wide holes were adopted as the standard size for golf holes the world over by the Royal and Ancient.

NEWBRIDGE, DUMFRIES AND GALLOWAY
The Twelve Apostles

The stone circle near the Dumfries village of Newbridge known as the Twelve Apostles is, at 88

metres (289 feet) in diameter at its widest, the largest stone circle on the Scottish mainland and remains amongst the largest in the whole of Britain. Despite its modern name, the group is originally thought to have once included as many as 20 individual stones.

NEW LANARK, SOUTH LANARKSHIRE
World Heritage Site

On the opening of a textile factory and mill in South Lanarkshire in the late 1700s, the industrialist David Dale and his son-in-law Robert Owen founded a whole new village for the millworkers at New Lanark on the Clyde. Providing good-quality housing and infrastructure, New Lanark became a socialist model for the Industrial Revolution and was renowned throughout Europe. It was designated a World Heritage Site in 2009.

NEWLANDS, SCOTTISH BORDERS
British Olympian Walter Rutherford

Golf has been contested at the Olympic Games only twice in

their history, namely in 1900 and 1904. At the 1900 Paris Games, Scotland's Walter Rutherford, born in Newlands in 1870, took the silver medal, losing out on the gold by just one point.

NORTH BERWICK, EAST LOTHIAN
The North Berwick Witch Trials

Dozens of people were implicated in a series of witch trials in the East Lothian town of North Berwick in the late 1500s, which originated in an apparent plot to raise a storm and shipwreck the Scottish King James VI and his bride Anne of Denmark on their return from their wedding in Copenhagen. Amongst the first to be tried was Gelie Duncan, a servant of a local chamberlain, who confessed to witchcraft under torture when her apparent gift for healing the sick aroused suspicion. Another of the accused, Agnes Simpson, a local midwife and healer, was even taken before the king himself for questioning. Eventually confessing to over fifty bizarre crimes – including relieving the pains of a woman in labour by suffering them herself, and even baptising a cat

– Simpson was strangled to death and burnt in January 1591.

PAISLEY, RENFREWSHIRE
The Paisley Witch Trial

The Paisley Witch Trial concerned 11-year-old Christian Shaw, the daughter of a local laird, who accused seven 'witches' – three men and four women – of casting a spell which possessed her, making her float through the air and vomit bones, feathers and rocks. Although the accused denied all of the charges brought against them, they were all nevertheless found guilty and sentenced to death. On 10 June 1697, the seven were taken to the Gallow Green in west Paisley where they were strangled and burnt. A memorial to those executed was unveiled in May 2008.

PENCAITLAND, EAST LOTHIAN
Ghost of Charles I

Also known as Fountainhall, Penkaet Castle in Pencaitland, south-east of Edinburgh, is said to be haunted by several ghosts, of which Charles I is just one. Supposedly, Charles' ghost is responsible for several unusual disturbances that have been reported in the bedroom at the castle that now houses Charles' bed, which was brought to Penkaet in 1923. Amongst many other stories of unexplained occurrences at the castle, the bedclothes of Charles' bed have often been found thrown back or disturbed as if slept in, even though the room has lain empty overnight.

PORTPATRICK, DUMFRIES AND GALLOWAY
The Southern Upland Way

The Southern Upland Way is the longest of Scotland's long-distance walking routes, stretching for 340 kilometres (212 miles) from Portpatrick near Stranraer to the North Sea at Cockburnspath in the Scottish Borders. As such, the route is the only officially designated coast-to-coast footpath in the UK.

PRESTONPANS, EAST LOTHIAN
The Battle of Prestonpans

Following an earlier skirmish at Highbridge near Fort William, the Battle of Prestonpans was the

first major conflict of the Second Jacobite Rising of 1745. The two sides – the Jacobites, led by Bonnie Prince Charlie, and more than 2,000 British government troops led by Sir John Cope, an experienced British Army officer – clashed for just ten minutes early in the morning of 21 September 1745, during which time Cope's troops were easily outmanoeuvred and forced to flee. With defeat inevitable, Cope and his men abandoned the battle, returning to the safety of a garrison at Berwick-upon-Tweed.

SEIL, ARGYLL AND BUTE
Britain's narrowest strait

The island of Seil in Scotland's Firth of Lorn stands just 6 metres (20 feet) from the Scottish mainland, forming the narrowest sea strait in the whole of the British Isles.

SHUNA, ARGYLL AND BUTE
Population: one

Shuna is one of several islands that stand in Loch Linnhe in western Scotland. At 1.5 square kilometres (0.6 square miles), it is also the largest of the four islands of Scotland with a resident population of just one.

SKERRYVORE, ARGYLL AND BUTE
Britain's tallest lighthouse

A remote reef roughly 19 kilometres (12 miles) south of the island of Tiree in the Inner Hebrides is the site of Scotland's – and Britain's – tallest lighthouse. Skerryvore (48 metres/156 feet), as it is known, was built over six years from 1838 to 1844 by Alan Stevenson, son of the renowned Scottish engineer Robert Stevenson (and uncle of the author Robert Louis Stevenson), atop a rocky outcrop barely 26 square metres (280 square feet) at low tide, from an unprecedented 4,300 tonnes of granite.

ST ANDREWS, FIFE
The life of St Andrew

According to Christian tradition, St Andrew was one of the first – if not indeed the very first – disciple of Jesus and, as his remains are thought to have been brought there sometime in the mid 700s, was chosen as the patron saint of Scotland in the tenth century.

The city of St Andrews in Fife, meanwhile, has borne his name since the twelfth century, if not earlier. Andrew is also one of the patron saints of Russia, Romania, Ukraine and, significantly, Greece, where he was crucified in the city of Patras on a crux decussata, an X-shaped cross, in the early first century AD.

Execution of Patrick Hamilton

On 29 February 1528, the Scottish clergyman and Protestant reformer Patrick Hamilton, son of a nephew of James IV, was executed for heresy at St Andrews. The previous year, Hamilton's controversial preaching had led the Archbishop of St Andrews to demand that he be tried for heresy and, as a result, Hamilton had fled to the continent. Nevertheless, fully aware of the consequences, Hamilton maintained his faith and soon returned to St Andrews to recommence his preaching, where he was subsequently tried, found guilty on 13 charges of heresy and sentenced to death. The same day as sentence was passed, Hamilton was taken out to St Salvator's Chapel in the city and burned at the stake.

Chariots of Fire film set

West Sands Beach was the setting for the memorable opening and closing scenes of Hugh Hudson's *Chariots Of Fire*, telling the story of a group of athletes preparing for the 1924 Paris Olympics. The film won four of the seven Oscars for which it was nominated at the 1981 Academy Awards, including Best Picture.

STIRLING
Stirling Old Bridge

Completed in *c.* 1500, Stirling's Old Bridge was for over 300 years the easternmost crossing point over Scotland's River Forth until the New Bridge, designed by Robert Stevenson, was opened in the nineteenth century.

Prime Minister Henry Campbell-Bannerman's constituency

The first Liberal prime minister of the twentieth century, Henry Campbell-Bannerman is also the only leader to have died at 10 Downing Street, a little under three weeks after his resignation due to ill health in April 1908. Born in Kelvinside in Glasgow, he represented the constituency of Stirling Burghs throughout his political career (1868–1908).

TIREE, ARGYLL AND BUTE
Vagrant seabird spotted

Ordinarily, the Ascension frigatebird is only found on Boatswainbird, a tiny 13-acre (52-hectare/0.02-square-mile) island off the coast of Ascension Island in the South Atlantic, itself around 1,600 kilometres (1,000 miles) from the coast of Africa. In July 1953, however, a frigatebird was found on Tiree in the Inner Hebrides – at the time, it was misidentified as a magnificent frigatebird of the tropical Atlantic and Pacific, yet a re-examination of the case in 2002 concluded that the specimen was in fact a juvenile Ascension frigatebird, the only such bird ever seen in Western Europe.

TURNBERRY, SOUTH AYRSHIRE
Birth of Robert the Bruce

Although the exact details of his birth are unclear, traditionally Robert the Bruce is said to have been born at Turnberry Castle on the Ayrshire coast in 1274. He was crowned Robert I in 1306, and throughout his 23-year reign is renowned for his opposition to Edward II's tenuous rule over Scotland, culminating in victory at the Battle of Bannockburn in 1314. He died in 1329, succeeded by his only son, David II.

WEST KILBRIDE, NORTH AYRSHIRE
see under East Kilbride, South Lanarkshire

WHAT'S IN A NAME?

Broom, Highland
Loch Broom takes its name from a Celtic word meaning 'dew' or 'rain', the origin of the Scots *bhraoin*, 'rain shower'.

Cavers, Scottish Borders
Perhaps derived from an Old English first name, Cafhere.

Dollar, Clackmannanshire
Derives from a Celtic word for a meadow.

Largo, Fife
The towns of Upper and Lower Largo in Fife derive their names from the Scots word *learg*, meaning 'slope'. The town of Largs in Ayrshire shares a similar meaning.

Muck, Highland
One of the smallest islands in the Inner Hebrides, deriving its name from the Gaelic word *muc*, meaning 'pig'.

Shin, Highland
Perhaps related to a Celtic word meaning 'charm', or 'enchanted'.

Stair, South Ayrshire
Meaning 'place at the stepping stones', from the Gaelic *stair*.

Tongue, Highland
Actually means 'tongue', in the sense of 'tongue of land', derived from the Scandinavian word *tunga*.

Wrath, Highland
The headland of Cape Wrath takes its name from the Scandinavian *hvarf*, meaning 'turning point'.

Yell, Shetland
Of obscure meaning, the name of Shetland's Yell island is nonetheless most likely Scandinavian in origin.

10

NORTHERN AND CENTRAL SCOTLAND

Perth and Kinross, Dundee, Angus, Aberdeen,
Aberdeenshire, Moray, Highland, Western Isles,
Orkney, Shetland

ABERDEEN

Nobel Laureate John Macleod

John James Rickard Macleod was born at Clunie in Perthshire in 1876. Having studied medicine at the University of Aberdeen, Macleod worked and studied at Leipzig, London, Ohio and Toronto before returning to Aberdeen as professor of physiology in 1928. He was awarded the Nobel Prize for Medicine with his associate Frederick Banting in 1923 for their work on the discovery of insulin.

The Aberdeen Bestiary

The Aberdeen Bestiary, one of the most remarkable examples of its kind, is thought to have been written sometime around 1200. Although its history and authorship are unknown, the bestiary is first recorded as part of Henry VIII's library at the Palace of Westminster in the mid 1500s and, as its name suggests, has been held in Aberdeen's Marischal College Library, now part of the University of Aberdeen, since the early seventeenth century. The book contains 100 highly decorated 'folios' in turn comprising illustrated and detailed descriptions of dozens of different creatures, plants, trees and precious stones. Like most bestiaries of similar times, descriptions of real animals are interspersed with those of mythical ones, including the *leocrota*, a cross between a lion and a stag described as 'the swiftest of all wild animals', the *caladrius*, a pure white bird with extraordinary healing powers, and the *amphisbaena*, a two-headed serpent whose eyes 'glow like lamps'.

Oscar-winner Annie Lennox

Born in Aberdeen in 1954, Annie Lennox became only the fourth Scottish Oscar winner ever when she won the award for Best Original Song for 'Into the West' in 2004. It was one of 11 Oscars taken home by *The Return of the King*, the final instalment in Peter Jackson's exceptional *The Lord of the Rings* film trilogy, and Lennox shared the award with the film's composer Howard Shore and screenwriter and lyricist Fran Walsh.

Football's first dugout

Aberdeen's Pittodrie Stadium was the first football ground in Britain to have a dugout at the side of the pitch, installed there in the 1920s at the request of the club's coach Donald Coleman. Pittodrie was amongst the first all-seated grounds in Britain, although Clydebank's Kilbowie Park, the home ground of Clydebank FC until 1996, was the first, in 1977.

Aberdeen, South Dakota

Founded in 1881, Aberdeen is the county seat of South Dakota's Brown County. With a population of over 26,000, it is also the largest of all of the places named Aberdeen in the US, ahead of a large port city on Mississippi's Tombigbee River, and towns in Idaho, Maryland, Washington and Ohio.

AONACH EAGACH, HIGHLAND
Braveheart film set

The opening sequence of Mel Gibson's multi-award-winning epic *Braveheart*, telling the story of William Wallace, was filmed at

Aonach Eagach, a mountainous ridge to the north of Glencoe in the Scottish Highlands. Despite being set in Scotland, however, most of the film's other battle sequences were in fact filmed in Ireland. It won five Oscars from a total of ten nominations in 1996, including both Best Picture and Best Director.

ARBROATH, ANGUS
The Arbroath smokie

The Arbroath smokie is a traditional dish of smoked salted haddock. Although probably descended from similar Scandinavian recipes, local lore has it that the dish was first conceived of following a fire in the town in which a barrel of salted haddock was accidentally 'cooked'. The dish was awarded Protected Geographical Indication status by the EU in 2004.

Remarkable football victory

In perhaps the biggest senior football victory of all time, on 12 September 1885 Arbroath beat Aberdeen Bon Accord 36–0 in a first-round Scottish Cup match at Arbroath's Gayfield Park, with an average of one goal every two and a half minutes. Remarkably, 13 of Arbroath's goals were scored by one player, John 'Jocky' Petrie. It is reported that Arbroath's goalkeeper Jim Milne had so little to do during the game that he spent most of the time sheltering from bad weather behind a spectator's umbrella.

BADBEA, HIGHLAND
The Highland Clearances

The former village of Badbea in Caithness was established in the late eighteenth century during the Highland Clearances, when landowners in the far north of Scotland forcibly removed tenants from their homes and turned the land over to more profitable sheep farming. Badbea was founded by evictees from several nearby settlements who were each given a plot of land, but were nonetheless left to clear the land and build their new houses themselves. The village steadily flourished over the years that followed, but its isolation and inaccessibility eventually proved its downfall and, having declined in the years leading up to the turn of the twentieth century, by 1911 it had been abandoned.

BALLATER, ABERDEENSHIRE
The Royal Bridge

Queen Victoria officially opened the Royal Bridge at Ballater in 1885. Situated in the heart of what is known as Royal Deeside, the area surrounding Ballater and nearby Braemar has long had connections to the royal family – as well as being the site of Balmoral Castle, the area also includes the Queen Mother's former estate of Birkhall, now owned by Prince Charles.

BARRA, WESTERN ISLES
Base of pirate Rory MacNeil

In the early seventeenth century, Rory MacNeil, then chief of the Clan MacNeil, gained a reputation as a pirate by raiding the ships that strayed past his home at Kisimul Castle off the island of Barra in the Outer Hebrides. Earning him the nickname 'Rory the Turbulent', the raids MacNeil carried out on the English ships were enough to gain the attention of Elizabeth I, who offered a reward for his capture and demanded the help of James VI of Scotland in resolving the problem. Consequently, in 1610, MacNeil was forcibly deposed,

and arrested and imprisoned in Edinburgh. Despite losing his lands, however, by claiming that the attacks he had made on Elizabeth's ships were revenge for the brutal treatment of James' mother, Mary, Queen of Scots, at the hands of the English, MacNeil was eventually granted a pardon by the king.

BEN NEVIS, HIGHLAND
Britain's highest point

Located in the western Grampian Mountains, Ben Nevis is the highest mountain in Scotland, Great Britain and the British Isles. It is thought to take its name from either the Scots Gaelic *nibheis*, meaning 'venomous', or else *nèamh-bhathais*, roughly equating to 'head in the clouds'. An estimated 125,000 climbers and walkers reach the mountain's 1,344-metre (4,409-foot) peak each year. It is one of only nine mountains in the whole of the British Isles to stand over 1,219 metres (4,000 feet) and – alongside Ben Macdui in Aberdeenshire – is one of just two in excess of 1,300 metres (4,265 feet), tall enough to be able to see across to Northern Ireland on a clear day.

BROUGHTY FERRY, DUNDEE
Titanic Officer David Blair

Originally appointed second officer on board the *Titanic*, Dundee-born David Blair is amongst the most notorious 'escapees' of the disaster, having been made to leave the ship at Southampton following a last-minute reshuffle of the crew – the late appointment of Chief Officer Henry Wilde demoted the previous Chief Officer William Murdoch to first officer and, as a result, First Officer Charles Lightoller took over Blair's position as second officer, effectively putting him out of a job. Tragically, Blair accidentally took the key to the ship's crow's nest locker with him as he left at Southampton and consequently the lookouts could not access the binoculars the locker contained, and were left to rely purely on their own eyesight to keep watch. In 2007, Blair's key was sold for £90,000 at auction in Devizes, Wiltshire.

THE BUTT OF LEWIS, WESTERN ISLES
Vagrant bird spotted

The first European sighting of a purple martin, the largest species of swallow native to North America, was recorded at the Butt of Lewis in September 2004. Native to the eastern and central USA, the bird usually winters in northern South America and the Amazon basin.

THE CAIRNGORMS
Britain's largest national park

Scotland's Cairngorms National Park was officially established in 2003, immediately becoming by far the largest national park in the whole of the British Isles; when the park's southern boundary was extended in 2010, the total area it covers increased by some 20 per cent to a total of 4,528 square kilometres (1,748 square miles), equivalent in size to almost two Lake Districts, or six per cent of the entire land area of Scotland. The Cairngorms is also the highest national park in Britain, with more than one-third of its land standing over 400 metres (1,300 feet), and is home to four of the five highest mountains in the British Isles.

CANNICH, HIGHLAND
The Cannich Puma

After two years of reported big cat sightings centred on the village of Cannich in the Scottish Highlands, in 1980 a live puma was caught by a local farmer who had rigged a trap on an area of his land the creature was known to frequent. The cat was subsequently taken to Kincraig's Highland Wildlife Park near Kingussie, where it lived in captivity until its death in 1985. The specimen, named 'Felicity', is now held at Inverness Museum.

CORRACHADH MÒR, HIGHLAND

Britain's westernmost point

Corrachadh Mòr on Highland's Ardnamurchan Peninsula is the westernmost point on mainland Great Britain, standing over 6 degrees longitude west of the Greenwich Meridian, and over 35 kilometres (22 miles) further west than Land's End.

CULLODEN, HIGHLAND

The Battle of Culloden

Fought early on the morning of 16 April 1746, the Battle of Culloden was not only the last battle of the Jacobite Uprising but also the last pitched battle ever fought on British soil. It proved a decisive victory for the British under the command of William Augustus, Duke of Cumberland and third son of George II, and irrevocably quashed the Jacobites' objective of restoring the Stuart line to the throne. Following the battle, the Jacobite leader Charles Edward Stuart, Bonnie Prince Charlie, fled to the Isle of Skye before going into exile in France, whilst many Jacobite prisoners were either executed or transported to the colonies.

DORNOCH, HIGHLAND

Wedding of Madonna

In 2000, Skibo Castle near the Highand town of Dornoch on the Moray Firth was at the centre of a media frenzy when it hosted the wedding of Madonna and Guy Ritchie on 22 December. The couple – whose son Rocco was born in August 2000 – separated in November 2008.

DUNDEE

Twinned with Nablus

The twinning association between Dundee and the Palestinian city of Nablus, around 60 kilometres

(38 miles) north of Jerusalem, was arranged amidst considerable local opposition in 1980. The agreement recognises and commemorates the extraordinary specialist medical treatment the then mayor of Nablus, Bassam Shaka'a, received in Dundee having been injured by a car bomb in the Middle East.

Dundee cake

Dating from the nineteenth century, Dundee cake is one of the most famous local dishes in Britain. Sometimes flavoured with whisky, the cake is a rich fruitcake traditionally topped with almonds.

RRS Discovery

The RRS *Discovery* was built in Dundee and launched in the Firth of Tay on 21 March 1901. The last three-masted wooden ship ever built in Britain, the *Discovery* was used by the explorer Robert Falcon Scott on his first successful voyage to Antarctica in January 1902 – she would not return to Britain until September 1904, having spent two years trapped in ice in Antarctica's McMurdo Sound.

Adhesive stamp invented

The Scottish inventor James Chalmers was born in Arbroath in 1782. He moved to Dundee in 1809, and after several years working as a printer and newspaper publisher began suggesting ideas for postal reform from the mid 1820s. Amongst his many innovations was the adhesive postage stamp, which he proposed in an essay written to London's General Post Office in 1838: the stamps (or 'slips'), he stated, should be 'rubbed on the back with a strong solution of gum, or other adhesive substance'.

Triple red card awarded

Although there are a surprising number of incidences of players receiving multiple red cards in a single game, one of the most memorable is that of Dean Windass, who received three red cards in quick succession whilst playing for Aberdeen in a disastrous Scottish League match against Dundee United at Tannadice Park on 9 November 1997. Windass, who was to leave Aberdeen at the end of the 1997–98 season, was initially sent off for a foul before being given two further red cards for verbally abusing the referee and then throwing a corner flag into the crowd. Aberdeen went on to lose 5–0, whilst Windass was given a six-match ban.

EAS A'CHUAL ALUINN, HIGHLAND
Britain's tallest waterfall

With a drop of 201 metres (658 feet), Eas a'Chual Aluinn in Highland is the highest waterfall in the British Isles. A so-called 'horsetail' waterfall (that is, one that keeps almost constant contact with the rock over which it falls), remarkably the water of Eas a'Chual Aluinn descends more than twice the height of the Big Ben clock tower of London's Palace of Westminster, and three times the height of Niagara Falls.

EDAY, ORKNEY
Base of pirate John Gow

Thought to have been born in Wick in the late 1690s, the pirate John Gow's short but nonetheless notorious career – which later inspired Sir Walter Scott's novel *The Pirate* – began whilst he was second mate on board a European trade ship named the *Caroline* in 1724. Here it appears Gow helped to arrange a mutiny in which he murdered the *Caroline*'s captain and assumed control, renaming the ship the *Revenge* before setting out on numerous raids throughout the western Mediterranean over the months that followed. With supplies on board growing low, however, Gow returned to his childhood home on Orkney in February 1725 where, despite posing as a wealthy tradesman named 'Smith' and renaming his ship the *George*, he and the *Revenge* were soon recognised by a merchant passing through the islands and he was eventually captured on the Calf of Eday, an islet in the North Orkneys, having run aground during a failed attempt to raid the island. Tried at the Old Bailey in London, Gow was found guilty of piracy and murder and hanged at Execution Dock on the Thames in 1725.

EILEAN MÒR, WESTERN ISLES
The Flannan Isles mystery

Despite taking place more than a century ago, the mystery of the lighthouse on Eilean Mòr, the largest of Scotland's Flannan Isles in the Outer Hebrides, continues to prove as baffling as ever. Nevertheless, the fact remains that some sort of untoward event seems to have taken place on the island in the early afternoon of 15 December 1900 which resulted in the disappearance of all three of the lighthouse's keepers, James Ducat, Thomas Marshall and Donald McArthur. Tentatively, it is presumed that one or more of the men must have been swept from the island into the sea by a freak wave or gale, with any survivors perhaps lost in an ill-fated rescue attempt; yet the eerie scene which the men left behind – the gate to the house was locked, one set of oilskins had been left behind, the lighthouse lamp was fully prepared and ready to be lit – combined with the island's rugged isolation, has since given rise to several more macabre and outlandish theories regarding the men's disappearance. The true events at Eilean Mòr that day, however, will never be known.

FAIR ISLE, SHETLAND
Refuge of vagrant birds

Due to its isolated location, Fair Isle, a 7.5-square-kilometre (3-square-mile) island situated halfway between Shetland and Orkney, is a notoriously fruitful site for spotting vagrant birds in the British Isles, and as such has been the location of a permanent bird observatory since 1948. Amongst the many and varied bird species to have been spotted on the island over the years are Britain's first ever American kestrel, the smallest species of falcon found in North America; rufous-tailed robin, usually found in the far north and east of Asia; hermit thrush, native to North America; Pechora pipit and Siberian rubythroat, usually found in the tundra of Russia; Cretzschmar's bunting, native to the eastern Mediterranean; lanceolated warbler, found in Japan; and Sykes' warbler, usually found in Arabia and Central Asia.

FORTINGALL, PERTHSHIRE
The Fortingall Yew

A yew tree standing in the churchyard of the Perthshire village of Fortingall is almost certainly the oldest tree in Europe. It is also likely that it is the oldest single living organism in the British Isles, with estimates at its age ranging from 3,000 to 5,000 years old. If accurate, the Fortingall yew would already have been 1,000 years old when the pyramids of Egypt were built, 3,000 years old at the time of the birth of Christ, and 4,000 years old at the time of the Norman Conquest.

FORT WILLIAM, HIGHLAND
William III

The fort from which Fort William takes its name was built by English parliamentary forces during Scotland's Royalist Rising of the early 1650s in defence against Scots loyal to Charles II. In 1690, the fort was strengthened and much improved, and named after William III (William of Orange), whilst in deference to his queen, Mary II, the town that developed around the fort became known as Maryburgh. Eventually, the whole town was later incorporated as Fort William, perhaps with additional reference to Prince William, the Duke of Cumberland, who fought against the Jacobite Rising at the Battle of Culloden in 1746.

INVERNESS, HIGHLAND
Football's record-breaking multiple postponements

A 1979 second-round cup tie between the now defunct Inverness Thistle FC and Falkirk was postponed some 29 times due to bad weather. Originally scheduled for 9 January, the match finally took place at Kingsmills Park in Inverness some 44 days later on 22 February, with Falkirk winning 4–0.

Inverness, Sweden

Inverness is the name of an area of Danderyd, a suburban municipality near to Stockholm in Sweden. At just 32 square kilometres (12 square miles), it is one of the smallest municipalities in the entire country, yet is by far the most affluent with an average income per capita of more than SKr 4,300,000 (roughly £400,000).

JOHN O'GROATS, HIGHLAND
Lands End to John o'Groats

Roughly 970 kilometres (600 miles) apart as the crow flies, the shortest distance by road from Land's End in Cornwall to John o'Groats in Caithness is almost half as long again, at a total of 1,407 kilometres (874 miles). Jokingly referred to as 'Le Jog', the route is a pinnacle for long-distance walkers and cyclists, although famously a whole host of different modes of transport have been used to make the journey in the past – amongst them a pogo stick, a skateboard, a motorised shopping trolley, a seven-seater bicycle, a replica horse-drawn World War One ambulance, and even a motorised toilet travelling at just 4 miles per hour. More recent attempts have seen the RAF Red Arrows display team complete the journey on Vespa scooters in 2010, and, in 2008, the entire journey was completed for the first time using the newly introduced concessionary travel pass for the over-60s.

Jan de Groot

The most northerly settlement on mainland Great Britain – as well as one of the most famous village names in the whole of Scotland – John o'Groats is in fact named after a Dutchman, a local sailor named Jan de Groot, who is believed to have lived in the town during the reign of James IV.

KILLIECRANKIE, PERTH AND KINROSS
The Battle of Killiecrankie

In 1688, the Catholic King James II was effectively ousted from the English throne by parliament, who invited the protestant Prince William of Orange and his wife Mary, James' daughter from his marriage to Anne Hyde, to claim the throne for themselves. In what became known as the Glorious Revolution, James fled to France the following year and was declared to have abdicated, allowing William III and Mary II to accede to the throne unopposed. Understandably, the incident sparked great unrest across the British Isles, including the Battle of Killiecrankie, the opening battle of Scotland's first Jacobite Rebellion – on 27 July 1689, James' Scottish supporters clashed with more than 3,000 government troops led by the experienced General Hugh Mackay. Although the Jacobites won the battle, their leader, Viscount Dundee, was killed and within weeks the rebellion was brought to an end.

KINCRAIG, HIGHLAND
Stronghold of the wildcat

The Scottish wildcat is Britain's only remaining native predatory cat and is the largest predatory mammal left in the wild here – it is roughly 50 per cent larger than the average domestic cat. Extinct in England and Wales since the mid 1800s, today Britain's entire population of wildcats is confined to the Scottish Highlands, with estimations at the number of individuals left in the wild ranging from 3,500 (including hybrids interbred with domestic cats) down to an estimated pure-bred population of just 400. A new survey to determine the wildcat's distribution was launched in 2008 at Kincraig's Highland Wildlife Park, where captive pure-bred wildcats are successfully reared and reintroduced to the wild.

KINROSS, PERTH AND KINROSS
Prime Minister Alec Douglas-Home's constituency

Born in 1903, Alec Douglas-Home was the first British prime minister to be born in the twentieth century. He served two constituencies during his time in parliament, namely Lanark (1931–45, 1950–51) and Kinross and West Perthshire (1963–74), during which time he became prime minister. He remains the last prime minister personally chosen by the monarch, and is the only prime minister of recent times to have been preceded and succeeded by different people with the same first name (Harold Macmillan and Harold Wilson).

KIRKWALL, ORKNEY
Peter Maxwell Davies' The Yellow Cake Revue

Written in protest to plans to mine uranium in the Orkney Islands, Sir Peter Maxell Davies' *Yellow Cake Revue* – including the popular solo piano piece 'Farewell To Stromness' – was first performed at Kirkwall's St Magnus Festival, which Davies founded in 1977, on 21 June 1980. Written for piano and voices, the 'yellow cake' alluded to in the title of the work is the name of a form of uranium.

KYLEAKIN, HIGHLAND
Haakon IV

The name of the village of Kyleakin on the Isle of Skye means 'strait of Haakon', and as such refers to the Norwegian King Haakon IV, said to have moored at the harbour there ahead of the Battle of Largs in October 1263. Although the battle itself was indecisive, in time Norway was to lose its hold on what were its *Súðreyjar*, the 'southern lands' of the Western Isles of Scotland, the Kintyre peninsula and Isle of Man.

LERWICK, SHETLAND
Up Helly Aa

The festival of Up Helly Aa is held every year in Lerwick in the Shetland Islands on the last Tuesday in January. The day's festivities culminate in a grand torchlit procession through the streets of the town by hundreds of participants, known as 'guizers', dressed in fancy dress and carrying flaming torches. At the end of the procession, led by the head guizer, or 'Guizer Jarl', a wooden longboat is burnt in the same way as it would have been at a Viking funeral, in tribute to the Shetland Islands' Nordic heritage.

Robert Stout, thirteenth premier of New Zealand

Sir Robert Stout was born in Lerwick in 1844. Having qualified as a teacher, he moved to Dunedin in New Zealand in 1863, where he continued teaching before training as a lawyer, later teaching law at Dunedin's Otago University. Stout was elected to parliament in 1875 as MP for Caversham, although he resigned four years later having served in Cabinet for a little over a year. He returned to politics in the 1880s and after just a month back in parliament became premier of New Zealand in August 1884, serving intermittently over the following three years. A long-time supporter of women's suffrage, Stout was instrumental in ensuring voting rights for women whilst serving in government under Prime Minister Richard Seddon. In 1893, New Zealand became the first country (although still a British colony) to allow women to vote.

LOSSIEMOUTH, MORAY
Saltopus discovered

Discovered in 1910, *Saltopus* ('hopping foot') was one of the smallest of all dinosaurs, a slim, bipedal carnivore that would likely have been under 1 metre (3.3 feet) in length. It also had hollow bones, making it lightweight and, presumably, a swift and agile sprinter. Dating from the Late Triassic period, around 220 million years ago, *Saltopus* is one of very few dinosaur species to have been discovered in Scotland.

MAINLAND, ORKNEY
World Heritage Site

Designated in 1999, the World Heritage Site known officially as the 'Heart of Neolithic Orkney' comprises four separate ancient monuments on the Mainland island of Orkney, dating from 3,000 to 2,000 BC. The site includes the multi-chambered cairn of Maes Howe, the stone circles of Stenness and the Ring of Brodgar, and the astonishing Stone Age settlement of Skara Brae, perhaps the best-preserved Neolithic village in Europe.

MEY, HIGHLAND
Former royal residence, the Castle of Mey

The most northerly inhabited castle on the British mainland, the Castle of Mey in the far north of Scotland dates from the mid 1500s. First owned by the earls of Caithness, the castle was purchased by the Queen Mother in 1952, who used Mey as a holiday home throughout her later life until her death in 2002.

LOCH MORAR, HIGHLAND
Britain's deepest lake

Situated 55 kilometres (35 miles) west of Loch Ness, Loch Morar in Highland reaches a maximum depth of −310 metres (−1,017 feet), almost twice the maximum depth of the English Channel. It is the deepest lake in the entire British Isles.

LOCH NESS, HIGHLAND
Britain's greatest lake

Loch Ness, at 56 square kilometres (21.7 square miles), is the second-largest loch in Scotland, and the fourth-largest lake in the whole of the UK; its average depth of −132 metres (−433 feet), meanwhile, is greater than that of any other British lake, and this loch alone holds more water than all of the lakes of England and Wales combined. Unusually, despite its size, Loch Ness contains just one island, and even this is believed to be an artificial island, or *crannog*, constructed in the Iron Age.

THE OUT SKERRIES, SHETLAND
Scotland's easternmost point

The Out Skerries are the easternmost of the Shetland Islands and so comprise the most easterly point in all of Scotland. The two largest islands, Housay (1.52 square kilometres/0.6 square miles) and Bruray (0.5 square kilometres/0.2 square miles), are also the only inhabited islands in the group, which also includes the nearby Grunay and Bound Skerry as well as several smaller islets and sea stacks. The islands' total population is just 76.

OUT STACK, SHETLAND
Britain's northernmost point

The Shetland Islands comprise the most northerly islands in the whole of the British Isles, with many of their number lying almost as close to mainland Norway as they do to mainland Scotland. Of the major islands, Unst is both the northernmost and, at 120 square kilometres (46 square miles), the third largest by area, and can claim to be the northernmost of all the inhabited islands in the whole of Britain; its tiny village of Skaw is, consequently, our most northerly settlement. Further north still, the nearby island of Muckle Flugga is the site of the most northerly lighthouse in Britain and, although uninhabited today, is nevertheless the northernmost habitable island, having recorded a resident population right up to the 1981 census. At the most extreme, however, is the tiny islet of Out Stack which, although little more than a bleak rocky outcrop – the 'full stop at the end of Britain', as it is known – would nonetheless be your last landfall ahead of the Arctic if heading due north from the top of the British Isles.

PERTH, PERTH AND KINROSS
The Gowrie Conspiracy

The Gowrie Conspiracy of 1600 was an attempt by John Ruthven,

3rd Earl of Gowrie, and his brother Alexander to kidnap King James VI of Scotland. Although several different accounts of the plot exist, the king's own version states that the brothers had lured him to Gowrie House in Perth on a false pretence yet on his arrival had locked him in a turret. Luckily, the king managed to raise the alarm to his companions waiting in the courtyard below and he escaped, whilst his would-be kidnappers were both killed.

Scotland's Jubilee city

To mark the Diamond Jubilee of Elizabeth II in 2012, three towns from across the UK – namely Chelmsford, Perth and St Asaph in Wales – were granted official city status by the crown, and as such Perth became Scotland's seventh city, and the last Scottish town to be raised to city status.

Perth Racecourse

Set within the grounds of Scone Palace, Perth Racecourse is the most northerly in Britain. It is also, at around 2 kilometres (1.25 miles) in length, one of the shortest.

POLTALLOCH, ARGYLL AND BUTE
The West Highland terrier

The West Highland white terrier – more commonly known simply as the 'Westie' – is one of Britain's most popular dog breeds, with over 8,000 individuals registered with the UK Kennel Club in 2007. Likely developed around Poltalloch in Argyll in the nineteenth century from the naturally white offspring of Cairn and Scottish terriers, West Highlands are hardy dogs, known for their tenacity and robust, cocky nature. The breed has twice taken Best in Show at Crufts, most recently in 1990.

RAASAY, HIGHLAND
Britain's deepest point

At 62 square kilometres (25 square miles), the island of Raasay immediately east of the Isle of Skye is the twenty-eighth-largest island in the British Isles. The island is surrounded by some of the deepest inshore waters in the whole of the British Isles, with the Inner Sound, the stretch of water separating Raasay from the Scottish mainland at Applecross, plummeting to a depth of −177 fathoms (−323 metres/−1,060 feet).

SCALLOWAY, SHETLAND
Scalloway Castle

Built on the orders of Patrick Stewart, 2nd Earl of Orkney, Scalloway Castle on Shetland's Mainland was completed in 1600. At the time, Scalloway was the capital of the Shetland Islands and from his castle Stewart could maintain his brutal and oppressive control over the islands until he was overthrown and imprisoned in Edinburgh in 1614. He was executed the following year.

SKYE, HIGHLAND
Virginia Woolf's To the Lighthouse

Published in 1927, Virginia Woolf's fifth novel *To the Lighthouse* is set over two separate days, ten years apart, in the summer home of the Ramsay family on the Isle of Skye in the Inner Hebrides. Although a difficult novel in some respects, containing very little action or dialogue, *To the Lighthouse* is considered nonetheless one of the best modernist novels of the twentieth century.

Skye terrier

The Skye terrier, identified by its low-held body and thick, long, grey or sandy-coloured coat, is one of the most distinctive of all terrier breeds, as well as being one of the oldest, perhaps dating back as far as the sixteenth century. Nevertheless, in 2006, the Skye was identified by the UK Kennel Club as the most endangered of all native British dog breeds, with only 30 individual dogs registered in 2005.

ST KILDA, WESTERN ISLES
The UK's westernmost extreme

Comprising a group of four larger islands as well as many smaller islets and stacks, the remote archipelago of St Kilda in the North Atlantic Ocean is one of the most isolated points in the whole of Western Europe, lying over 60 kilometres (37 miles) from its nearest landfall at North Uist in the Outer Hebrides. Despite the islands' extreme isolation and extraordinarily precipitous terrain – the 427-metre (1,400-foot) high sea cliffs on Hirta, the largest island, are the highest in the UK – St Kilda nevertheless recorded a resident population as late as 1930, and consequently is considered the westernmost habitable point in the whole of the United Kingdom. Only the North Atlantic stack at Rockall, 460 kilometres (285 miles) west of Scotland and a full 13 degrees west of the Greenwich Meridian, lies any further westward in the British Isles, although its ownership is disputed by the UK, Ireland, Iceland and the Faroe Islands.

STORNOWAY, WESTERN ISLES
Stornoway Castle

Stornoway Castle on Lewis was built around 1100 by the MacNicol family. Soon taken by Viking invaders, the castle belonged for many years to Lewis' MacLeod dynasty until it was destroyed in 1653 by Oliver Cromwell's troops. The last remnants of the castle were removed in the nineteenth century during construction of a pier in the town.

STRATHALLAN, PERTH AND KINROSS
Death of Áed of Scotland

The early Scottish King Áed was one of the sons of Kenneth I, often cited as the first king to rule a united Scottish kingdom in the ninth century. Taking over from his brother Constantine I following his death in 877, Áed's short reign was marred by his cousin Giric's rival claim to the throne, who, just one year after Áed's accession, killed him in battle at Strathallan.

STRONTIAN, HIGHLAND
Discovery of strontium

The alkaline metal strontium, chemical element number 38, derives its name from the Highland town of Strontian where its source mineral, strontianite, was first discovered. In the late 1790s, several scientists – including Adair Crawford, William Cruickshank and Thomas Charles Hope – each suggested that strontianite must contain some new metal previously unknown to science, which Hope, then professor of chemistry at the University of Glasgow, named *strontites*. It was not until 1808, however, that Sir Humphrey Davy isolated the first metallic samples of this new element using electrolysis in a London laboratory.

THE TAY
Britain's greatest river

The seventh-longest river in the UK, the 193-kilometre (119-mile) Tay is also the longest river lying entirely in Scotland, and moreover is thought to carry more water than any other river in the British Isles, with an average daily flow at Perth estimated at 175 cubic metres (38,500 gallons) per second. Remarkably for such a significant river, the Tay's exact source – a stream, Allt Coire Laoigh, south of the summit of Ben Lui in the southern Highlands – was not officially pinpointed until 2011.

The Tay Rail Bridge Disaster

The first Tay Rail Bridge, completed in 1878 and at the time the longest bridge in the world, was destroyed during a storm on 28 December 1879 in what remains one of the worst meteorological disasters ever to have occurred in the British Isles. Although the bridge was later criticised for its poor design and construction, and had likely already been weakened in earlier gales, it was a huge waterspout that formed during the storm that finally destroyed it, tearing through the central section of the bridge, tragically just as a passenger train was travelling across it. A total of 75 people died in the disaster, including the son-in-law of Thomas Bouch, the bridge's designer.

THURSO, HIGHLAND
Britain's most extreme station

Dating from the late nineteenth century, Thurso Rail Station is the northernmost National Rail station in the British Isles.

UIG, WESTERN ISLES
The Lewis Chessmen

The Lewis Chessmen, an extraordinary collection of around ninety chess pieces made from walrus ivory in *c.* 1200, were found buried in a sand dune near Uig on the Isle of Lewis in 1831. The fact that there are so many pieces in the collection, including several duplicates, suggests that the chessmen were made to be sold and were perhaps buried for safekeeping on Lewis by a merchant on passage from

Norway to Ireland, likely not long after they were made. Today, most of the chessmen are on display in London's British Museum with the remainder housed at Edinburgh's National Museum of Scotland.

WICK, HIGHLAND
Ebenezer Place

When Mackays Hotel was built in Wick in 1883, the council at the time remarkably deemed that the building's shortest side nonetheless constituted a street in its own right, and as a result it became necessary to give the street a name – ultimately, despite being just 206 centimetres (81 inches) in length, Ebenezer Place was created. Comprising nothing more than the old hotel building – whose address, unsurprisingly, is 1 Ebenezer Place – today the street is officially recognised as the shortest street in the world.

YTHAN, ABERDEENSHIRE
Stronghold of the water vole

Britain's largest vole, the water vole is one of the most endangered creatures in the British Isles. Once widespread throughout the country, the voles have vanished from over 90 per cent of sites since the 1950s, largely due to predation from the introduced American mink, and although its population has shown a slight resurgence in recent years, it remains a priority vulnerable species. One of its principal remaining strongholds – and the site of a successful breeding population – is Scotland's Cairngorm region, and a successful scheme completed in January 2009 to eradicate the mink from the entire catchment area of Aberdeenshire's River Ythan should go a long way towards securing the vole's survival in this area at least.

NORTHERN IRELAND

BALLYNOE, COUNTY DOWN
Ballynoe Stone Circle

The Ballynoe Stone Circle near Downpatrick in Northern Ireland comprises over fifty large stones set closely together in a circle over 30 metres (100 feet) across, with several separate pairs of stones placed at varying distances around the outside. Excavations at the site have unearthed two stone tombs or cists beneath a large mound inside the ring, which were found to contain cremated bones.

BELFAST
Falls Road and Shankhill Road

The neighbouring Falls Road and Shankill Road in west Belfast have become infamous for their association with the troubles which devastated Northern Ireland in the second half of the twentieth century. Whilst Falls Road is predominantly Catholic, Shankill Road is mostly Protestant and for decades the two thoroughfares have been separated by so-called 'peace lines', reinforced barriers intended to prevent and discourage further sectarian violence.

Twinned with Nashville

Nashville was founded as Fort Nashborough in 1779 by the American pioneers James Robertson and John Donelson, both of whom were of Scots-Irish lineage and had ancestral links to Northern Ireland; indeed, many of the city's earliest settlers – including the Antrim-born parents of the future US President Andrew Jackson – were of similar descent. Fittingly, then, Belfast, the capital of Northern Ireland, and Nashville, the capital of Tennessee, have been official twin cities since 1994, with the annual Belfast

Nashville Songwriters Festival commemorating the association today.

Queen's University

Founded in 1845, the main building of Belfast's Queen's University was one of several buildings in the city designed by the English architect Sir Charles Lanyon. It was officially opened by Queen Victoria and Prince Albert in 1849 when, owing to a city-wide outbreak of cholera at the time, it was one of only a few buildings that the royal couple were permitted to enter during their trip. On opening, just 90 students were admitted to the university, whilst today there are more than 20,000.

The Northern Bank robbery

In December 2004, the biggest cash robbery in Northern Ireland's history took place at the central branch of the Northern Bank in Belfast. On the night of 19 December, gangs of armed men dressed as police officers entered the homes of two of the bank's employees, holding both them and their families at gunpoint. As they had been requested, both of the employees returned to work as usual the following day and

remained there until after the bank had closed, at which point they were made to allow members of the gang to enter the bank and give them access to the cash store. The robbers made off with £26.5 million in a mixture of used and unusual sterling banknotes, US dollars and euros, the vast majority of which remain unrecovered.

HMHS Britannic

Built by Harland & Wolff in Belfast and launched in February 1914, the *Britannic* was intended to be a transatlantic passenger liner, one of the largest of the White Star Line and sister ship to the *Titanic*. Following the outbreak of World War One, however, what would have been the HMS *Britannic* became the HMHS, requisitioned as a hospital ship and sent to the eastern Mediterranean to transport wounded troops back to Great Britain. On 21 November 1916, halfway into her sixth journey to the Mediterranean, she struck a mine in the Cyclades islands off Greece and sank with the loss of 30 lives.

Portable defibrillator invented

Having earlier pioneered emergency mobile coronary

care units (MCCUs) for cardiac patients, Professor Frank Pantridge of Belfast's Queen's University and Royal Victoria Hospital went on to invent the portable defibrillator in the 1960s. The device, which administers a safe electrical jolt to the heart in order to restore its natural rhythm, originally comprised two car batteries and weighed 70 kilograms (154 pounds) when it was first installed in a Belfast ambulance in 1965. Thanks to numerous refinements over the years, however, much more lightweight defibrillators are now fitted to all new ambulances, and even smaller AEDs (automated external defibrillators) are now common first-aid appliances.

COMBER, COUNTY DOWN
Thomas Andrews, builder of the Titanic

Born in Comber in County Down in 1873, Thomas Andrews Jr. was a renowned shipbuilder in charge of overseeing construction of the *Titanic* at the Harland & Wolff shipyards in Belfast. He took his place on the *Titanic*'s maiden voyage with the intention of noting any problems with the ship that could be rectified in the future. Having helped dozens of

passengers into the lifeboats after the iceberg hit, Andrews was last seen alone in the ship's first-class smoking room. His body was never recovered.

CROM, COUNTY FERMANAGH
The Great Yew

The extraordinary 800-year-old yew trees of the Crom Estate in County Fermanagh are some of the most remarkable trees in the whole of Northern Ireland, as well as certainly being amongst the oldest. Crom's Great Yew near Crom Castle appears to be a single tree but is in actual fact comprised of two yew trees – one male and one female – which have grown and become entwined together over the centuries.

DERRY/LONDONDERRY, COUNTY DERRY/ LONDONDERRY
Friel's Translations debuts

Perhaps the most well-known work by the Irish playwright Brian Friel, *Translations* debuted at the Guildhall Theatre on 23 September 1980. Set in the early nineteenth century in, like several of his works, the Irish village of Ballybeg, the play was first performed by Friel's own Field Day Theatre Company which he established in 1980 with the actor Stephen Rea, who appeared in the first performance. The 1980 production also featured future Hollywood star Liam Neeson and Ray McAnally, who later won BAFTAs for his roles in *The Mission* (1986) and *My Left Foot* (1989).

'The Londonderry Air'

The 'Londonderry Air' is a popular Irish folk tune and the unofficial national anthem of Northern Ireland, used as such at various events including the Commonwealth Games. The piece, which has no lyrics, is a transcription of one of many melodies collected by the eighteenth-century Irish folk music enthusiast Jane Ross and was first published in 1855. Despite having no words, the tune has been used as the basis of many hymns and songs over the years, most notably 'Danny Boy', written in 1913.

Londonderry, Chile

Londonderry Island is one of the southernmost islands in the Tierra del Fuego group lying off the tip of South America. Whilst the archipelago itself is divided between Chile and Argentina, Londonderry is owned solely by Chile and forms part of the country's Magallanes region, which extends as far south as Chile's Antarctic territory.

DRUMSKINNY, COUNTY FERMANAGH
The Drumskinny Stones

The stone circle at Drumskinny in Fermanagh originally contained over thirty stones (several of which have since been replaced) arranged in a circle 13 metres (42 feet) in diameter. The site, much like the similar yet much larger and more widely dispersed site at Beaghmore in County Tyrone, also contains a stone row and cairn, and is thought to date from *c.* 2000 BC.

DUNAVERNEY, COUNTY ANTRIM
The Dunaverney flesh-hook discovered

The Dunaverney flesh-hook, comprising three decorated bronze tubes that would have presumably been used to remove cooked meat from a cauldron at ceremonial feasts, was found in Garry Bog in Dunaverney, Antrim, in 1829. One of the most significant antiquities ever found in Ireland, the flesh-hook dates from around 12,000 years ago. Two of the tubes it comprises are adorned with birds – one with swans, the other with a pair of ravens – which would presumably have had some kind of symbolic significance to Bronze Age culture.

DUNNAMORE, COUNTY TYRONE
The Beaghmore Stone Circles

The astonishing network of stone circles, rows and cairns that comprise the Beaghmore system near the village of Dunnamore in County Tyrone was discovered under peat deposits in the 1940s. In all, over one thousand stones comprising more than twenty individual monuments have since been uncovered, estimated to date from the early Bronze Age, *c.* 2000–1500 BC. Although the stones' purpose is impossible to ascertain for sure, it is likely that some are meant to correspond to the movements of the sun and moon, whilst others are presumably burial mounds.

THE GIANT'S CAUSEWAY, COUNTY ANTRIM
World Heritage Site

One of only four natural World Heritage Sites in the UK – and the only site in Northern Ireland – the Giant's Causeway near Portballintrae in Antrim was officially appointed in 1986. Comprising a mass of some 40,000 predominantly six-sided interlocking basalt columns formed by an ancient volcanic eruption millions of years ago, according to local legend the causeway was built as a means of reaching Scotland by the mythical giant Finn McCool.

KILROOT, COUNTY ANTRIM
Parish of writer Jonathan Swift

Jonathan Swift was born in Dublin in 1667. Having studied at Dublin University and receiving a Masters degree from Oxford in 1692, Swift was ordained into the Church of Ireland and appointed prebend (a position roughly equivalent to a canon) of Kilroot, Antrim, in 1694. Subsequently, Swift returned to Dublin and held the position of dean of St Patrick's Cathedral from 1713 until his death in 1745. It was at Dublin that he wrote much of his most well-known work, including his *Drapier's Letters* (1724–25), the satirical essay *A Modest Proposal* (1729) and *Gulliver's Travels* (1726).

MAGHERAVEELY, COUNTY FERMANAGH
Stronghold of Britain's only crayfish

The white-clawed crayfish is the only native British species of freshwater crayfish. Once widely distributed in rivers across the British Isles, over the last thirty years the species has suffered a huge decline in numbers due to competition from the larger and more aggressive American signal crayfish, an accidentally introduced species that has since overwhelmed the white-claws in many waterways throughout the country. Although still found at a number of sites across the British Isles, the white-claws' numbers continue to decline and the surviving population at Magheraveely Marl Loughs in Northern Ireland, along with those at locations in the Peak District and Lake District, is one of the most important in the UK.

MALLUSK, COUNTY ANTRIM
John Ballance, fourteenth premier of New Zealand

Born in Antrim in 1839, John Ballance emigrated to New Zealand in 1866. His political career began in 1875 when he was elected to parliament as MP for Rangitikei, later serving in Cabinet as (amongst numerous other roles) treasurer, minister for education and minister for defence. Having become increasingly disillusioned with the work of the premiers under whom he had served, however, Ballance established his own group of like-minded politicians and led a newly formed Liberal Party to success at the 1890 New Zealand elections, becoming leader of both the country's first Liberal government and its first with allegiance to a single party. Although he died suddenly just three years later, the party Ballance had formed held office until 1912.

MANGER, COUNTY FERMANAGH
The UK's westernmost point

Fermanagh is the westernmost of the counties of Northern Ireland, and as such contains the westernmost inhabited point in the whole of the UK, namely Manger (or Manger Bog), a townland in the far west of the obsolete parish of Inishmacsaint and once home to a manned crossing point on the Irish-Northern Irish border.

Manger lies even further west than Donegal, and almost as far west as the Irish cities of Cork and Limerick.

MAZE, COUNTY DOWN
The Good Friday releases

One of the final stages of Northern Ireland's 1998 Good Friday Agreement went ahead on 28 July 2000, with the early release of 52 Republican and 26 paramilitary prisoners from County Down's Maze Prison. The men, the last of 428 prisoners whose release was arranged in the agreement, were also amongst the last inmates of the Maze itself, which was closed the following September.

LOUGH NEAGH
Largest lake in British Isles

At 392 square kilometres (151 square miles), Northern Ireland's Lough Neagh is the largest lake in the British Isles and, at more than twice the size of Lake Garda, is one of the largest in all of Western Europe. Situated centrally in Northern Ireland, the lough touches on five of the country's six counties, with only County Fermanagh lacking a Lough Neagh shoreline. Remarkably, despite its size, the lough has a relatively shallow average depth of just −9 metres (−30 feet).

Stronghold of the pollan

Pollan is a silvery, herring-like subspecies of freshwater whitefish related to those usually found in Arctic waters, suggesting that the creature became isolated in the waterways of Ireland at the end of the last Ice Age. Indeed, the pollan's population in Northern Ireland represents 90 per cent of its entire distribution in the British Isles and, outside of the Republic of Ireland, the fish is found nowhere else in Western Europe. Although still locally numerous in Lough Neagh, recently other populations of pollan have decreased to such an extent that the species is now listed as endangered.

RATHLIN, COUNTY ANTRIM
Population: 75

Rathlin is the northernmost point of Northern Ireland and is the country's only inhabited offshore island. L-shaped and no more than a mile wide at any point, Rathlin is the site of a popular RSPB nature reserve and lies around 9 kilometres (5.5 miles) from the mainland at Ballycastle in County Antrim, and a little over 25 kilometres (15 miles) from Scotland's Kintyre peninsula. Once home to more than 1,000 people, a population of just 75 was recorded in 2001.

SLIEVE DONARD, COUNTY DOWN
The peak of Northern Ireland

At 850 metres (2,786 feet), Slieve Donard is the highest mountain in Northern Ireland, situated roughly halfway between the towns of Newcastle and Kilkeel in the Mourne Mountains. Named after St Donard, a compatriot

of St Patrick, Slieve Donard is comfortably the tallest Northern Irish peak, standing over 80 metres (260 feet) taller than the second highest, Slieve Commedagh.

STRABANE, COUNTY TYRONE
Ireland's tallest structure

Constructed in 1963, the 305.5-metre (1,002-foot) steel mast of the Strabane transmitting station near County Tyrone's border with Donegal is the tallest structure in the whole of Ireland; Ireland's tallest habitable building is marked by the 94-metre (308-foot) spire of St John's Cathedral in Limerick, built in 1861.

WHAT'S IN A NAME?

British, County Antrim
Known as *Briotás* in Irish, the name means 'wooden fence', or 'palisade'.

Clare, County Armagh
A common place name in Ireland, Clare derives from the Irish *clár*, meaning 'plain'.

County Down, Northern Ireland
One of the six counties of Northern Ireland, Down derives its name from the Irish word for 'fort', *dún*.

Lack, County Fermanagh
Known in Irish as *An Leac*, 'the flagstone'.

Maze, County Antrim
Known as *An Mhaigh*, meaning 'the plain' in Irish.

Tempo, County Fermanagh
Known as *An tiompú Deiseal* in Irish, the name means 'right-hand turn'.

THE REPUBLIC
OF IRELAND

AUGHRIM, COUNTY GALWAY
The Battle of Aughrim

Like Scotland's first Jacobite Rebellion, Ireland's seventeenth-century Williamite Wars were a series of skirmishes fought between Irish supporters loyal to the deposed James II of England and government forces loyal to William of Orange, who was by then William III. As well as being one of the last battles in the whole campaign, the Battle of Aughrim, fought on 12 July 1691, is today considered the bloodiest battle ever to have been fought on Irish soil, with around one in every five of the 38,000 troops involved being killed. A decisive victory for William's supporters, Aughrim effectively ended the Jacobite cause in Ireland.

BALLINESKER, COUNTY WEXFORD
Saving Private Ryan film set

The extraordinary opening Omaha landings sequence of Steven Spielberg's acclaimed World War Two drama *Saving Private Ryan* (1998) was filmed on the beaches of Ballinesker in south-east Ireland. The scene took two months to film, featured 1,500 extras, and cost almost $12 million – the film went on to gross $480 million at the worldwide box office, and won five out of the 11 Oscars for which it was nominated, including Spielberg's second for Best Director.

BALLYCROY, COUNTY MAYO
THE BURREN, COUNTY CLARE
CONNEMARA, COUNTY GALWAY
GLENVEAGH, COUNTY DONEGAL
THE WICKLOW MOUNTAINS, COUNTY WICKLOW
Ireland's national parks

The Republic of Ireland's six national parks together cover 621 square kilometres (240 square miles), an area just slightly larger than that of the New Forest, and which accounts for less than one per cent of the country's entire land area. With the exception of Killarney National Park in County Kerry (see separate entry), they have all been established since the 1980s, with the most recently established park – The Burren in County Clare, created in 1998 – also being the smallest, at roughly 15 square kilometres (5.8 square miles). By far the largest, meanwhile, is the Wicklow Mountains National Park, whose area was extended in 2009 to a total of 205 square kilometres (79 square miles).

BALLYMAN, COUNTY KILDARE
The Curragh

Situated near Ballyman, halfway between Kildare and Newbridge in the centre of County Kildare, The Curragh is Ireland's largest racecourse and, at over two and a half miles in length, is one of the longest in Europe. Sharing its name with the 5,000-acre plain on which it stands, the name 'Curragh' comes from the Irish word *cuirreach*, literally meaning 'racecourse'. It is home to the five Irish classics, namely the Irish 1,000 and 2,000 Guineas, Derby, Oaks and St Leger.

BEALNABLATH, COUNTY CORK
Assassination of Michael Collins

The Irish revolutionary leader and statesman Michael Collins was shot and killed in a violent ambush in the tiny hamlet of Bealnablath near Crookstown, Cork, on 22 August 1922 at the outset of the Irish Civil War. Despite travelling with a convoy of several other people, remarkably Collins was the only fatality, commemorated by a memorial cross later erected in the village.

BOHOLA, COUNTY MAYO
Mayor of New York William O'Dwyer

Born in 1890 in the tiny County Mayo village of Bohola, William O'Dwyer emigrated to New York in 1910. After serving in the New York police, he worked for many years as a lawyer before being elected district attorney in 1939. He became New York City's hundredth mayor in 1945, but resigned amidst a police scandal and facing ill health in 1950. Having spent many of his final years in Mexico, including a period serving as ambassador under President Truman, O'Dwyer died in New York on 24 November 1964. He is buried in Arlington National Cemetery.

BRÚ NA BÓINNE, COUNTY MEATH
World Heritage Site

Officially designated the 'Archaeological Ensemble of the Bend of the Boyne', the prehistoric Brú na Bóinne collection of sites in Meath became Ireland's first World Heritage Site in 1993. Predating both Stonehenge and the pyramids of Egypt, the site features a multitude of graves, tombs, artworks and standing stones, and as such is one of the largest and most important ancient sites in all of Europe.

THE BURREN, COUNTY CLARE
see under Ballycroy, County Mayo

CARRANTUOHILL, COUNTY KERRY
Ireland's highest mountain

Known in Irish as Corrán Tuathail, 'the inverted crescent' or 'sickle', Carrantuohill (1,038 metres/3,406 feet) is Ireland's highest mountain and the highest peak in County Kerry's Macgillycuddy's Reeks, the 20-kilometre (12-mile) chain of mountains that also includes Ireland's only other mountains in excess of 1,000 metres.

CARRICK-ON-SUIR, COUNTY TIPPERARY
Irish Olympian Tom Kiely

The Irish athlete Tom Kiely was born in Carrick-on-Suir in 1869. At the 1904 Olympic Games in St Louis, Kiley won gold in the men's decathlon, but as Ireland was not independent at the time, his victory was assigned to Great

Britain; Kiely's medal was the only gold won by Britain in 1904, but nevertheless it ensures Great Britain's status as the only country in the world to have won a gold medal at every modern Olympic Games.

CLARE ISLAND, COUNTY MAYO

Base of pirate Grace O'Malley

A legendary figure in Irish history – and perhaps the most famous female pirate in British folklore – Grace O'Malley, Gráinne Ní Mháille, was born in Ireland in *c.* 1530. Her reputation for piracy probably dates from the 1560s when, from her family's home on Clare Island in County Mayo, O'Malley would often use her father's ships and troops to raid passing ships and demand payment in return for safe passage through the waters overseen by her family. In her later years, however, O'Malley became better known for her part in the Irish struggle against the ever-encroaching English occupation and, in particular, against Sir Richard Bingham, the English governor of Connacht. In 1593, she even secured a meeting

with Elizabeth I in Greenwich to discuss Bingham's role in Ireland, likewise managing to arrange for the release of her son, Tiboid, whom Bingham had had kidnapped and imprisoned. O'Malley remained an important figure in the fight to oust the English from Ireland right up to her death in *c.* 1603.

CLIFDEN, COUNTY GALWAY

Aviation pioneers Alcock and Brown

Captain John Alcock and Lieutenant Arthur Whitten Brown crash-landed in a bog near the Galway town of Clifden early on the morning of 15 June 1919, having made the first ever non-stop transatlantic air crossing in a modified World War One bomber. The 3,040-kilometre (1,890-mile) flight from St John's in Newfoundland took just under 16 hours, averaging a speed of 185 kilometres per hour (115 miles per hour), and won Alcock and Brown a £10,000 *Daily Mail* aviation prize for the first transatlantic flight under 72 hours. Both men were later knighted by George V.

CONEY, COUNTY SLIGO
Population: six

Thought to have given its name to the much larger island in Brooklyn, New York, Coney Island in Sligo Bay had a population of just six in the 2006 Irish census, having once been home to more than 100 people at the end of the nineteenth century. One of just 15 islands in the whole of the Republic of Ireland with a population of less than ten, Coney Island, or Inishmulclohy, is County Sligo's only inhabited offshore island.

CONNEMARA, COUNTY GALWAY
see under Ballycroy, County Mayo

DUBLIN, COUNTY DUBLIN
The Spire of Dublin

Considered the tallest sculpture in the world – the Statue of Liberty is barely half its height, Rio de Janeiro's Christ the Redeemer less than a third – the Spire of Dublin is a 120-metre (390-foot) monument standing on the city's central O'Connell Street. Conical in shape, the base of the Spire is 3 metres (10 feet) in diameter, tapering up to a tip of just 15 centimetres (6 inches). The extraordinary structure, officially titled the Monument of Light, stands on the former site of Nelson's Pillar, Ireland's equivalent to London's Nelson's Column, which was destroyed by an IRA bomb in 1966.

'The Soldier's Song'

'Amhrán na bhFiann', 'The Soldier's Song', is the national anthem of Ireland. Written by the Dublin-born songwriters Peadar Kearney and Patrick Heeney in 1907, it was not until 1923 that the song was translated into Irish by Liam Ó Rinn, replacing 'God Save The King' to become the official national anthem of the Irish Free State in 1926.

Dublin, Ohio

There are over a dozen different places named Dublin in the United States, of which the largest by far is found in Ohio. Although the city, which straddles the borders of three state counties, has a population in excess of 41,000 today, even as recently as 1970 Dublin was still only a small town of less than 700 residents. Its subsequent boom was initiated by the completion of the I-270 freeway in 1975, which connected the town to Cincinnati, Cleveland and Columbus, and inevitably led to the granting of official city status in 1987.

Assassination of Lord Frederick Cavendish

Son of the 7th Duke of Devonshire, Frederick Charles Cavendish MP was made Chief Secretary of Ireland in 1882. On 6 May, having just that day taken the oath of office at Dublin Castle, Cavendish and Irish Office Permanent Undersecretary Thomas Henry Burke were walking in Dublin's Phoenix Park when they were set upon by members of the Irish National Invincibles, an extreme nationalist group, who stabbed both men to death. The Phoenix Park Murders as they became known caused a national outcry, and Cavendish's subsequent burial at Edensor in Derbyshire, close to the Duke of Devonshire's family home of Chatsworth House, was attended by 300 members of parliament and a further 30,000 mourners.

Ireland's literary Nobel Laureates

As of 2012, roughly half of all of Ireland's Nobel Laureates have been awarded the prize for literature. Of these, three were born in Dublin. W. B. Yeats was born in the suburb of Sandymount in 1865, and became the first Irishman to win a Nobel Prize in 1923 for his 'inspired poetry which... gives expression to the spirit of a nation'. Two years later, the 1925 prize was awarded to George Bernard Shaw, who remains the only person to have won both a Nobel Prize and an Oscar (Best Adapted Screenplay for *Pygmalion*, 1938). Samuel Beckett, finally, was born in Foxrock in Dublin in 1906, and was awarded the prize in 1969.

US actress Maureen O'Hara

Perhaps best known for her films starring opposite John Wayne, including *Rio Grande* (1950) and *The Quiet Man* (1952), the actress Maureen O'Hara was born in Ranelagh in Dublin in 1920. First cast in Hitchcock's *Jamaica Inn* in 1939, O'Hara soon became a popular Hollywood actress, appearing opposite

Charles Laughton as Esmeralda in *The Hunchback of Notre Dame* (1939), opposite Tyrone Power in the Oscar-nominated *The Black Swan* (1942), and opposite Walter Pidgeon in John Ford's *How Green Was My Valley* (1941). She became an official US citizen in 1946, and after a career spanning seven decades, officially retired from acting in 2000.

Dublin's Viking leader expelled

Following the Battle of Glenn Máma in December 999, the Irish king of Munster, Brian Boru, attacked the city of Dublin and, early in 1000, expelled the city's Viking leader Sigtrygg Silkbeard – Sigtrygg was only permitted to return once he had agreed to serve under Brian's control. Soon afterwards, Brian, who was now in control of half of Ireland, turned his attention to the province of Meath and on his victory there in 1002 took the title of Ard Rí, High King of Ireland.

Act of Union passed in Ireland

Certainly the most important political event of its time, the Act of Union – joining what had been until then the two separate kingdoms of Great Britain and Ireland – was passed in 1800, first by Britain on 2 July and then by the Irish parliament in Dublin on 1 August. The act came into effect on 1 January 1801, creating the United Kingdom of Great Britain and Ireland with its new Union flag now incorporating the red diagonal cross of St Patrick, whilst one hundred Irish MPs were henceforth entitled to stand in the House of Commons. Although the act's origins are somewhat questionable – peerages and other honours were offered as bribes to secure votes in its favour, whilst Prime Minister William Pitt the Younger arguably saw it more as a means of offsetting an otherwise dangerous alliance between Ireland and France – it nevertheless remains in force, albeit partially amended, in the UK.

Victoria's final tour of Ireland

Just one year before she died, Queen Victoria made her fourth and final official visit to Ireland, arriving on 3 April 1900. The visit, which followed Victoria's establishment of the Irish Guards and was ostensibly intended to recognise the Irish contribution to the Boer War, was both celebrated and vehemently opposed, with many Nationalist protests taking place throughout the Queen's stay. Nevertheless, the trip allowed for perhaps the last cinematic footage of Victoria to be filmed as she rode in an open carriage through Dublin's Phoenix Park.

Delvin vs Reilly

On 30 July 1761, Richard Nugent MP, Lord Delvin, was challenged to a duel by a Captain George Reilly in the music rooms of Marlborough Gardens in Dublin after Delvin acted 'improperly' to a woman in Reilly's company and refused to apologise for his conduct. One account of the duel states that, despite a great show of bravado, Delvin did not know that his sword was meant to be taken out of its scabbard before being used and, perhaps as a consequence, he was promptly run through by Reilly. He died from his injuries a week later on 6 August, aged just 19.

Bank of Ireland robbery

On 26 February 2009, a gang of six criminals kidnapped a junior Bank of Ireland employee's girlfriend, her mother and her five-year-old nephew and held them hostage overnight, whilst he was made to collect cash totalling €7.6 million (roughly £6.7 million) from the bank's central branch in Dublin's College Green the following day. The cash, held in four laundry bags, was taken to Clontarf Road railway station in Dublin and given over to a member of the gang, after which the hostages were released and, finally, the Irish police were informed of the incident. In the weeks that followed, several members of the gang were apprehended and arrested, and much of the cash was recovered. The theft remains the biggest bank robbery ever committed in Ireland.

James Joyce's Ulysses

One of the most discussed and controversial novels of the twentieth century, James Joyce's masterpiece *Ulysses* is set in Dublin on 16 June 1904, and is loosely based on Homer's *Odyssey*. Despite the events of the novel taking place over the course of one day and largely involving only the single principal character,

Leopold Bloom, *Ulysses* runs to 250,000 words.

Handel's Messiah

Written in a little over three weeks in the summer of 1741, Handel's masterpiece oratorio *Messiah* – with its familiar 'Hallelujah' chorus – is one of the most popular choral pieces in all classical music. Based on a libretto written by Handel's frequent collaborator Charles Jennens, *Messiah* premiered in Dublin's Music Hall on 13 April 1742 where, at the request of the then dean of St Patrick's Cathedral (and author of *Gulliver's Travels*), Jonathan Swift, it was performed under the title of *A Sacred Oratorio*, as Swift, like many religious clerics at the time, was wary of such religiously themed material being performed in a theatre.

O'Casey's Juno and the Paycock premieres

Set in Dublin during the Irish Civil War, Sean O'Casey's *Juno and the Paycock* premiered at Dublin's Abbey Theatre on 15 March 1924. The play, the second part of O'Casey's Dublin Trilogy

alongside *The Shadow of a Gunman* (1923) and *The Plough and the Stars* (1926), was adapted for cinema in 1930 by Alfred Hitchcock and even became an albeit poorly received Broadway musical, *Juno*, in 1959. It remains one of O'Casey's most popular and frequently performed works.

Oscar-winner George Bernard Shaw

Better known as a playwright, George Bernard Shaw won the 1938 Oscar for Best Adapted Screenplay for his adaptation of his own play *Pygmalion*, becoming the first Irish-born Oscar winner. He had earlier won the Nobel Prize for Literature in 1925.

Yeats first edition auctioned

A rare first edition of 'Easter, 1916', one of the most controversial works of the Irish poet W. B. Yeats, was sold at auction in Dublin in October 2003 for €7,100 (roughly £4,950 at the time). Written in the aftermath of the Irish Easter Rising, only three such first editions of the poem, dating from 1917, are known to exist from an initial print of just 25 – Yeats had been reluctant to publish the poem more widely, fearing that its political content could have provoked further unrest. The poem was not printed again for another three years.

Use of hypodermic needles pioneered

It was at Dublin's Meath Hospital in the mid 1840s that the Irish physician Francis Rynd pioneered the use of a hollow needle to administer medication hypodermically, directly into the bloodstream of his patients. Rynd's methods were published in the *Dublin Medical Press* in 1845, although the concoctions he injected would certainly not be employed today – he used, for instance, a solution of morphia and creosote to treat neuralgia patients. Subsequently, in 1855, Edinburgh's Alexander Wood became the first doctor to use a hypodermic syringe, developed by the French physician Charles Pravaz in 1853.

The Dublin Olympics

Dublin has twice bid for the Olympic Games, losing out in 1936 to Berlin and in 1940 (when London also launched an unsuccessful bid) to Tokyo. Japan, however, went on to turn down the 1940 games due to the Second Sino-Japanese War, whilst the games themselves – like those of 1944 – were eventually cancelled because of World War Two.

Murder of Veronica Guerin

On 26 June 1996 the Irish journalist Veronica Guerin was shot and killed by a group of drug dealers as she waited in her car at a road junction near Newlands Cross in South Dublin. An acclaimed film of her life, starring a Golden-Globe-nominated Cate Blanchett in the title role, was released in 2003.

THE GLEN OF IMAAL, COUNTY WICKLOW
Glen of Imaal terrier

Irish Glen of Imaal terriers – or 'Glens' as they are otherwise known – date from the seventeenth century, and although amongst the least known of terrier breeds, are nevertheless somewhat easily recognisable thanks to a noticeably stocky body and characteristically short, stumpy legs. Like the Skye terrier, the Glen of Imaal is one of the most vulnerable of all British breeds – in 2007 there were more giant pandas in the world than pure-bred Glens – forcing recent steps to be taken in order to ensure its survival.

GLENVEAGH, COUNTY DONEGAL
see under Ballycroy, County Mayo

INNISFREE, COUNTY SLIGO
Yeats' 'Lake Isle of Innisfree'

The uninhabited island of Innisfree, or Inis Fraoigh, is one of 22 islands in County Sligo's Lough Gill. W. B. Yeats' poem dedicated to it, 'Lake Isle of Innisfree', was first published in 1890 and was written whilst Yeats was in London. Feeling homesick for Ireland, and partly inspired by the American writer Henry David Thoreau – whose time spent in isolation in a log cabin in Massachusetts was detailed in his 1854 book *Walden* – Yeats' 12-line poem expresses a desire to depart for the peace and solitude of the island; it opens, 'I will arise and go now, and go to Innisfree / And a small cabin build

there [...] / And I shall have some peace'.

KELLS, COUNTY KILKENNY
Grand National winner Red Rum

On 3 May 1965, three-time Grand National winner Red Rum was born at Rossenarra Stud in Kells, County Kilkenny. Bred by Martyn McEnery, Red Rum was put up for sale by owner Lurline Brotherton (whose horse Freebooter had won the 1950 National) and bought by former taxi driver and used-car salesman Donald 'Ginger' McCain in 1972, who famously trained the horse in Sefton, Merseyside, by running it on the sands of nearby Southport Beach. Red Rum ran in a total of five consecutive Grand Nationals in the 1970s (winning in 1973, 1974 and 1977) and was due to run in a sixth in 1978 but was removed from the race the day before on grounds of ill health. Red Rum never raced again and died in 1995. McCain, meanwhile, went on to become one of only two trainers to have achieved four Grand National wins when Amberleigh House won the 2004 race, 31 years after Red Rum's first victory.

KERRYCURIHY, COUNTY CORK

The Desmond Rebellions

Ireland's Desmond Rebellions of the mid to late 1500s were a series of uprisings largely responding to the prospect of English governance in the province of Munster. The first rebellion lasted from 1569 to 1573 and was instigated by James Fitzmaurice Fitzgerald, a cousin of the earl of Desmond, who began by attacking Kerrycurihy and several other known English settlements throughout the province, driving the English from their lands. Soon afterwards, Fitzmaurice attacked both Kilkenny and the city of Cork before Sir Henry Sidney, Elizabeth I's lord deputy in Ireland, retaliated and dispersed the insurgents. After attempting a second rebellion with the support of Spanish and Italian troops in 1579 Fitzmaurice was killed, and by 1583 the Desmond Rebellions were over.

KILKEA, COUNTY KILDARE

Birthplace of Ernest Shackleton

The tiny village of Kilkea in County Kildare was in 1874 the birthplace of the renowned explorer Sir Ernest Shackleton. Following an early career in the Royal Navy, Shackleton first joined Robert Falcon Scott's expedition to the Antarctic in 1901 before embarking on his own expedition in 1908, which reached within 150 kilometres (90 miles) of the South Pole. Later expeditions in 1914–16 and 1920 were, however, less successful and Shackleton died of a heart attack on the island of South Georgia in 1922.

KILKENNY, COUNTY KILKENNY

'Kilkenny cats'

To 'fight like Kilkenny cats' means to fight ferociously, often describing two parties who fight until they have mutually exhausted each other. The phrase's history is unclear, although various explanations have nonetheless been suggested over the years, including a story of two cats that fought each other to death, eating each other up until only their tails were left behind. Use of the phrase to describe two warring sides, however, is likely rooted in the bitter border disputes common throughout Ireland in the seventeenth and eighteenth centuries.

The Kilkenny Witch Trial

One of the earliest witch trials in the British Isles was that of Alice Kyteler, a Flemish-Irish noblewoman, which took place in Kilkenny in 1324. Kyteler was accused of witchcraft by several of her own children who were apparently dismayed to discover that they would receive less money after her death than the son she had borne by her first husband. In all, 12 people – including Kyteler's first-born son, William Outlaw – were implicated in the trial. Although found guilty, Kyteler escaped punishment and managed to flee to England, yet many of her associates were less fortunate and indeed Kyteler's own maidservant, Petronella de Meath, was flogged and burnt at the stake in 1324, the first recorded death by burning for heresy in Irish history.

KILLARNEY, COUNTY KERRY
First national park in the British Isles

When Muckross House and its surrounding estate were gifted to the Irish state in 1932 by the US Senator Arthur Vincent, the British Isles' first ever national park came into existence. Since its establishment, Killarney National Park, as it became known, has since been vastly extended and now covers a total area of 102 square kilometres (39.5 square miles), making it the third-largest national park in Ireland. It is of immense ecological importance, featuring the largest expanse of untouched native Irish woodland in the entire country, and is home to Ireland's only wild population of red deer.

LIMERICK, COUNTY LIMERICK
The Living Bridge

Joining two distinct sections of the University of Limerick across the River Shannon, the Living Bridge won a European RIBA Award in 2008. Part designed by those responsible for Gateshead's Millennium Bridge, its striking design incorporates several wider 'platforms' along the bridge's length intended to be used as meeting places or as exterior teaching or performance areas. At 350 metres (1,150 feet), it is moreover the longest pedestrian bridge in Ireland.

LISCANNOR, COUNTY CLARE
Birth of John Philip Holland

John Philip Holland was born on 29 February 1840 in the tiny village of Lisconnor on Ireland's west coast. The marine engineer was renowned for his design of submersibles, including the first submarine ever used by the Royal Navy. He lived and worked in Ireland until 1873, when he emigrated to America. Two years later, he submitted his first, albeit unsuccessful, submarine design to the US Navy; after more than twenty-five years' further work, the US Navy finally commissioned the USS *Holland* in 1900. The design was adopted by the Royal Navy in the same year, and Britain's *Holland 1* was launched in 1901.

MIZEN HEAD, COUNTY CORK
The Mizen to Malin Trail

The Irish equivalent of Great Britain's Land's End to John o'Groats route, Ireland's Mizen to Malin trail covers a south-to-north distance by road of around 610 kilometres (380 miles), or 466 kilometres (289 miles) as the crow flies, linking Mizen Head in County Cork to Malin Head in County Donegal.

MULLAGHMORE, COUNTY SLIGO
Assassination of Lord Mountbatten

Whilst sailing in Donegal Bay during a stay at his holiday home in Mullaghmore on 27 August 1979, Lord Louis Mountbatten, 1st Earl Mountbatten of Burma, was killed by a bomb placed on his boat *Shadow V* by the IRA. The terrible attack also claimed the lives of Ireland's Baroness Brabourne and her 14-year-old grandson.

OUGHTERARD, COUNTY KILDARE
O'Connell vs d'Esterre

One of the most significant figures in Irish political history, Daniel O'Connell was known variously as 'The Liberator', for his efforts to repeal the 1800 Act of Union and regain home rule for Ireland, and 'The Emancipator', in recognition of his successful campaign to allow Irish Catholics the right to sit in the Houses of Parliament. In 1815, he was challenged to a duel by John d'Esterre, a member of the Dublin Corporation (the city's administrative board) after delivering a speech criticising the corporation. On 1 February, the men met at Ougtherard in the north of County Kildare, where d'Esterre, despite being a noted duellist, was shot in the hip and died soon afterwards. Distraught at having killed a man, however, O'Connell went on to pay an allowance supporting d'Esterre's daughter and her family for the rest of his life. He died in 1847.

PORTMARNOCK, COUNTY DUBLIN
The life of St Marnock

Portmarnock, north of Dublin, takes its name from the fifth-century Irish bishop St Marnock, or Mernoc, who was a disciple of St Columba. St Marnock also gives his name to several towns and places in Scotland, including Kilmarnock, Dalmarnock, a suburb of Glasgow, and Inchmarnock, an island in the Sound of Bute.

RATHCOOLE, SOUTH DUBLIN
Irish Olympian Michelle de Bruin

Born Michelle Smith in Rathcoole in South Dublin in 1969, the swimmer Michelle de Bruin remains Ireland's most successful Olympian. Having failed by some margin to win a medal at both the Seoul and Barcelona Games in 1988 and 1992 respectively, at Atlanta in 1996 Smith exhibited an astonishing improvement in her performance, taking home a total of four medals including a record three golds in the women's 400-metre freestyle and 400-metre and 200-metre individual medleys. Her remarkable improvement, however, led to a series of doping allegations and when a tampered urine sample was submitted in 1998 she was banned from competition for four years.

THE SHANNON
The British Isles' longest river

The River Shannon is not only the longest river in Ireland, but the longest in the entire British Isles. Rising on the slopes of Cuilcagh Mountain in County Cavan at a spot known as the Shannon Pot, the river flows through 11 Irish counties before reaching the Atlantic at Limerick, some 360 kilometres (224 miles) away.

SHEEGOREY, COUNTY ROSCOMMON
The Gaelic Chieftain

Overlooking Ireland's N4 motorway near the tiny village of Sheegorey in Roscommon stands *The Gaelic Chieftain*, an extraordinary metal sculpture of a figure on horseback comprised of dozens of individual metal planes welded together. Designed by the Northern Irish sculptor and artist Maurice Harron, the work commemorates and stands above the site of the sixteenth-century Battle of Curlew Pass, fought between the Gaelic Irish and the English in 1599 as part of the Nine Years' War. The statue was officially dedicated in 1999, the year of the four-hundredth anniversary of the battle.

SKELLIG MICHAEL, COUNTY KERRY
World Heritage Site

Skellig Michael was appointed a World Heritage Site in 1996. Despite being one of the most isolated islands in the entire British Isles, lying 12 kilometres (7 miles) offshore from the Irish mainland in the Atlantic Ocean, for six centuries the island was home to a major Irish monastic community centred around a Celtic monastery built on the island's 230-metre (755-foot) summit in the seventh century.

TEARAGHT ISLAND, COUNTY KERRY
Ireland's westernmost point

Kerry is Ireland's westernmost county, as well as being its fifth largest by area. Dunmore Head on Kerry's Dingle Peninsula is the westernmost point on the mainland, whilst the nearby Blasket Islands, Na Blascaodal, contain Tearaght Island, the westernmost point in Ireland, the British Isles, and, excluding Iceland, the whole of Western Europe.

TRALEE, COUNTY KERRY
The Kerry blue terrier

Originally bred for herding, hunting and other sports, the Kerry blue terrier has an unclear ancestry but is likely related to the Bedlington terrier, Irish terrier and perhaps even the Portuguese water dog, although one somewhat romantic account of the breed's history is that it developed from a Russian 'blue dog' which was rescued from a ship wrecked in Tralee Bay. It is an uncommon breed, but is nonetheless easily identifiable as one of the larger terriers, with long, straight front legs, a soft curly coat and square-shaped face and head. A Kerry blue took Best in Show at Crufts in 2000.

WATERFORD, COUNTY WATERFORD
Death of Ivar of Waterford, 1000

Waterford is the smallest and oldest of Ireland's five cities, founded by Viking settlers in 914. One of the city's earliest kings, Ivar of Waterford died in 1000 and is remembered both for expelling the Viking King Sigtrygg Silkbeard from his throne in Dublin in 994 (as Brian Boru would do six years later), and as the father of Ragnall of Waterford, who built Reginald's Tower in the city in 1003. The tower, which likely takes its name from Ragnall mac Gillemaire, one of the city's last kings who was imprisoned there by Anglo-Norman invaders in 1170, is

today the oldest civic building in the whole of Ireland.

THE WICKLOW MOUNTAINS, COUNTY WICKLOW
see under Ballycroy, County Mayo

WOODSTOWN, COUNTY WATERFORD
Viking village discovered

Construction of a bypass in the Waterford village of Woodstown was halted in 2003 when preliminary work hinted at the existence of an entire Viking village – based around a large fort and complete with seemingly distinct industrial, commercial and residential areas – a little below the ground. Later and ongoing excavations uncovered weaponry, ships' nails, glass, amber, silver ingots and dozens of lead weights that would likely have been used in trading and metal processing. Moreover, preliminary radiocarbon tests carried out at the site suggested that it may even have been originally settled as early as the fifth century by native Irish tribes, before being resettled by the Vikings around 400 years later.

WHAT'S IN A NAME?

Clara, County Offaly
Also known as Clóirtheach, meaning 'level place'.

Clash, County Tipperary
From the Irish *clais*, meaning 'ravine'.

Convoy, County Donegal
Known as Convoigh in Irish, meaning 'hound plain'.

Cork, County Cork
Ireland's second city, Cork derives its name from the Irish *corcach*, 'swamp'.

Curry, County Sligo
Derives from the Irish for 'weir', *cora*.

Drum, County Monaghan
Known also as Droim, derived from the Irish *druim*, meaning 'ridge'.

Golden, County Tipperary
Known also as An Gabhailín, from the Irish for 'little fork'.

Kill, County Kildare
Related to the Irish word *cill*, meaning 'church', which also appears in the name of County Kildare itself.

Letter, County Kerry
Derives from the Irish *leiter*, meaning 'hillside'.

Screen, County Wexford
Presumably comes from the Irish word for 'shrine'.

Swords, Dublin
Likely related to the word 'sward', used of an open grassy area.

Tara, County Meath
Means 'conspicuous place'.

Trim, County Meath
Known in Irish as Balle Átha Troim, meaning 'ford of the elder-trees'.

SUBJECT INDEX

I. GEOGRAPHY

Land's Ends – The Extreme Points of the British Isles
Corrachadh Mòr, Highland / Lady Park Wood, Monmouthshire / Land's End, Cornwall / Les Minquiers, Jersey / Lowestoft, Suffolk / Manger, County Fermanagh / Marshall Meadows, Northumberland / Mull of Galloway, Dumfries and Galloway / The Out Skerries, Shetland / Out Stack, Shetland / St Kilda, Western Isles / The Scilly Isles / Tearaght Island, County Kerry

The High Life – The Highest Peaks and Points of the British Isles
Beacon Hill, Norfolk / Ben Nevis, Highland / Carrantuohill, County Kerry / The Cheviot, Northumberland / Cross Fell, Cumbria / The Spire of Dublin, Dublin / The Fens, East Anglia / Guy's Hospital, Southwark / Les Platons, Jersey / Scafell Pike, Cumbria / Shard London Bridge, Southwark / Skelton, Cumbria / Slieve Donard, County Down / Snowdon, Gwynedd / Strabane, County Tyrone

The British Isles – Islands of the British Isles with Fewer Than 100 Inhabitants
Brownsea, Dorset / Caldey, Pembrokeshire / The Calf of Man / Coney, County Sligo / Lundy, Devon / Piel Island, Cumbria / Rathlin, County Antrim / St Agnes, Scilly Isles / Shuna, Argyll and Bute

Waterworld – Rivers, Lakes and Waterways
Loch Awe, Argyll and Bute / Coton in the Elms, Derbyshire / Eas a'Chual Aluinn, Highland / Loch Lomond, Highland / Loch Morar, Highland / Loch Ness, Highland / Lough Neagh / Raasay, Highland / Seil, Argyll and Bute / The Severn / The Shannon / The Tay / The Thames / Windermere, Cumbria

Stormy Weather – Meteorological and Natural Disasters
Birmingham – The Birmingham tornado / Bishop's Castle – 5.1 magnitude earthquake / Boscastle, Cornwall – The Boscastle floods / Farnborough, Hampshire – The Great Storm, 1987 / Great Yarmouth, Norfolk – 6.1

magnitude earthquake / Harwich, Essex – The Great Storm, 1703 / Kempston, Bedfordshire – Devastating Home Counties tornado / Lewes, East Sussex – Devastating avalanche / Llyn Peninsula – The Llyn Earthquake / London – The Great Smog / Lynmouth, Devon – The Lynmouth floods / Ryde, Isle of Wight – Remarkable waterspout recorded / The Tay – The Tay Rail Bridge Disaster / Widecombe-in-the-Moor, Devon – Rare 'ball lightning' attack

Park-keeping – The National Parks of the British Isles
Ballycroy, County Mayo / The Broads / The Brecon Beacons / The Burren, County Clare / The Cairngorms / Connemara, County Galway / Dartmoor, Devon / Exmoor / Glenveagh, County Donegal / Killarney, County Kerry / The Lake District / Loch Lomond and The Trossachs, Scotland / The New Forest, Hampshire / The North York Moors / Northumberland National Park / The Pembrokeshire Coast / The Peak District / Snowdonia / The South Downs / The Wicklow Mountains, County Wicklow / The Yorkshire Dales

Walk This Way – Walks and Routes
Canterbury, Kent – The Pilgrim's Way / Edale, Derbyshire – The Pennine Way / Ilchester, Somerset – The Fosse Way / John o'Groats, Highland – Land's End to John o'Groats / Knighton, Powys – The Offa's Dyke Path / Minehead, Somerset – The South West Coast Path / Mizen Head, County Cork – The Mizen to Malin Trail / Portpatrick, Dumfries and Galloway – The Southern Upland Way / Isle of Man – Raad ny Foillan

Streets Ahead – Famous Streets and Roads
Belfast – Falls Road and Shankhill Road / Bridge, City of London – Pudding Lane / Edinburgh – The Royal Mile / Exeter, Devon – Parliament Street / Harlech, Gwynedd – Ffordd Penllech / Lincoln, Lincolnshire – Steep Hill / Liverpool, Merseyside – Penny Lane / Manchester – Sir Matt Busby Way / Newcastle-upon-Tyne, Tyne and Wear – Grey Street / Stratford-on-Avon, Warwickshire – Chapel Street / Swindon, Wiltshire – The Magic Roundabout / West Overton, Wiltshire – The Ridgeway / Wick, Highland – Ebenezer Place / York, North Yorkshire – The Shambles

Off the Map – Ghost and Destroyed Towns
Badbea, Highland – The Highland Clearances / Bothwellhaugh, North Lanarkshire – Abandoned colliery village / Hampton-on-Sea, Kent – Lost to the sea / Heathrow, London - The village cleared for the airport / Kenfig, Bridgend – The village lost to the sands / Mardale Green, Cumbria – The

drowned village of Mardale Green / Tide Mills, East Sussex – Eighteenth-century village abandoned / Tyneham, Dorset – Commandeered 'in the national interest' / Wharram Percy, North Yorkshire – Extraordinary abandoned mediaeval village

State of the Nation – British City Names in the USA
Aberdeen, South Dakota / Bangor, Maine / Birmingham, Alabama / Dover, Delaware / Dublin, Ohio / Lincoln, Nebraska / London, Ohio / Manchester, New Hampshire / Oxford, Ohio / Richmond, Virginia / Worcester, Massachusetts

World Map – British Place Names Around the World
Bristol Island, South Georgia / Edinburgh, Tristan da Cunha / Greenwich, South Shetland Islands / Inverness, Sweden / Jura, Argyll and Bute – Jura, France / London, Kiribati / Londonderry, Chile / Middlesex, Belize / Plymouth, Montserrat / Portsmouth, Dominica / Scarborough, Tobago

2. CULTURE AND CUSTOMS

Common Heritage – World Heritage Sites in the British Isles
Avebury, Wiltshire – Avebury Stone Circle / Bath, Somerset / Blaenavon, – Torfaen / Brú na Bóinne, County Meath / Durham, County Durham – Durham Cathedral / The Giant's Causeway, County Antrim / Ironbridge, Shropshire / Mainland, Orkney / New Lanark, South Lanarkshire / Pontcysyllte Aqueduct, Wrexham / Skellig Michael, County Kerry / Studley Royal Park, North Yorkshire

Tales of Two Cities – Twin and Sister Cities
Belfast – Nashville / Bradford, West Yorkshire – Skopje / Bristol – Tbilisi / Cardiff – Xiamen / Coventry, West Midlands – Belgrade / Dundee – Nablus / Harrogate, North Yorkshire – Wellington / Kingston-upon-Hull, East Yorkshire – Freetown / Manchester – St Petersburg / Newcastle-upon-Tyne, Tyne and Wear – Bergen / Northampton – Ljubljana / Whitby, North Yorkshire – Nuku'alofa / Whitwell, Rutland – Paris

What's in a Name? – Places Named After Famous People
Alexandria, West Dumbarton – Alexander Smollett / Beddgelert, Gwynedd – Gelert and Llewellyn the Great / Camden, London – William Camden / Fleetwood, Lancashire – Created by Peter Hesketh-Fleetwood / Fort William,

Highland – William III / Glamorgan – Morgan ab Owain / John o'Groats, Highland – Jan de Groot / Kingstanding, Birmingham – Charles I / Kyleakin, Highland – Haakon IV / Queen Charlton, Somerset – Catherine Parr / Queenborough, Kent – Philippa of Hainault / Saltaire, West Yorkshire – Sir Titus Salt

Custom Made – Unusual Local Customs and Traditions
Allendale, Northumberland – Tar Barrelling / Ashton-under-Lyme, Greater Manchester – The Black Knight Pageant / Bacup, Lancashire – The Nutters Dance / Bourne, Lincolnshire – The Bourne Running Auction / Chedzoy, Somerset – The Chedzoy Candle Auction / Gawthorpe, West Yorkshire – The Coal Carrying Championships / Haxey, Lincolnshire – The Haxey Hood / Leighton Buzzard, Bedfordshire – The Wilkes Walk / Lerwick, Shetland – Up Helly Aa / Ramsbottom, Lancashire – The Black Pudding Throwing Championship / Saddleworth, Greater Manchester – Rushbearing / Shebbear, Devon – Turning the Devil's Stone / St Briavels, Gloucestershire – The Bread and Cheese Dole / St Columb Major, Cornwall – Hurling / Tissington, Derbyshire – Well Dressing / Ufton Nervet, Berkshire – The Ufton Dole / Urswick, Cumbria – Rushbearing / Whittlesey, Cambridgeshire – The Straw Bear

Moonrakers and Janners – Regional Nicknames
Birmingham – Brummies / Hartlepool, Durham – Monkey Hangers / Lincolnshire – Yellowbellies / Liverpool, Merseyside – Scousers / London – Cockneys / Newcastle-upon-Tyne, Tyne and Wear – Geordies / Plymouth, Devon – Janners / Sunderland, Tyne and Wear – Mackems / Bishops Cannings, Wiltshire – Moonrakers

Local Speciality – Traditional Local Dishes
Arbroath, Angus – The Arbroath Smokie / Bakewell, Derbyshire – Bakewell pudding / Bedford, Bedfordshire – Bedfordshire Clangers / Chorley, Lancashire – Chorley cakes / Dundee cake / Edinburgh rock / Eton, Berkshire – Eton mess / Exeter pudding / Grantham, Lincolnshire – Grantham Gingerbread / Helston, Cornwall – Helston pudding / Kendal, Cumbria – Kendal mint cake / Pontefract, West Yorkshire – Pontefract cakes / Richmond-upon-Thames – Maids of honour / Southwell, Nottinghamshire – The Bramley apple / Chailey, East Sussex – Sussex Pond Pudding / Tregaron Ceredigion – Tregaron broth

Heroes and Villains – Urban Legends and Folk Heroes
Alloway, South Ayrshire – Tam o'Shanter / Bennane Head, South Ayrshire – Sawney Bean / Carlisle, Cumbria – Adam Bell / Knaresborough, North Yorkshire – Mother Shipton / Leicester, Leicestershire – Black Annis / Old Ford, London – Spring-heeled Jack / Pauntley, Gloucestershire – Dick Whittington / Windsor, Berkshire – Herne the Hunter / Zennor, Cornwall – Matthew Trewhella and the mermaid of Zennor

All Round – Stone Circles
Avebury, Wiltshire / Ballynoe, County Down / Beaghmore, County Tyrone / Bodmin Moor, Cornwall – The Hurlers / Boroughbridge, North Yorkshire – The Devil's Arrows / Castlerigg, Cumbria / Chipping Norton, Oxfordshire – The King's Men / Drumskinny, County Fermanagh / Langwathby, Cumbria – Long Meg and Her Daughters / Newbridge, Dumfries and Galloway – The Twelve Apostles / Postbridge, Devon – The Grey Wethers / Stanton-in-Peak, Derbyshire – The Nine Ladies

Country Music – National Anthems of the British Isles
Douglas, Isle of Man – 'Arrane Ashoonagh' / Dublin – 'The Soldier's Song'/ 'Flower of Scotland' / Guernsey, Channel Islands – 'Sarnia Cherie' / Jersey, Channel Islands – 'Ma Normandie' and 'Island Home' / Londonderry, Northern-Ireland – 'The Londonderry Air' / Morwenstow, Cornwall – 'The Song of the Western Men' / Pontypridd, Wales, Rhondda Cynon Taff – 'Land of My Fathers'

Turns of Phrase – Words and Phrases
Aldgate, London – Aldgate draught / Bath, Somerset – Get yourself to Bath / Bridport, Dorset – Stabbed with a Bridport dagger / Bristol – Bristol fashion / Coventry, West Midlands – Sent to Coventry / Dover, Kent – When Dover and Calais meet / Dunstable, Bedfordshire – Downright Dunstable / The Forth Bridge – Painting the Forth Bridge / Grantham, Lincolnshire – Grantham gruel / Great Dunmow, Essex – To eat Dunmow bacon / Jedburgh, Scottish Borders – Jedburgh justice / Kilkenny, County Kilkenny – Kilkenny cats / Lincoln – The Devil over Lincoln / Newcastle-upon-Tyne, Tyne and Wear – Carrying coals to Newcastle / Newgate, London – Newgate fashion / The Thames, London – Setting fire to the Thames

3. PEOPLE

Big Fish, Small Pond – Famous Sons of Small Towns
Burnham Thorpe, Norfolk – Admiral Nelson / East Budleigh, Devon – Walter Raleigh / East Knoyle, Wiltshire – Christopher Wren / Kilkea, Kildare – Ernest Shackleton / Marton, North Yorkshire – Captain Cook / Mytholmroyd, West Yorkshire – Ted Hughes / Tremadog, Gwynedd – Lawrence of Arabia / Wantage, Oxfordshire – Alfred The Great / Woolsthorpe-by-Colsterworth, Lincolnshire – Isaac Newton / Wylam, Northumberland – George Stephenson

Multiple Births – Shared Birthplaces of Notable Britons
Ashford, Kent – Malcolm Sargent and Frederick Forsyth / Bury St Edmunds, Suffolk – Sir Peter Hall and Bob Hoskins / Coventry, West Midlands – Frank Whittle and Philip Larkin / Kingston-upon-Hull, East Yorkshire – William Wilberforce and Amy Johnson / Portsmouth, Hampshire – Isambard Kingdom Brunel and Charles Dickens / Salford, Greater Manchester – James Prescott Joule and Peter Maxwell Davies / Scarborough, North Yorkshire – Charles Laughton and Ben Kingsley / Swansea – Dylan Thomas and Princess Lilian of Sweden / Torquay, Devon – Sir Richard Burton and Agatha Christie / York, North Yorkshire - Guy Fawkes and W. H. Auden

Without a Trace – Last Sightings of Famous Missing Persons
Aust, Gloucestershire – Disappearance of Richey Edwards / The (Owain) Glyndwr Rising / Eilean Mòr, Western Isles – The Flannan Isles mystery / Newhaven, East Sussex – Disappearance of Lord Lucan / Seaton Carew, Durham – Disappearance of John Darwin / Sunningdale, Berkshire – Disappearance of Agatha Christie / Tower of London – The Princes in the Tower

Playing the Jack – Jack the Ripper Suspects
Ashby-de-la-Zouch, Leicestershire – Frederick Bailey Deeming / Camden, London – Walter Sickert / Colchester, Essex – Sir William Gull / Glasgow – Thomas Neill Cream / St Albans, Hertfordshire – Mary Pearcey / Stourbridge, Worcestershire – William Bury / Wimbourne Minster, Dorset – Montague Druitt / Windsor, Berkshire – Prince Albert Victor

A Night to Remember – Passengers and Crew of the *Titanic*
Benson, Oxfordshire – *Titanic* lookout Reginald Lee / Broughty Ferry, Dundee – *Titanic* Officer David Blair / Chorley, Lancashire – *Titanic* Officer

Charles Lightoller / Colne, Lancashire – *Titanic* bandleader Wallace Hartley / Comber, Down – Thomas Andrews, builder of the *Titanic* / Farncombe, Surrey – *Titanic* victim Jack Philips / Hanley, Staffordshire – *Titanic* Captain Edward Smith / Leeds, West Yorkshire – *Titanic* victim Father Thomas Byles / Melksham, Wiltshire – *Titanic* victim Sidney Goodwin / Scarborough, North Yorkshire – *Titanic* Officer James Paul Moody / Wirksworth, Derbyshire – *Titanic* survivor Lawrence Beesley

Duel Personalities – Duels
Cawston, Norfolk – Hobart vs Le Neve / Dublin – Delvin vs Reilly / Gosport, Hampshire – Hawkey vs Seton / Hoxton, London – Ben Jonson vs Gabriel Spenser / Kircaldy, Fife – Landale vs Morgan / Oughterard, Kildare – O'Connell vs d'Esterre / Winster, Derbyshire – Cuddie vs Brittlebank

Murder Most Foul – Assassinations in British History
Bealnablath, County Cork – Michael Collins / Canterbury, Kent – Thomas Becket / Dublin – Lord Frederick Cavendish / Edinburgh – Lord Darnley / Enfield, London – Ross McWhirter / The Houses of Parliament, London – Spencer Percival / London Bridge, London – Georgi Markov / Mullaghmore, County Sligo – Lord Mountbatten / Newlands Cross, South Dublin – Veronica Guerin / Piccadilly, London – Alexander Litvinenko / Portsmouth, Hampshire – Duke of Buckingham

On Pain of Death – Executions
Chelmsford, Essex – The Peasants' Revolt and execution of Thomas Baker / Edinburgh – William Burke / Fotheringhay, Northamptonshire – Mary, Queen of Scots / Liverpool, Merseyside – Peter Anthony Allen / Shrewsbury, Shropshire – Dafydd ap Gruffydd / The Solent – Admiral John Byng / York, North Yorkshire – Dick Turpin

A Nobel Cause – Nobel Prize Winners
Aberdeen – John MacLeod / Bury, West Sussex – John Galsworthy / Cambridge, Cambridgeshire – J. J. Thomson / Clay Cross, Derbyshire – Arthur Henderson / Dublin – Ireland's literary Nobel Laureates / Haggerston, London – Randal Cremer / Liverpool, Merseyside – Ronald Ross / Oxford – John Hicks / West Hampstead, London – Doris Lessing

American-English – Notable Americans Born in the British Isles
Blackpool, Lancashire – US actor John Mahoney / Bohola, County Mayo – Mayor of New York William O'Dwyer / Bristol – America's first female doctor,

Elizabeth Blackwell / Ceres, Fife – US statesman James Wilson / Dernhall, Cheshire – US General Charles Lee / Down Hatherley, Gloucestershire – American statesman Button Gwinnett / Dublin – US actress Maureen O'Hara / Dublin – Irish American Independence signatories / Gifford, East Lothian – US statesman John Witherspoon / Liverpool, Merseyside, – US statesman Robert Morris / Llandaff, Cardiff – US statesman Francis Lewis / East Finchley, London – Jerry Springer / Eltham, London – US entertainer Bob Hope / Hackney, London – US actress Jessica Tandy / Hereford, Herefordhire – US entertainer Frank Oz / Poplar, London – US actress Angela Lansbury / Shaftesbury, Dorset – US architect Richard Upjohn / Thetford, Norfolk – US campaigner Thomas Paine

Saints Days – Places Named After Saints
Bury St Edmunds, Suffolk / East Kilbride, South Lanarkshire / Kirkcudbright, Dumfries and Galloway / Merthyr Dyfan, Vale of Glamorgan / Merthyr Tydfil, Merthyr / Portmarnock, Dublin County / St Albans, Hertfordshire / St Andrews, Fife / St Bees, Cumbria / St Briavels, Gloucestershire / St Helier, Jersey / St Ives, Cornwall / St Neots, Cambridgeshire / West Kilbride, North Ayrshire

Pirate Coast – British Pirates
Barra, Western Isles – Rory MacNeill / Clare Island, County Mayo – Grace O'Malley / Eday, Orkney – John Gow / Exmouth, Devon – William Kyd / Fowey, Cornwall – Hankyn Seelander / Jersey, Channel Islands – Eustace the Monk / Leith, Edinburgh – Thomas Green

4. HISTORY AND POLITICS

Millennium – Centennial Years in British History
1000
Burton-upon-Trent, Staffordshire – Founding of Burton Abbey / Chester, Cheshire – Æthelred the Unready attacks Scotland/ Dublin – Dublin's Viking leader expelled/ Rochester, Kent – Viking raids / Scarborough, North Yorkshire – Scarborough chapel / St Dunstan-in-the-West, London – Church of St Dunstan founded / Waterford – Death of Ivar of Waterford / Wherwell, Hampshire – Death of Queen Ælfthryth

1100
Biddenden, Kent – The Biddenden Maids / Gloucester – Founding of Gloucester Cathedral / Lostwithiel, Cornwall – Restormel Castle /

Northampton, Northamptonshire – The Holy Sepulchre / Stornoway, Western Isles – Stornoway Castle / Thirsk, North Yorkshire – Thirsk Castle / Tower of London's first prisoner / Upper Canterton, Hampshire – Death of William II / Westminster Abbey – Coronation of Henry I / York, North Yorkshire – Death of Thomas of Bayeux

1200

Aberdeen – *The Aberdeen Bestiary* / Areley Kings, Worcestershire – Layamon's *Brut* / Battle, East Sussex – Death of Odo of Canterbury / Framlingham, Suffolk – Framlingham Castle built / Lincoln – The Battle of Lincoln / Old Temple House, Holborn – Death of Hugh of Lincoln / Uig, Western Isles – The Lewis Chessmen / Westminster Abbey – Coronation of Isabella of Angoulême

1300

Brotherton, North Yorkshire – Birth of Thomas Brotherton / Caerlaverock, Dumfries and Galloway – Edward I takes Caerlaverock Castle / Gloucester – Robert of Gloucester's *Chronicle* / Goldsmiths' Hall, City of London – Hallmarking established / Hereford – The Hereford Mappa Mundi / The Farne Islands, Northumberland – The House of Farne / Newenden, Kent – Edward II's game of *'creag'* / Trapp, Carmarthenshire – Carreg Cennen Castle completed / Westminster Abbey – The Coronation Chair

1400

Anglesey – Birth of Owen Tudor / Cirencester, Gloucestershire – The Epiphany Rising / Glyndyfrdwy, Denbighshire – Owain Glyndwr proclaimed Prince of Wales / Newcastle – Newcastle county corporate formed / Staindrop, County Durham – Birth of Richard Neville / Westminster Abbey – Death of Chaucer

1500

Blickling, Norfolk – The fate of George Boleyn / Cawood, North Yorkshire – Death of Thomas Rotherham, Archbishop of York / Deritend, Birmingham – Birth of Biblical pioneer John Rogers / Fleet Street, City of London – Early printing press established / Hatfield, Hertfordshire – Death of Edmund, son of Henry VII / Sevenoaks, Kent – Death of John Morton, Archbishop of Canterbury / Stirling – Stirling Old Bridge / Stourton, Staffordshire – Birth of Reginald Pole, Archbishop of Canterbury / Willimoteswick, Northumberland – Birth of Nicholas Ridley / Wisbech, Cambridgeshire – Death of John Alcock

1600

Dunfermline, Fife – Birth of Charles I / East India House, City of London – East India Company founded / Edinburgh – Birth of John Ogilby / Oxford – Early performance of *Hamlet* / Perth, Perth and Kinross – The Gowrie Conspiracy / Ravenglass, Cumbria – Death of notorious trickster Tom Skelton / Scalloway, Shetland – Scalloway Castle

1700

Leith, Edinburgh – The Darien Scheme / Myddle, Shropshire – Gough's *History of Myddle* / Plymouth, Devon – Voyages of Edmond Halley / The Scilly Isles – *A New Voyage to Carolina* / Westminster – Death of John Dryden / Windsor, Berkshire – Death of William, Duke of Gloucester

1800

Dublin – Act of Union passed in Ireland / East Dereham, Norfolk – Parish of English writer William Cowper / Glasgow – The Glasgow Police Act / Lacock, Wiltshire – Photography pioneer Fox Talbot / Slough, Berkshire – Herschel discovers infrared / Theatre Royal, Covent Garden – Attempted assassination of the king / York, North Yorkshire – Birth of astronomer William Parsons

1900

Brantwood, Cumbria – Death of scholar John Ruskin / Brighton, East Sussex – Birthplace of Gilbert Ryle / Cambridge – Mendel's hybridisation rediscovered / Dublin – Victoria's final tour of Ireland / Farringdon Street, Clerkenwell – Labour Party founded / Hitchin, Hertfordshire – Birth of the Queen Mother / Jersey, Channel Islands – Milestone language bill passed / Manchester – Churchill's parliamentary debut

2000

Bankside – The Tate Modern opens / Bletchley, Buckinghamshire – Enigma machine stolen / Dornoch, Highland – Wedding of Madonna / Longbridge, Birmingham – Final Longbridge Mini produced / Maze, Antrim – The Good Friday releases / Midhurst, West Sussex – Death of Alec Guinness / Milton Keynes, Buckinghamshire – Extraordinary *Harry Potter* pre-orders / Preston, Lancashire – Trial of murderer Harold Shipman / Ramsey, Isle of Man – *Solway Harvester* disaster / Wembley Arena, Wembley – Prime Minister Tony Blair heckled / Wotton Underwood, Buckinghamshire – Death of John Gielgud

Hatched, Matched and Dispatched – Royal Births, Marriages and Deaths
Births: Caernarfon, Gwynedd – Edward II / Dunfermline, Fife – Birthplace of Scottish kings Alexander I, David II, James I, Charles I / Islip, Oxfordshire – Edward the Confessor / Monmouth, Monmouthshire – Henry V / Pembroke, Pembrokeshire – Henry VII / Selby, North Yorkshire – Henry I / St James' Palace, Westminster – London's royal birthplaces / Turnberry, South Ayrshire – Robert the Bruce / Wantage, Oxfordshire – Alfred the Great / Winchester, Hampshire – Henry III / Marriages: Arundel, West Sussex – Henry IV / Canterbury, Kent – Henry III / Dover, Kent – James II / Grafton Regis, Northamptonshire – Edward IV / Greenwich, London – First marriage of Henry VIII / Marlborough, Wiltshire – King John / Portsmouth, Hampshire – Charles II / Titchfield, Hampshire – Henry VI / York, North Yorkshire – Edward III / Deaths: Abington, South Lanarkshire – Cuilén of Scotland / Berkeley, Gloucestershire – The life and death of Edward II / Burgh-by-Sands, Cumbria – Edward I / Corfe Castle, Dorset – Edward the Martyr / Gainsborough, Lincolnshire – Sweyn Forkbeard / Kensington Palace – London's last royal days / Newark, Nottinghamshire – King John / Pucklechurch, Gloucestershire – Edmund I / Sandringham, Norfolk – George V / Strathallen, Perth and Kinross – Aed of Scotland / Upper Canterton, Hampshire – William II / Wherwell, Hampshire – Queen Ælfthryth

Ghosts of the Past – Places Haunted by British Royal Ghosts
Berkeley, Gloucestershire – Edward II / Blickling, Norfolk – The fate of George Boleyn / Borthwick, Midlothian – Mary, Queen of Scots / Bradgate Park, Leicestershire – Lady Jane Grey / Kensington Palace, London – London's last royal days / Owlpen, Gloucestershire – Margaret of Anjou / Pencaitland, East Lothian – Charles I / Snape, North Yorkshire – Catherine Parr / Sudbury, Derbyshire – Queen Adelaide / Windsor, Berkshire – Ghosts of Henry VIII, Elizabeth I, Charles I, and many more

Victoriana – Places Officially Opened By Queen Victoria
Ballater, Aberdeenshire – The Royal Bridge / Belfast – Queen's University / Berwick-upon-Tweed, Northumberland – The Royal Border Bridge / Egham, Surrey – Royal Holloway, UCL, The Founder's Building / Glasgow City Chambers / Hyde Park, – The Great Exhibition / Leeds, West Yorkshire – Town Hall / The Manchester Ship Canal / The Royal Albert Hall, Kensington – The Central Hall of Arts and Sciences / The Royal Courts of Justice, Westminster – The English High Court

In Residence – Royal Residences

Audley End, Essex – Audley End House / Brighton, East Sussex – Royal Pavilion / Carisbrooke, Isle of Wight – Carisbrooke Castle / Chelmsford, Essex – Beaulieu Palace / Dunfermline, Fife – Dunfermline Palace / East Cowes, Isle of Wight – Osborne House / Hamilton, South Lanarkshire – Cadzow Castle / Kings Langley, Hertfordshire – Kings Langley Palace / Laverstock, Wiltshire – Clarendon Palace / Linlithgow, West Lothian – Linlithgow Palace / Mey, Highland – Castle of Mey / Oxford – Beaumont Palace

Prime Locations – Constituencies of Britain's Twentieth-century Prime Ministers

Bewdley, Worcestershire – Stanley Baldwin / Bexley, London – Ted Heath / Bromley, London – Harold Macmillan / Caernarfon, Gwynedd – David Lloyd George / Cardiff – James Callaghan / East Fife – H. H. Asquith / Edgbaston, Birmingham – Neville Chamberlain / Epping, Essex – Winston Churchill / Finchley, London – Margaret Thatcher / Glasgow – Andrew Bonar Law / Huntingdon, Cambridgeshire – John Major / Huyton, Lancashire – Harold Wilson / Kinross, Perth and Kinross – Alec Douglas-Home / Limehouse, London – Clement Attlee / Manchester – Arthur Balfour / Seaham, Durham – Ramsay MacDonald / Sedgefield, County Durham – Tony Blair / Stirling – Henry Campbell-Bannerman / Warwick, Warwickshire – Anthony Eden

The Political World – British-born World Prime Ministers

Barry, Vale of Glamorgan – Julia Gillard, Prime Minister of Australia / Crosshouse, East Ayrshire – Andrew Fisher, fifth prime minister of Australia / Eccleston, Merseyside – Richard Seddon, fifteenth prime minister of New Zealand / Edinburgh – Edward Stafford and Thomas Mackenzie, premiers of New Zealand / Glasgow – John A. Macdonald, first prime minister of Canada / Kidderminster, Worcestershire – Walter Nash, twenty-seventh prime minister of New Zealand / Lerwick, Shetland – Robert Stout, thirteenth prime minister of New Zealand / Mallusk, Antrim – John Ballance, fifteenth prime minister of New Zealand / Newport, Isle of Wight – Henry Sewell, first premier of New Zealand / South Shields, Tyne and Wear – William Fox, second premier of New Zealand

Means of Demonstration – Protests and Campaigns

Brecon, Powys – The Glyndwr Rising / Buckingham Palace, London – Fathers 4 Justice / Chelmsford, Essex – The Peasants' Revolt and execution of Thomas Baker / Cirencester, Gloucestershire – The Epiphany Rising / Epsom, Surrey

– The suffragette movement / Jarrow, Tyne and Wear – The Jarrow March / Kerrycurihy, County Cork – The Desmond Rebellion / Sampford Courtenay, Devon – The Prayer Book Rebellion / St Keverne, Cornwall – The Cornish Rebellion / Tolpuddle, Dorset – The Tolpuddle Martyrs / Wymondham, Norfolk – Kett's Rebellion / York, North Yorkshire – The Pilgrimage of Grace

Finders Keepers – Historical Artefacts and Antiquities Discovered in Britain
Attleborough, Norfolk – Bronze Age Settlement unearthed / Dunaverney, Antrim – The Dunaverney flesh-hook / Ferrybridge, West Yorkshire – Ancient burial site unearthed / Harnham, Wiltshire – Stone Age site / Langstone, Hampshire – The Langstone longboat / Newark, Nottinghamshire – Iron Age artefact discovered / Snodland, Kent – Roman hoard unearthed / St Asaph, Denbighshire – Ancient Roman coin discovered / Staffordshire – The Moorlands Pan / Whiteball, Somerset – Britain's oldest shoe / Wickford, Essex – Remarkable Stone Age camp unearthed / Woodstown, Waterford – Viking village discovered

Battle of Britain – British Battlefields
Aughrim, County Galway – The Battle of Aughrim / Culloden, Highland – The Battle of Culloden / Dunbar, East Lothian – The Battle of Dunbar / East Stoke, Nottinghamshire – The Battle of Stoke Field / Killiecrankie, Perth and Kinross – The Battle of Killiecrankie / The Battle of Lincoln / Maldon, Essex – The Battle of Maldon / Prestonpans, East Lothian – The Battle of Prestonpans / Towton, North Yorkshire – The Battle of Towton / Worcester, Wosrcetershire – The Battle of Worcester

Invasions – Sites of Invasions of Britain
Deal, Kent – Invasion of Perkin Warbeck / Guernsey, The Channel Islands – The Nazi occupations / The Isle of Wight – French invasion and the Siege of Carisbrooke / Lindisfarne, Northumberland – Early Viking invasion / Pevensey, East Sussex – Invasion of William of Normandy, 1066 / Riccal, North Yorkshire – Norse invasion of Britain / Richborough, Kent – Roman invasion of Britain / Thetford, Norfolk – The Great Heathen Army invades / Walmer, Kent – Invasion of Julius Caesar

Bewitched – Locations of Famous Witch Trials
Bideford, Devon / Guernsey, Channel Islands / Kilkenny / North Berwick, East Lothian / Paisley, Renfrewshire / Pendle Hill, Lancashire / Samlesbury, Lancashire / Warboys, Cambridgeshire

Heist – Notable British Robberies and Thefts
Belfast – The Northern Bank robbery / Dublin – Bank of Ireland robbery / Heathrow Airport – Brink's-MAT robbery / Knightsbridge, London – Knightsbridge safe deposit robbery / Ledburn, Buckinghamshire – The Great Train Robbery / Millennium Dome, Greenwich – 'Millennium Star' attempted robbery / Salford, Greater Manchester – Notorious Midland Bank robbery / Tonbridge, Kent – Securitas robbery

Take a Leap – Events of 29 February
Cambridge – The discovery of pulsars (1968) / Kensington – Actor Joss Ackland (1928) / Lisconnor, County Clare – Birth of John Philip Holland (1840) / Long Crendon, Buckinghamshire – Death of Ruth Pitter (1992) / Manchester – Birth of John Byrom (1692) / St Andrews, Fife – Execution of Patrick Hamilton (1528) / Thatched House Lodge, London – Birth of James Robert Bruce Ogilvy (1964) / Westminster, London – The end of Prince Harry's tour of duty (2008)

Christmas Days – Events of 25 December
Cockermouth, Cumbria – Birth of Dorothy Wordsworth / Oxford – Orlando Gibbons' baptism / Sandringham, Norfolk – First royal Christmas message 1932 / Sutton, Surrey – Quentin Crisp / Welbeck, Nottinghamshire – Death of William Cavendish, 1st Duke of Newcastle / Westminster Abbey, London – Coronation of William the Conqueror, 1066 / Windsor, Berkshire – Popularisation of the Christmas tree in Britain

On the Road – Feats and Firsts in British Transport
Aldermaston, Berkshire – Britain's first petrol station / Brighton, East Sussex – Pioneering electric railway / Clifden, County Galway – Aviation pioneers Alcock and Brown / Croydon – Croydon Airport / East Peckham, Kent – Britain's first speeding ticket / Farnborough, Hampshire – Britain's first powered flight / Flax Bourton, Somerset – Britain's first breath test / London – Britain's first traffic lights / Plymouth, Devon – The first transatlantic flight / Tanfield, Durham – The world's oldest rail bridge / Thurso, Highland – Britain's most extreme station / Wolverhampton, West Midlands – Britain's first traffic lights

Shipshape – Notable British Ships
Belfast – HMHS *Britannic* / Bristol – SS *Great Western,* SS *Great Eastern* / Chatham, Kent – HMS *Victory* / Clydebank, West Dunbartonshire – RMS

Lusitania / Dumbarton, West Dunbartonshire – *The Cutty Sark* / Dundee – RRS *Discovery* / Sunderland, Tyne and Wear – HMS *Investigator* / Wallsend, Tyne and Wear – RMS *Carpathia* / Whitby, North Yorkshire – HMS *Endeavour*

Last, But Not Least – Famous Lasts

Filton, Gloucestershire – The Concorde's final flight / Fishguard, Pembrokeshire – The last invasion of Britain / Gloucester – Last coronation outside of London / Perth, Perth and Kinross – Prime Minister Alec Douglas-Home's constituency / Wells, Somerset – Britain's last trenches survivor / Wembley Stadium, London – The Beatles' last concert

5. ARTS AND ENTERTAINMENT

All the World's a Stage – Places Mentioned in Shakespeare

Ampthill, Bedfordshire – *Henry VIII* (III.ii) / Banbury, Oxfordshire – *The Merry Wives of Windsor* (I.i) / Brentford, London – *The Merry Wives of Windsor* (IV.ii) / Iona, Argyll and Bute – *Macbeth* (II.iv) / Goodwin Sands, off Kent, English Channel – *The Merchant of Venice* (III.i) / Inchcolm, Fife – *Macbeth* (I.ii) / Pontefract, West Yorkshire – *Richard III* (III.iii) / Salisbury, Wiltshire – *King Lear* (II.ii) / Tewkesbury, Gloucestershire – *Henry IV, Part 2* (II.iv) / Ware, Hertfordshire – *Twelfth Night* (III.ii) / Winchester, Hampshire – *Troilus and Cressida* (V.x)

Page Turners – Settings and Inspirations for Famous Books

Bath, Somerset – *Northanger Abbey, Persuasion* / Cooling, Kent – Dicken's *Great Expectations* / Dublin – James Joyce's *Ulysses* / Great Yarmouth, Norfolk – Dicken's *David Copperfield* / Leith, Edinburgh – Irvine Welsh's *Trainspotting* / London – George Orwell's *1984* / Ottershaw, Surrey – H. G. Wells' *War of the Worlds* / Skye, Highland – Virginia Woolf's *To the Lighthouse* / Stonyhurst, Derbyshire – Conan Doyle's *The Hound of the Baskervilles* / Top Withens, North Yorkshire – Emily Brontë's *Wuthering Heights* / Whitby, North Yorkshire – Bram Stoker's *Dracula*

English Verse – Places Mentioned in Famous Poems

Dover, Kent – Arnold's 'Dover Beach' / Duddon, Cumbria – Wordsworth's 'River Duddon' sonnets / Grange, Cumbria – Southey's 'Cataract of Lodore'/ Grantchester, Cambridgeshire – Brooke's 'The Old Vicarage, Grantchester' / Innisfree, County Sligo – Yeats' 'Lake Isle of Innisfree' / Newstead,

Nottinghamshire – Byron's 'Elegy On Newstead Abbey' / Reading, Berkshire – Wilde's Ballad of Reading Gaol / Slough, Berkshire – Betjeman's 'Slough' / Stoke Poges, Buckinghamshire – Gray's 'Elegy'

Holy Orders – British Clergymen Writers
Bemerton, Wiltshire – Parish of Welsh writer George Herbert / Boldre, Hampshire – Parish of writer William Gilpin / East Dereham, Norfolk – Parish of English writer William Cowper / Eastleach, Gloucestershire – Parish of writer John Keble / Emneth, Cambridgeshire – Parish of *Thomas the Tank Engine* writer W. V. Awdry / Ford End, Essex – Parish of writer Arthur Shearly Cripps / Kilroot, Antrim – Parish of writer Jonathan Swift / Morwenstow, Cornwall – 'The Song of the Western Men' writer Robert Stephen Hawker / Netheravon, Wiltshire – Parish of writer Sydney Smith / Oxford – Lewis Carroll's early religious studies / St Dunstan-in-the-West, City of London – Parish of English poet John Donne

Opening Night – Premiere Performances
Birmingham – Holst's *The Planets* debuts / Bournemouth, Dorset – *Lokshin's 1st Symphony* / Bristol – *Guys & Dolls* premieres / Cambridge – Harold Pinter's *The Birthday Party* debuts / Chichester, West Sussex – Peter Shaffer's *The Royal Hunt of the Sun* debuts / Coventry, West Midlands – Britten's *War Requiem* debuts / Derry, Londonderry – Friel's *Translations* debuts / Dublin – Handel's *Messiah* / Glasgow – Extraordinary *Opus Clavicembalisticum* debuts / Dublin – O'Casey's *Juno and the Paycock* premieres / Edinburgh – Stoppard's *Rosencrantz and Guildenstern Are Dead* debuts / Gloucester – Vaughan William's epic *Fantasia* / Kirkwall, Orkney – Peter Maxwell Davies' *The Yellow Cake Revue* / Leeds, West Yorkshire – Vaughan Williams' *A Sea Symphony* / Liverpool, Merseyside – Elgar's *Pomp and Circumstance Marches* debut / Liverpool, Merseyside – *Blood Brothers*, *Shirley Valentine* / Manchester – Bax's *November Woods* premieres / Manchester – Du Maurier's *The Years Between* / Newcastle-upon-Tyne, Tyne and Wear – Shaw's *Caesar and Cleopatra* debuts / Northampton – Christie's *The Mousetrap* debuts / Royal Opera House, Covent Garden – Vaughan Williams' *The Pilgrim's Progress* debuts / Scarborough, North Yorkshire – Ayckbourn's *Relatively Speaking* debuts

Brit Flicks – Oscar-Winning Movies Filmed In Britain
Aonach Eagach, Highland – *Braveheart* / Ballinesker, Wexford – *Saving Private Ryan* / Bamburgh, Northumberland – *Becket* / Barnet, Hertfordshire

– *Gosford Park* / Ely, Cambridgeshire – *The King's Speech* / Farnham, Surrey – *Gladiator* / Hambleden, Buckinghamshire – *Sleepy Hollow* / Holkham, Norfolk – *Shakespeare In Love* / Loughborough, Leicestershire – *The Hours* / Plymouth, Devon – *Sense and Sensibility* / Redcar, North Yorkshire – *Atonement* / Repton, Derbyshire – *Goodbye Mr Chips* / Sheffield, South Yorkshire – *The Full Monty* / St Andrews, Fife – *Chariots of Fire*

And the Winner Is... – British Oscar Winners

Aberdeen – Annie Lennox / Croydon, London – David Lean and Peggy Ashcroft / Dublin – George Bernard Shaw / Edinburgh – Sean Connery / Glasgow – Peter Capaldi / Haslemere, Surrey – Rachel Portman / Ilford – Maggie Smith / Neath, Neath Port Talbot – Ray Milland / Norwich, Norfolk – Stuart Craig / Preston, Lancashire – Nick Park / Scarborough, North Yorkshire – Charles Laughton / Stockport, Greater Manchester – Wendy Hiller / Watford, Hertfordshire – T. E. B. Clarke / York, North Yorkshire – John Barry

Public Art – Sculptures and Other Public Works of Art

Aldeburgh, Suffolk – *Scallop* / Cheltenham, Gloucestershire – *The Minotaur and the Hare* / Gateshead, Tyne and Wear – *Angel of the North* / Glasgow – Bud Neill memorial unveiled (*Lobey Dosser and Rank Bajin*) / Horsham, West Sussex – The *Rising Universe* / Manchester – *The B of the Bang* / Reading, Berkshire – *The Maiwand Lion Memorial* / Sheegorey, County Roscommon – *The Gaelic Chieftain* / Woking, Surrey – *Tripod*

Still Life – Statues

Ashington, Northumberland – Jackie Milburn / Birmingham – Tony Hancock / Cambridge – Charles Darwin / Cardiff – Tasker Watkins / Corwen, Denbighshire – Owain Glyndwr / Douglas, Isle of Man – George Formby / Hawick, Scottish Borders – James Thomson / Ipswich, Suffolk – Alexander Obolensky / Morecambe, Lancashire – Eric Morecambe / Salisbury, Wiltshire – Canon Ezra Baya Lawiri / Stratford-on-Avon, Warwickshire – The Gower Memorial / York, North Yorkshire – Roman Emperor Constantine the Great

The Build-up – Buildings Awarded Royal Institute of British Architects' Awards

30 St Mary Axe, City of London – The Gherkin / Cambridge – The Cambridge Accordia / Edinburgh – The Scottish Parliament Building / Gateshead, Tyne and Wear – The Sage Gateshead / Leicester – The Curve Theatre / Limerick,

County Limerick – The Living Bridge / Manchester – The Civil Justice Centre / Penzance, Cornwall – The Exchange / Portsmouth, Hampshire – Aspex / Stockton-on-Tees, County Durham – The Infinity Bridge

Going, Going, Gone – Auction Lots

Aylsham, Norfolk – Churchill's ashtray auctioned / Christie's, Westminster – *On the Origin of Species* auctioned / Cirencester, Gloucestershire – Remarkable Jane Austen auction / Devizes, Wiltshire – Twentieth-century disaster memorabilia auctioned / Dorchester, Dorset – Dickens' business card auctioned / Dublin – Yeats first edition auctioned / Glasgow – Rare whisky auctioned / Ludlow, Shropshire – Adolf Hitler autograph auctioned / Midgham, Berkshire – Rare Beatles album auctioned / Oxford – Rare signed books auctioned / Penzance, Cornwall – Remarkable Churchill auction / Plymouth, Devon – Charlie Chaplin costume auctioned / Pontrilas, Herefordshire – Dickens' diamond ring auctioned

6. SCIENCE AND NATURE

Elementary – Chemical Elements Discovered In Britain

The British Museum, Bloomsbury – Niobium / Calne, Wiltshire – Oxygen / Edinburgh – Nitrogen / Low Mill, Cumbria – Early studies of platinum / The Royal Institution, Mayfair – Humphrey Davy's chemical elements / Strontian, Highland – Strontium / Terling, Essex – Argon / University College London, London – Discovery of the noble gases / Westminster, London – The platinum metals

Eureka! – Inventions and Inventors

Albury, Surrey – William Oughtred's slide rule / Belfast – Portable defibrillator / Crowmarsh Gifford, Oxfordshire – Jethro Tull's seed drill / Dublin – Hypodermic needle / Dundee – Adhesive stamp / Great Yarmouth, Norfolk – Fire extinguisher / Newtown, Powys – Mail order shopping / Stanhill, Lancashire – Spinning jenny / Swansea – Fuel cell

First Aid – Medical Feats and Firsts

Berkeley, Gloucestershire – Smallpox pioneer Edward Jenner / Birmingham – Discovery of digitalis / Cambridge – Importance of vitamins explained / Dublin – Use of hypodermic needles pioneered / Edinburgh – Anaesthesia pioneered / Glasgow – Lister's early antisepsis measures / Oldham, Greater Manchester – World's first 'test tube baby' born / Oxford – Bacon's early optical research / Portsmouth, Hampshire – James Lind's experimental voyage / St Bartholomew's, London – William Harvey's circulatory research

Fossil Records – Dinosaurs and Prehistoric Animals
Brighstone, Isle of Wight – *Eotyrannus* / Ewenny, Vale of Glamorgan – *Morganucodon* / Lossiemouth, Moray – *Saltopus* / Lyme Regis, Dorset – Plesiosaur / Minchinhampton, Gloucestershire – *Proceratosaurus* / Oxford – *Eustreptospondylus* / Peterborough, Cambridgeshire – *Sarcolestes* / Sutton, Suffolk – *Hyracotherium* / Walliswood, Surrey – *Baryonyx* / West Runton, Norfolk – The Runton Elephant

Under Threat – Strongholds of Endangered Species
Aysgarth, North Yorkshire – Stronghold of the dormouse / Chichester, West Sussex – The greater mouse-eared bat / Formby, Merseyside – Stronghold of the red squirrel / Kincraig, Highland – Stronghold of the wildcat / Lough Neagh, Northern Ireland – Stronghold of the pollan / Magheraveely, Fermanagh – Stronghold of Britain's only crayfish / The New Forest, Hampshire – Stronghold of Britain's reptiles / Swaffham, Norfolk – Last known sighting of a great bustard in Britain / Ythan, Aberdeenshire – Stronghold of the water vole

Flying Solo – Vagrant Birds in the British Isles
Ardnave, Argyll and Bute / Billingham, Durham / Butt of Lewis, Western Isles / Calf of Man, Isle of Man / Dinas Head, Pembrokeshire / Druridge Bay, Northumberland / Dungeness, Kent / Fair Isle, Shetland / Farne Islands, Northumberland / Flamborough Head, East Yorkshire / Kenidjack, Cornwall / Kilrenny, Fife / Nanjizal, Cornwall / Sladesbridge, Cornwall / Spurn, East Yorkshire / The Scilly Isles / Tiree, Argyll and Bute

Special Branches – Notable Trees
Boscobel, Shropshire – The Royal Oak / Crom, County Fermanagh – The Great Yew / Fortingall, Perthshire – The Fortingall Yew / Hatfield, Hertfordshire – The Queen Elizabeth Oak / Llangernyw, Conwy – St Digain's Yew / Manthorpe, Lincolnshire – The Bowthorpe Oak / Runnymede, Berkshire – The Ankerwyke Yew / Sherwood Forest, Nottinghamshire – The Major Oak / Southwell, Nottinghamshire – The Bramley apple / Tolpuddle, Devon – The Tolpuddle Martyrs

British Bulldog – Dog Breeds Originating in Britain
Airedale, West Yorkshire – Airedale terrier / Bedlington, Northumberland – Bedlington terrier / Bradford, West Yorkshire – The Yorkshire terrier / Glen of Imaal, County Wicklow – The Glen of Imaal terrier / Tralee, County Kerry – The Kerry blue terrier / Manchester – The Manchester terrier / Norwich – The Norwich terrier / Patterdale, Cumbria – The Patterdale terrier / Poltalloch, Argyll and Bute – The West Highland terrier / Sealyham, Dyfed – The Sealyham terrier / Skye, Highland – Skye terrier

Wild Life – Big Cat Sightings In Britain
Bournemouth, Dorset – The Bournemouth Puma / Cannich, Highland – The Cannich Puma / Cottenham, Cambridgeshire – The Fen Tiger / Coylton, South Ayrshire – The Galloway Puma / East Farndon, Northamptonshire – The Northamptonshire 'Black Beast' / Foel, Powys – The Welsh Panther / Great Witchingham, Norfolk – The Norfolk Lynx / Helensburgh, Argyll and Bute – The Helensburgh Panther / Hemingby, Lincolnshire – The Hemingby Panther / High Wycombe, Buckinghamshire – The Beast of Bucks / Llangadog, Carmarthenshire –The Carmarthenshire Cat / Trellech, Monmouthshire – Remarkable big cat attack / Winston, County Durham – The Durham Puma

7. SPORT AND LEISURE

Home Turf – Sporting Venues
Aberdeen – Pittodrie Stadium / Cardiff – The SWALEC Stadium / Chester, Cheshire – Deva Stadium / Henley-on-Thames, Oxfordshire – The Oxford–Cambridge Boat Race / Musselburgh, East Lothian – Musselburgh Links Golf Course / Rugby, Warwickshire – Rugby School / Silverstone, Northamptonshire – Britain's longest racetrack / South Shields, Tyne and Wear – The Great North Run / Swindon – The FA's first floodlights / West Bromwich, West Midlands – Britain's highest football ground / Wootton, Kent – Britain's shortest racetrack

Let the Games Begin – British Olympic and Commonwealth Games Venues
Birmingham – The Birmingham Olympics / Cardiff – The Cardiff Commonwealth Games / Chipping Campden, Gloucestershire – The Cotswold Olimpicks / Dublin – The Dublin Olympics / Edinburgh – The Edinburgh Commonwealth Games / Glasgow – The Glasgow Commonwealth Games / Douglas, Isle of Man – Commonwealth Games success / London – The London Olympics / Manchester – The Manchester Commonwealth Games

/ Much Wenlock, Shropshire – The Wenlock Olympian Games / Stoke Mandeville, Buckinghamshire – The Stoke Mandeville Games

Going for Gold – Olympic Medallists
Bayswater, London – Kitty McKane / Camberley, Surrey – Malcolm Cooper / Cardiff – Paul Radmilovic / Carrick-on-Suir, Tipperary – Tom Kiely / Chepstow, Monmouthshire – Richard Meade / Edinburgh – Chris Hoy / Macclesfield, Cheshire – Ben Ainslie / Marlow, Buckinghamshire – Steve Redgrave / Newlands, Scottish Borders – Walter Rutherford / Oldham, Greater Manchester – Henry Taylor / Pembury, Kent – Kelly Holmes / Rathcoole, South Dublin – Michelle de Bruin

Games of Two Halves – Football Feats and Facts
Aberdeen – Football's first dugout / Arbroath, Angus – Remarkable football victory / Derby – Derby County's woeful league performance / Dundee – Triple red card awarded / Inverness, Highland – Football's record-breaking multiple postponements / Kingston-upon-Hull, East Yorkshire – England's first penalty shoot-out / Loughborough, Leicestershire – Loughborough FC's farewell season / Luton, Bedfordshire – Joe Payne and the ten-goal game / Motherwell, North Lanarkshire – Football's fastest hat-trick / Reading, Berkshire – Football mascot sent off / Sheffield, South Yorkshire – Unique football ground records / St Albans, Hertfordshire – Tree disrupts play at football match / Sunderland, Tyne and Wear – Extraordinary goalkeeper's goal / Tunbridge Wells, Kent – Record-breaking penalty shoot-out contested / Wembley Stadium, London – The White Horse Final

National Interest – Horse Racing Feats and Facts
Andoversford, Gloucestershire – Grand National winner Mr Frisk / Ayr, South Ayrshire – Ayr Racecourse / Ballymany, Kildare – The Curragh / Beverley, East Yorkshire – Grand National winner Peter Simple / Cartmel, Cumbria – Britain's shortest racecourse / Chester, Cheshire – Britain's oldest racecourse / Compton, Berkshire – Grand National winner Foinavon / Exeter, Devon – Exeter Racecourse / Kells, Kilkenny – Grand National winner Red Rum / Lawrenny, Pembrokeshire – Grand National winner Kirkland / Perth, Perth and Kinross – Perth Racecourse / Pontefract, West Yorkshire – Pontefract Racecourse / Sedgefield, Durham – Sedgefield Racecourse

Have you enjoyed this book?
If so, why not write a review on your favourite website?

If you're interested in finding out more about our books,
follow us on Twitter: **@Summersdale**

Thanks very much for buying this Summersdale book.

www.summersdale.com